Theology and Lived Christianity

David M. Hammond, editor

*The Annual Publication
of the College Theology Society*

Volume 45

TWENTY-THIRD PUBLICATIONS
BAYARD ◉ Mystic, CT 06355

Co-published by the College Theology Society and

Twenty-Third Publications/ Bayard
185 Willow Street
P.O. Box 180
Mystic, CT 06355
(860) 536-2611
(800) 321-0411

ISBN:1-58595-020-3
Library of Congress Catalog Card Number: 00-131185
Printed in the U.S.A.

For

David Harvey Smith, M.D.
Healer, Thinker, Pilgrim

Acknowledgments

I am grateful to all the reviewers of the essays sent to me for consideration. Their timely and insightful responses were an essential part of the editorial process. My thanks also to all who submitted papers. They have shown great patience and cooperation as the volume moved forward. I am grateful to Mrs. Nancy Wagner, Graduate Assistant in the Department of Philosophy and Theology at Wheeling Jesuit University, for very valuable assistance in the early stages. Dan Connors at Twenty-Third Publications was a great help and encouragement. My gratitude also goes to the Board of Directors of the College Theology Society for the honor of this assignment. Gary Macy, last year's editor, gave me detailed and invaluable advice that saved hours of trial and error. Finally, I wish to express my loving thanks to my wife Robyn whose generosity made it possible for me to spend the extra time in my office editing this volume.

David M. Hammond
Wheeling Jesuit University
December 29, 1999 (Feast of St. Thomas Becket)

Table of Contents

Part III
The World of Mediation: Embodied Holiness

Part IV
Prayer and Transformation

Introduction

For several decades now, a renewed attention to the local Church as well as the recovery of the image of the Church as the people of God have encouraged theologians to pay closer heed to the concrete forms, expressions, devotional practices and other cultural embodiments of the Christian faith. In theory this new appreciation for the role of culture in the ongoing constitution of the Church followed easily enough from the widely popularized idea that the Church was not to be reduced to its hierarchical ministers; the faith, we learned, was present in the whole people of God. In practice, however, attending to the Christian faith as it is actually lived is quite an arduous task and will require more time, for it is one thing to acknowledge that an earlier theology did not find much value in the lived dimension of Christianity and another to reorient the theologian's attention, to discover the relevant questions, to ask about what is observed in such lived experience, to master the tools needed to answer such questions and finally to integrate these findings within a larger theological whole. The task is large and difficult but it is an essential part of the university's vocation "to dialogue with and learn from any culture."[1] The essays in this volume, most of which were delivered at the Forty-Fifth Annual Convention of the College Theology Society held at Saint Norbert's College in Green Bay, Wisconsin, June 3-6, 1999, are part of that dialogue.

A theology attentive to lived Christianity will need to know what the faithful think about the elements of their life-world, what sorts of meanings are being communicated to particular populations through specific devotions, customs, or practices. A certain level of self-understanding on the part of the theologian will also be required if we are to listen respectfully to the meanings and values communicated in the lived experience of Christians. On these and related issues theology is presently trying to find its way.

In the background of many of the essays in this volume is the need for a generous hermeneutic of symbolic meaning that flows from a self-critical theological method aware of and willing to take responsibility for its own presuppositions. This is especially important for an age of reform and renewal, for there is danger in the unacknowledged assumptions of a theology that has not taken up the challenge of thinking with the people. A current problem that besets most academic work is the modern separation of expert culture and traditional culture. In a plenary address at an earlier convention of the College Theology Society, Francis Schüssler Fiorenza pointed out that, although theologians are not the primary culprits of this modern separation, they do need to become more conscious of the pressures of contemporary academia and to search out ways of resisting the alienation of the two spheres.[2] Theologians who want to understand popular religion and the various lived expressions of Christianity must be careful to avoid assuming as normative modernity's separation of expert and traditional cultures. It would not be counted theological progress if the prejudices of liberal academia were simply to replace what it often dismisses as popular naïveté.

Theology reflects on experience but does not replace it and should not impede it. If one of the primary tasks of theology is to understand the symbolic world of the ordinary believer, that effort must begin with attentiveness to what is in fact happening in and among the people, for while we may speculate about what a particular practice seems to mean, verifying such interpretations is all but impossible if we have paid insufficient attention to the people, practices, and things that we interpret.

Theology must sometimes criticize and correct lived Christianity in light of the gospel. It must do so, however, without infringing on the rights of the non-theological members of the Body. The anthropologist Victor Turner once observed how hard it is for a modern academic inquirer to grasp the mentality of those in a pre-modern culture.[3] Postconciliar theologians have too often verified this observation by failing to understand the mentality of their own fellow Christians. Theologians and others should be as critical of the attitudes toward traditional culture taken for granted by contemporary academic culture as they are of harmful aspects of popular religion. Regrettably, some educated Christians often show less sympathy and understanding toward "the others" within their own Church than they do toward those of other faiths.

The essays in Part I of this volume address methodological issues in the study of lived Christianity. Roberto Goizueta's challenge to the theological community, forcefully articulated in his plenary address, here entitled "A Ressourcement from the Margins: U.S. Latino Popular Catholicism as Lived Religion," is both epistemological and religious. When theology separates form from content a false spiritualizing of Christianity blinds inquirers to the power of the form and discourages questions of embodied truth. A distrust of appearances, signs, and actual bodies weakens the theologian's solidarity with the people whose sense of religious truth is not primarily spiritual but incarnate. Do we respect the faith of the people enough to take seriously their demand not merely for meaning but for truth? Goizueta challenges theologians in modern and postmodern contexts to rethink the value they normally give (or too often fail to give) to religious common sense.

Theology alone is not adequate to the Church's task of communicating the gospel and transforming the world. If theology is to make its proper contribution to the Church's mission, the lines of communication between theology and the human sciences must be open. The turn to experience is here to stay but we are far from its full implementation in theology. In his plenary address, "Lived Research on Lived Religion," Fredric Roberts reports on a large, multiyear project under his direction. The early findings of the Metropolitan Detroit and Lansing Congregation Study Project already reveal how important it is to pay attention to the people in the pews; we don't necessarily know what they are thinking. Important and difficult, for if we are convinced of the need to consult the faithful, then how do we do it? Roberts' analysis of the diverse and often unexpected "knowledge encounters" in local congregations certifies the complexity of religious life in the church next door. Moreover, his discovery of the widespread use of "church consultants" suggests a lesson for theologians: we must continue to find ways of making our work accessible and useful to pastors and ordinary churchgoers. The expert culture of academic theology must communicate with the traditional cultures of the local Church.

One does not understand what one does not notice, and what one is likely to notice will depend on several factors, including a sensitivity to those who are different. The more we know of the vast diversity of Christianity, the better disposed will we be toward identifying the meaning and truth to be found in practices that we do not share. A mind well-stocked with a broad knowledge of diverse religious practices is more likely to catch on to what is happening in new cultural situations. The more we know, to paraphrase Jesus, the more we will learn (Matthew 25:29).

If this is true, an essential component of the theologian's sensitivity training for lived Christianity is the study of history: it provides nuance to theory and puts flesh on ideas. In Part II, "Retrieving Traditions of Lived Christianity," four diverse studies remind us of the theological benefits of good historical scholarship. Circumstance has always required missionaries to think on their feet about the encounter between faith and culture. What impedes the hearing of the gospel? What will promote it? They must take culture seriously and reflect explicitly on it if only because the cultures they encounter are so different from their own. In "The Inculturation of Christianity in Asia: From Francis Xavier to Matteo Ricci," Ronald Modras reminds us of the early Jesuit missionaries' arduous pioneering efforts to understand a Chinese way of life in the seventeenth century. Ricci is no doubt a dramatic example of what it takes to be received into an initially alien culture; he is also an illustration of the affinities of Renaissance humanism and seventeenth-century Confucian culture. To some degree, what Ricci brought with him from Renaissance Italy prepared him to discover and value what he encountered in China. In "Alexandre de Rhodes' Mission in Vietnam: Evangelization and Inculturation," Peter Phan presents a taste of his extensive research into a much less well known but more successful Jesuit missionary whose work in Vietnam almost four hundred years ago continues to bear fruit today in a vital Vietnamese Catholicism. The adequacy of our interpretation of lived Christianity today depends on an imaginative transposition of the insights gleaned from the efforts of these exemplary missionaries.

Philip Thompson presents a reading of the early Baptists that retrieves their sense of community and sacrament. In "Practicing the Freedom of God: Formation in Early Baptist Life," Thompson's examination of popular religious expressions (hymns, catechisms, sermons) discloses a strong ecclesial self-understanding in early Baptist history. The essay indicates that recent individualist notions of Baptist identity are thus in need of correction by way of historical retrieval; it also makes a contribution to ecumenical dialogue.

Lived religion is not, of course, to be romanticized any more than it is to be dismissed as superstition. The common sense of the simple believer can be mixed not only with common nonsense but with unacknowledged complicity in

structural evil. In "Claude Heithaus and the Integration of
Saint Louis University: The Mystical Body of Christ and
Jesuit Politics," Daniel Van Slyke tells the story of a prophetic Jesuit professor of archaeology who became a pioneer of
integration. Lived Catholicism of early twentieth-century
America was shamefully implicated in a massive institutional sin and yet the theology of the Mystical Body of Christ,
recommended by Pope Pius XII's encyclical, provided
Claude Heithaus with the theological resources to oppose
the evil of racism within his own university.

In Part III, four scholars from very different perspectives
all address the role of embodied meaning in lived
Christianity. Scholars are, by profession, print-oriented;
these explorations of the meanings incarnate in bodies, artistic images, gestures, and the natural world alert us to the
vast non-textual dimension of lived Christianity. In "'Your
Face Is My Only Homeland': A Psychological Perspective on
Thérèse of Lisieux and Devotion to the Holy Face," Mary
Frohlich demonstrates the value of theology's listening to
the relevant social sciences, in this case psychoanalytic object
relations theory. Frohlich also shows that, in the case of
Thérèse, holiness and mental illness are not so easily separated in a concrete life. Holiness resides at times inextricably
within the wounds of real human beings, socially and culturally located. Holiness or illness, faith or "superstition,"
spirit or flesh, theology or the social sciences, the Church as
institution or the Church as Mystery, a human Jesus or a
divine Christ—such false dichotomies confuse rather than
clarify.

Anthony Godzieba' s "Caravaggio, Theologian: Baroque
Piety and Poiesis in a Forgotten Chapter of the History of
Catholic Theology" reminds us that, in a Catholic sacramental imagination at least, no culture is devoid of redemptive
recovery. In his retrieval of the unjustly maligned Baroque
period Godzieba reinvigorates the theological imagination
with an analysis of the deeply sacramental vision of

Caravaggio. Art is a dimension of lived Christianity and the vast majority of great paintings were, until a few hundred years ago, created with the explicit intention of helping people to pray. Besides being an important lesson in the blind spots that continue to hamper the telling of the history of theology, Godzieba's lively essay proves that the text-oriented theological world is thirsting for the refreshment that great religious art can provide.

Anthropological fieldwork is another avenue that can uncover forms of incarnate meaning embedded in the physical, material, and bodily dimensions of religion. Michael Steltenkamp's essay, "New Age, Environmentalism, and Liturgical Inculturation," draws on his missionary activity among the Lakota Sioux, his perceptive insights into the cultural function of New Age practices, and his appreciation for the current environmental consciousness. Steltenkamp's training as an anthropologist has encouraged him to raise questions about how an earlier Catholic subculture had carried meanings and addressed needs that are increasingly being served by a medley of popular practices. Steltenkamp argues that flexible liturgical adaptation, combined with a willingness to learn from the devotional life of an earlier Catholic generation, offers an opportunity to inculturate Christianity today in ways that will affirm what is good in popular culture.

Theresa Lysaught's reflections on "Eucharist as Basic Training: The Body as Nexus of Liturgy and Ethics" investigate the ways in which Christian bodies are produced through regular, routine movement, posture, and gesture in worship. We train as disciples not merely cognitively and affectively but physically. Although careful not to reduce the liturgy to didactic or instrumental catechesis, Lysaught explores the connection between our formation as bodies and our moral formation in the life in the Body of Christ.

Part IV, "Prayer and Transformation," retrieves two classics that focus on the connection between the personal and the cosmic. Not everything is culturally particular; there are the universal experiences of struggle, meaning, suffering, and death even though they are lived out in diverse circumstances. No matter the cultural form of Christianity, the simple fact is that people pray to God for help. Edward Jeremy Miller retrieves a classic theological tradition that interprets the human desire for divine help during times of trouble in his essay "Praying When Troubled: Retrieving Boethius and Aquinas." Theology is likely to engage the lived Christianity of many undergraduates when life raises the question of meaningful and efficacious prayer. Aquinas' answer, building on Boethius, brings together the cosmic and the personal, revealing the intimate relationship between lived Christianity and systematic understanding. Miller intends the article to be of service to teachers of theology who regularly find themselves faced with pastoral questions or even crises among their students.

In the final essay, "'Do We Drink From An Empty Well?' The Spiritual Exercises and Social Sin," Maria Malkiewicz reads Loyola's spiritual classic in an effort to determine whether Jon Sobrino's critique is correct: does our awareness of structural evil require us to alter this classic of spirituality? The perpetuation of a faulty or inadequate tradition for its own sake, simply because it is traditional, is obviously contrary to the gospel. Malkiewicz's reading of the Exercises, however, shows that the foundation and First Week should be retained while integrating the new cultural context made clear to us in the recent literature of liberation theology. In the process of her sympathetic reading of the Exercises Malkiewicz presents a nuanced relationship between the recognition of personal guilt and the reality of social sin.

A theology sensitive to lived Christianity will be careful to make explicit its assumptions and procedures. It will be attentive to cultural forms not normally encountered in the university and take seriously the need for competent interdisciplinary study in any effort to understand and respect ordinary religious people. Such a theology will foster that which is worth preserving in devotional practices or behaviors and not naïvely assume that the bookish culture of the intellectual is normative for the Church. It will read history to prepare itself for diverse contemporary encounters with cultures. Always mindful of the incarnational anchor of Christian faith, it will give embodiment and incarnate meaning the significance it deserves. Retrieval of the classics will provide depth to its reflections on the relationship between a prayerful life of faith and the ongoing need to think it through. My hope is that the reader will find that these essays in different ways contribute to such a theology of lived Christianity.

David M. Hammond
Wheeling Jesuit University
December 29, 1999

Notes

1. *Ex Corde Ecclesiae,* # 43. For a valuable discussion of the relationship between *Ex Corde Ecclesiae* and *Fides et Ratio,* the Pope's encyclical on faith and reason, see William Portier, "Reason's 'Rightful Autonomy in *Fides et Ratio* and the Continuous Renewal of Catholic Higher Education in the United States," *Communio* 26 (1999), 541-556.

2. In an explication of Habermas's theory Fiorenza warns that an interpretation of fundamentalism that does not take these issues into account is in danger of missing the challenge that fundamentalism poses. See "Roman Catholic Fundamentalism: A Challenge to Theology" in *The Struggle over the Past: Fundamentalism in the Modern World,* ed. William Shea (Lanham, MD: University Press of America, 1993), 231-254.

3. Victor Turner, *The Ritual Process: Structure and Anti-Structure* (Chicago: Aldine, 1969), 2-3.

Part I
METHOD: HOW SHOULD
WE PROCEED?

A Ressourcement from the Margins: U.S. Latino Popular Catholicism as Lived Religion

Roberto S. Goizueta
Professor of Theology
Boston College

In July 1996, Abbot Guillermo Schulemburg of the Basilica of Our Lady of Guadalupe in Mexico City resigned from his post. A few days earlier, the Mexican media had quoted him as suggesting that Juan Diego, the indigenous man to whom *La Morenita* had appeared on December 9, 1531, was "not a reality." The national uprising that ensued had forced the Abbot's resignation.

This paper is a product of my own struggle to understand not only that event but many similar experiences I have had as I have walked with, or accompanied the U.S. Latino Catholic community in order to encounter there, in what Orlando Espín has called the "faith of the people,"[1] the God who, I believe, is revealed in the Crucified and Risen Christ, in the body of Christ. I walk with my community not only as a fellow Catholic, Christian, and Latino, but also as a professional theologian. This paper represents reflections on the intersection of these identities and, especially, on the ways in which—in my own experience—the contemporary, professional (or academic) theological enterprise is itself challenged by the lived religion of the poor, especially the lived religion of U.S. Hispanic and Latin American Catholics.

Before examining U.S. Hispanic popular Catholicism directly, therefore, I should spell out, even if only briefly, the specific features of contemporary theology that, I believe, must be questioned in the light of the lived faith of the people. For those features are obstacles to a full appreciation of U.S. Hispanic popular Catholicism. (I want to emphasize that what I am questioning here is not only those theologies that explicitly prescind from any consideration of popular Catholicism; I am also questioning my own theology and other theologies that claim as their starting point a preferential option for the poor.)

In short, my own experience over the past fifteen years has led me to ask whether, though of immense help for understanding popular Catholicism from the outside, modern and postmodern theologies are, in the end, capable of leading to a full appreciation of popular Catholicism as a lived faith that is neither modern nor postmodern. I would like to focus, especially, on the modern (and, by derivation, postmodern) separation of form and content, or sign and signified, as impeding such an appreciation and, therefore, impeding our ability to make a preferential option for the poor, our ability to walk in solidarity with the poor. Whatever our explicit intentions, that separation ultimately results in a privileging of the immaterial and abstract over the material and concrete, and a privileging of theoretical analysis over "common sense" knowledge without acknowledging the necessary, intrinsic connections between the poles in each case. In turn, such an epistemological separation obscures the fundamental character of praxis as reception of revealed truth and response to that revelation, rather than the action of an autonomous, self-constituting subject. Finally, the failure to understand praxis as fundamentally reception-response obscures the normative character of the Crucified and Risen Jesus Christ encountered by the poor, especially by Latin Americans and U.S. Latinos/as.

The Separation of Form and Content

Peter Casarella has described the separation of sign and signified as:

> a modern tendency to view the truth of the visible world with suspicion by conceiving of an idealized, self-contained, and logically precise theoretical screen. Or, in Husserl's words: "Immediately with Galileo...begins the surreptitious substitution of idealized nature for prescientifically intuited nature." In Galileo's wake, appearances of the non-idealized, "objective" world were well on their way to becoming mere appearances....we moderns are still heirs to his distrust of appearances. Unless our bare perception of an event in the natural world is accompanied by a complex, non-intuitive explanation, we fear that we have not gotten to the bottom of things. Non-technical views are thought of as "superficial," which literally means "skimming the surface." Faith in the power of the scientific viewpoint compels us to take our distance from the appearance as appearance. If we really want to understand the world, we need an explanation that will unmask the illusion of what we perceive with our own eyes.[2]

Indeed, those of us influenced by liberationist and contextual theological methods have, perhaps more than anyone, accepted the modern distrust of appearances and the presupposition that "appearances deceive."[3] While helpful and, indeed, necessary for unmasking oppressive ideologies and social structures, such suspicion can, however, become an epistemological absolute—what begins as a suspicion that appearances are real ends as a presupposition that they in fact are not. Any Christian theology, however, that assumes not only a suspicion but, indeed, a rejection of appearances as an aprioristic epistemological standpoint cannot ultimately appreciate a lived religion that presupposes an intrinsic relationship between appearance and reality, sign and signified, form and content. And, I will argue, U.S. Latino popular Catholicism is precisely such a lived religion. Thus, theologians like myself spend years trying to "get behind" the symbols and rituals of popular religion, trying to understand what they "really" mean, something that, to the people themselves, appears intuitively evident. As theologians, however, we have come to assume that *nothing* is intuitively evident; intuition cannot be trusted since it cannot "get behind" mere appearances. As Casarella notes: "Bare observation and effective moral action based upon a firm grasp of what is most essential about the real emerge as quaintly quixotic quests."[4]

Once appearance and reality are thus separated, the theological enterprise is quickly reduced to the methodological task of developing the appropriate intellectual instruments for demonstrating and analyzing that separation. As important as that task is, however, when the theological enterprise is simply *reduced* to methodology, the possibility that appearances may in fact disclose the real is precluded *a priori*:

> once the differentiation of a methodological standpoint is taken as an adequate substitute for what Lonergan calls "the mutual enrichment" of common sense by the self-disclosure of God, then method's edifice of a purely reflective consciousness becomes idolatrous. Taken as an end in itself, methodological reflection—no matter how rigorous and self-correcting—obscures the appearance of truth. When method dominates without attention to the disclosure of truth, theology suffers.[5]

When method dominates, the very possibility of disclosure,

as the appearance of the real, is itself precluded from the outset; we can spend our entire lives deconstructing the appearances without ever, in fact, "getting behind" them. The
postmodern assertion that there is, in fact, nothing at all
"behind" the appearances—there is no "there" there—
appears as simply the logical conclusion of the modern separation of the appearance and the real. Ultimately, then, the
reduction of theology to methodology absolves the theologian of ever having to commit him or herself to a particular
truth, or to any truth at all, as that which encounters us in history, makes an ultimate claim on our lives, and demands total
commitment. Insofar as any "truth" can be affirmed, it will
necessarily be only an abstract "truth" that, because it is not
intrinsically linked to a particular appearance or form, is presumed to have an existence independent of such concrete
forms. Thus, underlying the separation of form and content is
a fundamental distrust of physical, material, concrete reality.

Conversely, any religious faith that assumes that what
presents itself as true may in fact *be* true will be either dismissed outright or politely tolerated as the "simple" (read,
"naïve") faith of "the people." Theologians like myself are
likely to suggest that, if "the people" really understood what
is "behind" their religious practices, what their symbols and
rituals *really* mean, they would know that their real concern
is not God, or Jesus Christ, or Guadalupe, or Juan Diego, but
the universal "human" need for "cultural identity," or
"human dignity," or "liberation," or "self-empowerment,"
all of which could just as easily be expressed—and are, in
fact, expressed—in a myriad of other forms, other rituals,
other religions.

My own tendency toward such a "reading" of popular
religion became evident to me as I reflected on the Mexican
people's reactions to the Abbot's reported statements about
Juan Diego. Like that of so many other Latino theologians,
my reaction to the Mexican people's anger was to smile sym-
pathetically while, nevertheless, remaining convinced that

whether or not Juan Diego is real ultimately does not matter; what matters is the people's *belief* in Juan Diego, since it is the belief that is empowering and liberating; it is the *belief* that makes Juan Diego "real." It is not Juan Diego that matters; what matters is what he represents, e.g., the value of indigenous culture and *mestizaje*, the dignity of the poor. Eventually, however, I have had to confront the undeniable fact that, for the people themselves, what matters most is precisely the reality of *Juan Diego*—hence their visceral reaction to the Abbot's statement. What matters to them is not what Juan Diego "represents"; what matters is Juan Diego himself.

The vehemence with which the Mexican people rose up to defend Juan Diego points, moreover, to a further problem presented by the separation of form and content, sign and signified, and the consequent absolutization of theological method: in the wake of that separation, it becomes difficult, if not impossible, to conceive of the true, or the real, as anything but a mere human construction. (Hence, the modern separation of sign and signified leads inexorably to the postmodern deconstruction of the self-as-mere-appearance.) The sign becomes, not the disclosure of a truth which we *receive*, in which *act of reception* we find meaning; rather, the sign is itself the way in which we *construct* meaning for ourselves, the way in which we literally constitute ourselves and our world. As Thomas Merton once wrote: "If reality is something we interpret and act on to suit our own concept of ourselves, we 'respond' to nothing."[6] Thus, rather than understanding the construction of meaning as necessarily linked to the disclosure of truth, to revelation, truth-as-disclosed is simply reduced to meaning-as-constructed, and the truth question is elided altogether. Since the sign is not itself a disclosive and transformative "real presence," but only points to some presumed reality outside of and behind the sign, the sign itself is interchangeable with other signs, other forms of conveying the same "reality," which has no intrinsic connection to any particular sign. Thus, it should not matter to the Mexican people whether Juan Diego is real or not, since, after all, it is not Juan Diego himself who is real but our *belief* in Juan Diego as a sign that we ourselves have produced over the course of generations in order to construct meaning for ourselves. Juan Diego is merely an instrument, a vehicle for constructing and conveying that meaning. What matters is not Juan Diego but ourselves, our own need for identity, our own sense of dignity, our own need for liberation.

Now, this may be a necessary aspect of the faith of the people but, I would submit, it is clearly not *sufficient* to explain the people's own understanding of their faith. We cannot simply dismiss politely the Mexican people's reaction to the Abbot. We must begin to ask whether Guadalupe matters not just because of what she represents, but because she is Guadalupe, she is who she says she is; whether Jesus Christ saves us not just because of what he represents (e.g., "the victory of life over death") but because he is Jesus Christ. If the content of revelation (the "what") is not intrinsically related to the particular form of revelation, then the form itself is relativized precisely as "revelation," as the inbreaking, the irruption of the real in our world. Religion is then reduced to infinitely interchangeable symbols and rituals, all of which can be used as instruments or vehicles to convey meaning, to represent some value. Hence the reactions I have at times received from Mexican *abuelitas* and other Hispanics in parishes when, out of habit, I have referred to the gospels as "narratives." The *abuelitas* have not always been convinced. Not that the Gospels are not narratives; they are not convinced that the Gospels are *only* narratives. They are not convinced, in other words, that the Gospels point to the same "reality" that other religious narratives point to and can thus be interchanged with those other narratives. Despite my own intellectual inclination to the contrary, I have come to the realization that what matters to the people with whom I have worked in the community and in the parishes is precisely the reality of the *Gospels*, the reality of *Juan Diego*, the reality of *Guadalupe*, the reality of *Jesus Christ*.

What do we theologians do with the inescapable fact that, while we are concerned with the "liberation" of the poor, or with the promotion of "justice," the poor themselves are so often more concerned with Jesus on the Cross, or Our Lady of Guadalupe, or the healing waters of Chimayó, or *La Dolorosa*, or San Martín de Porres? Our tendency has been, I think, to interpret these popular religious practices, this lived religion, as *themselves* liberative, empowering, and, consequently, valuable—or, when distorted, as oppressive. Thus, I myself have written on popular religion as an implicit source of that human dignity and self-worth that are the foundation of any genuine liberation. Yet our focus remains "praxis," "experience," "popular religion," "justice," "freedom," etc., while the focus of the people themselves is Jesus Christ, Guadalupe, San Martín, etc., as the sources of their own identity, their own praxis, their own experience, their own justice, their own liberation. Do I simply dismiss this belief as naïve, uneducated, or, in Peter Casarella's words, "quaintly quixotic"? Or do I allow my own presuppositions to be confronted by the privileged wisdom of the poor?

The Preferential Option for the Lived Religion of the Poor

The separation of the real from its particular, concrete historical form is, I submit, utterly alien to the lived faith of the poor and, specifically, alien to Latin American and U.S. Latino popular Catholicism. Consequently, the preferential option for the poor *itself* demands that the theologian reject such a separation. As elaborated by liberation theologians like Gustavo Gutiérrez, the option for the poor implies and presupposes an intrinsic connection between sign and signified, between the real and the appearance, between the true and its disclosure. For Gutiérrez, that unity is embodied in the Word of God, the Crucified and Risen Christ.

Inspired by the work of Gutiérrez and other Latin American theologians, U.S. Latino/a theologians have sought to incarnate the theological method of Latin American liberation theology in the sociohistorical context of the U.S. Latino community, i.e., we have sought to articulate a theology that takes as its starting point a preferential option for the marginalized community of Latinos and Latinas in the United States. Like Latin American liberation theology, U.S. Latino/a theology thus represents an understanding of the theological task as, in the well-known phrase of Gustavo Gutiérrez, "critical reflection on Christian praxis in the light of the Word,"[7] more specifically, a critical reflection on the Christian praxis of our U.S. Hispanic communities in the light of the Word. That reflection has surfaced several themes that distinguish the praxis of U.S. Latino communities as marginalized communities. Two such central themes, for instance, are the experience of *mestizaje* (racial-cultural mixture) and popular religion.

In the remainder of this paper, I would like to focus on this latter theme, popular religion and, more specifically, popular Catholicism, to suggest that, as a defining characteristic of U.S. Hispanic Christian praxis, "the faith of the people," or the "lived religion" of the poor, itself represents a challenge to our own theologies and, indeed, to all theologies grounded in a preferential option for the poor, particularly those Christian theologies that understand themselves as "critical reflection on Christian praxis in the light of the Word." The faith of the people calls me to an intellectual and religious conversion that subverts the very foundations of the Christian theological enterprise as I have known it and, arguably, as most of us have known it in modern, or postmodern Western cultures. What I will thus suggest is that U.S. Latino popular Catholicism, the lived religion of the poor, is ultimately incomprehensible for those of us schooled in modern and postmodern theological methods, unless we

ourselves are converted to a radically different way of "seeing."

By emphasizing the significance of popular Catholicism
precisely as a central aspect of "Christian praxis," that is, as
a defining characteristic of the praxis of the poor, U.S.
Latino/a theologians have broadened and deepened the
understanding of praxis beyond the more explicitly sociopolitical understanding of Christian praxis emphasized in the
early years of Latin American liberation theology. Indeed,
Latin American liberation theologians themselves have
increasingly embraced this broader understanding, giving
increased attention to popular religion, the lived religion of
the poor, as a "praxis" that grounds theological reflection.
Thus, "Christian praxis" is understood to include not only
sociopolitical action but also the lived faith, spirituality, ritual practices, and devotional life that, together with the struggle for social justice, are necessary, intrinsically interrelated
dimensions of Christian discipleship. As Gustavo Gutiérrez
insists, sociopolitical action must itself be grounded in an
attitude of worship and thanksgiving for the gratuitous,
unmerited love that God has offered us in the person of Jesus
Christ:

> We in Latin America are also convinced...that in
> the liberation process we are capable of creating our
> own idols for ourselves. For example, the idol of
> justice: it might seem strange to say this but justice
> can become an idol if it is not placed in the context
> of gratuity.... Gratuity is the framework for justice
> and gives it meaning in history. Social justice, no
> matter how important it is—and it is—can also be
> an idol, and we have to purify ourselves of this to
> affirm very clearly that only God suffices and to
> give justice itself the fullness of its meaning.[8]

Hence, as critical reflection on Christian praxis *in the light of
the Word* (with a capital "W"), the theological enterprise

always stands under the judgment of that Word, that is, theology and praxis must conform to the Word, for the latter is the foundation of both theological reflection and praxis. "'God first loved us' (1 John 4:19)," writes Gutiérrez, "[e]verything starts from there. The gift of God's love is the source of our being and puts its impress on our lives.... From gratuitousness also comes the language of symbols....In their religious celebrations, whether at especially important moments or in the circumstances of everyday life, the poor turn to the Lord with the trustfulness and spontaneity of a child who speaks to its father and tells him of its suffering and hopes.... The other is our way for reaching God, but our relationship with God is a precondition for encounter and true communion with the other."[9] The poor understand, argues Gutiérrez, that, before we can choose God or others, God has already chosen us. Christian praxis is, at bottom, a praxis of grateful reception and response; before praxis is the action of a historical agent, it is the action of a recipient; before it is action-as-doing, it is action-as-receiving. More specifically, we become historical agents precisely in the praxis of reception and response. "'God first loved us'.... Everything starts from there." Our childlike openness to and reception of God's love is the precondition for any truly liberative praxis; the latter is but the eucharistic, or grateful response to the former. Gutiérrez at no time opposes contemplative receptivity to social activity; on the contrary, he understands both contemplation and action as intrinsically related dimensions of *praxis*.[10]

The increased attention to popular religion *as praxis*, as the starting point of theology, brings to light those aspects of Gutiérrez's method too often under-appreciated in the past, namely, the specifically *Christian* aspects of his definition of theology: "*critical* reflection on *Christian* praxis in the light of the *Word*." That is, the life of faith, or "lived religion," is itself central to theology and "praxis." Moreover, the life of faith itself has a transcendent source, "the Word."

Having appropriated Gutiérrez's emphasis on praxis and his relegation of theology to a "second step," however, many of us have tended to underestimate the significance of the adjective "*Christian* praxis" and, especially, the significance of the last phrase "in the light of the Word." "A hasty and simplistic interpretation of the liberationist perspective," writes Gutiérrez, "has led some to affirm that its dominant, if not exclusive, themes are commitment, the social dimension of faith, the denunciation of injustices, and others of a similar nature. It is said that the liberationist impulse leaves little room for grasping the necessity of personal conversion as a condition for Christian life.... Such an interpretation and criticism are simply caricatures. One need only have contact with the Christians in question to appreciate the complexity of their approach and the depth of their spiritual experience."[11] What grounds theology is not praxis as such but praxis *as encountered by God's Word*: "The ultimate criteria come from revealed truth, which we accept in faith, and not from praxis itself. It is meaningless—it would, among other things, be a tautology—to say that praxis is to be criticized 'in the light of praxis'."[12] For Gutiérrez, such an acceptance in faith always implies a total commitment of the whole person, it implies a praxis of faith whose "inescapable context" is "the massive social, economic, and political marginalization of the majority of the earth's people."[13]

Taken in its entirety, therefore, Gutiérrez's definition of theology presents the Christian theologian with a methodological paradox: the more profoundly we accompany the poor, the more profoundly we identify with the Christian praxis of the poor and reflect critically on that praxis in the light of the Word, the more we are confronted with a lived faith that takes as its starting point, not praxis *per se*, but the gratuitous Word of God, Jesus Christ himself (including the entire communion of saints at whose center Christ stands). As received by us in and through our lives of discipleship, our lives of Christian praxis, the gratuitous Word of God is "a precondition for encounter and true communion with the other." In Gutiérrez's words, "everything starts from there." That is, the more we direct our gaze to the poor, the more they re-direct our gaze away from them and ourselves onto God and what God has done and continues to do for us: "the gratuitousness of God's love is the framework within which the requirement of practicing justice is to be located."[14]

Gutiérrez's point—and the problem it poses for me as a theologian trained in modern and postmodern methodologies—is illustrated by a seemingly ordinary experience that continues to haunt me. Several years ago, on the feast of Our Lady of Guadalupe, I remember chatting with an elderly Mexican *abuelita* on our way out of church. In the course of our conversation, I inquired about her fervent devotion to *La Morenita*. "Why," I asked, "is Our Lady of Guadalupe so special to you?" Pausing for a few seconds, she smiled and responded with two words: "Se quedó" ("She stayed"). Having written and lectured extensively on the theological, cultural, and epistemological significance of Our Lady of Guadalupe, I must admit that I was somewhat stunned by the brevity of the woman's response: "Se quedó."

The more I have reflected on those two words, however, the more I have come to appreciate the challenge that the religious faith of the poor represents for me as a theologian and, especially, as a *Christian* theologian. To allow those words to enter fully into my mind and heart is to be confronted by the radical demands of a truth which, even now, I can only barely glimpse; a truth so profoundly alien to my own way of thinking, as a professional theologian, that even its vague outlines appear otherworldly and, indeed, threatening. During the past few years, I have wrestled for hours with those two words. Finally, out of sheer exhaustion, I have come to rest in their uneasy presence and my reflections have yielded to prayer. This spiritual journey has compelled me to ask some soul-searching questions, a journey that I have undertaken only half-heartedly, at the unwitting bidding of an elderly Mexican woman, a journey that reflects, I think, the challenge that U.S. Latino popular Catholicism poses for the Church, for theology, for the professional theologian, and for the Christian.

What Gutiérrez and the *abuelita* have in common is: 1) their belief in a divine love, a divine praxis, that is the *source* and goal of our own praxis, which is in turn an act of *reception* and *response* to that source, and 2) their affirmation that the fullness of that divine love, that divine praxis, becomes visible, or tangible in history in a particular form. Theology and praxis have their source in *the Word* who, together with the communion of saints at whose center He stands, remains with us and *therefore* empowers us to go on. Our ability to act as historical agents, our freedom, our very identity are themselves given us by the God who loved us first, the God who is fully revealed in the wounded body of the Crucified and Risen Christ, in his Mother, in the communion of saints. Echoing Gutiérrez's words, Jon Sobrino observes:

> To be encountered by the Lord is the experience of the love of God. Indeed it is the experience of the fact that love is the reality that discloses to us, and makes us able to be, what we are. It is God's coming to meet us, simply because God loves us, that renders us capable of defining our very selves as who we are, in order, in our turn, to go forth to meet others.... Without a true encounter with God, there can be no true encounter with the poor.... To have genuine love for our sisters and brothers, we must have an experience of the God who first loved us.[15]

The preferential option for the poor accords a privileged status to the *faith* of the poor and in so doing, paradoxically redirects our attention from that faith itself to a *divine* praxis which is the *source* of our own experience, the source of our own praxis, the source of our own life. The grounds for the preferential option for the poor, then, are ultimately *theologi-*

cal: "Gutiérrez insists on commitment to the poor and on the epistemological privilege of their vantage point on *theological* grounds, namely, the special care of the God of the Bible for the poor and God's choice of the oppressed as the favored instrument for the accomplishment of the divine will in history."[16] "The ultimate basis of God's preference for the poor," argues Gutiérrez, "is to be found in God's own goodness and not in any analysis of society or in human compassion, however pertinent these reasons may be."[17] Our ability to recognize, receive, and embrace, in the Crucified and Risen Christ, the concrete, unrepeatable form of God's love as the source of our very identity is inseparable from the ability to embody that love in our social praxis; these are two inseparable dimensions of "Christian praxis" as a praxis of reception and response.

To speak of the act of faith as a response may be belaboring the obvious. Admittedly, Christian theologians have, from the very beginning, understood the act of faith as "response." The principal influence for many contemporary theologians, however, has been modern praxis-based or postmodern contextual methodologies (here, I would include U.S. Hispanic theologians). These methodologies have not only taken historical praxis as their starting point but, at times, have presupposed a particular, modern Western definition of praxis as autonomous agency, which itself is often understood instrumentally. (I have elsewhere argued that even the postmodern deconstruction of the agent-subject presupposes what it claims to reject.)[18] Praxis-based and contextual methodologies have, of course, revolutionized Christian theology by demonstrating not only the ethical but also the *theological* and *epistemological* necessity of a preferential option for the poor. These methods have also underscored the necessarily sociopolitical dimension of our response to God's gratuitous love. What I would now like to suggest, however, is that the option for the poor is itself short-circuited and, indeed, distorted when it is not undertaken, as Gutiérrez demands, "in the light of the Word." That is, we become incapable of recognizing and, *a fortiori*, of affirming a faith and a theology which are neither rationalistic nor conceptualistic but truly incarnational, sacramental in the sense that form and content, sign and signified, are intrinsically related.

For the lived faith of the poor, specifically popular Catholicism, is precisely a faith lived in the light of the Word which, as such, demands a theological reflection itself illumined by that light. These are a faith and a theology for which historical praxis, context, and experience are always themselves incorporated into a divine praxis: orthopraxis presupposes a Theo-praxis and, more specifically, a Christo-praxis. Thus, the praxis on which theology is based is itself derived from and in-formed by the Word who is received as grace, as gift; it is a praxis incorporated from the outset into a communion of saints which, though mystical and spiritual, is also palpable, visible, and real. In Latino popular Catholicism, therefore, the person is in constant, dynamic interaction with the communion of saints, which has the Crucified and Risen Christ at its center, and which, from the outset, shapes and forms the person's praxis. "God loved us first."

Such an understanding of the lived faith of the poor calls into question any separation of form and content, sign and signified, the real and the appearance. For Gutiérrez, "the light of the Word" forms our theology and praxis, which, in turn, must themselves—precisely as *Christian* theology and praxis—con-form to the Word. If I am correct in observing that many theologians, like myself, influenced by liberationist methods have, at least by default, underestimated the importance of the explicitly Christian and explicitly responsive dimensions of Gutiérrez's own definition of theology, we have, at the same time, thereby severed the intrinsic connection between the content of Christian revelation ("love," "freedom," "justice") and its concrete, particular, sociohistorical form (the Word), the intrinsic connection between the sign and the signified. As a result, we read popular Catholicism—a faith-praxis in which, I would suggest, form and content are inseparable—through a nominalist modern, or deconstructivist postmodern lens that distorts and, ultimately, depreciates the lived religion of the poor. More specifically, we have failed to appreciate fully popular Catholicism's *pre*-modern (for lack of a better term) understanding of human action as fundamentally reception and response (hence, relational by definition), and, therefore, popular Catholicism's *pre*-modern understanding of the normative character of the *form* of revelation. I would argue, in other words, that "the faith of the people" as a "lived religion" is fundamentally a praxis of, in Hans Urs von Balthasar's phrase, "seeing the Form." "The content...," contends von Balthasar, "does not lie behind the form (*Gestalt*), but within it. Whoever is not capable of seeing and 'reading' the form will, by the same token, fail to perceive the content. Whoever is not illumined by the form will see no light in the content either."[19] The Latino theologian Alejandro García-Rivera explains the act of "seeing the form" as follows:

> "Seeing" the form, like the act of hearing, is not a selective or controlling act, but an act of surrender to that which is "seen". ...what is being received is the form of that which is other. The reception of that which is other makes unique demands. To receive that which is other means that the other must be received wholly. That which is other can only be experienced in its fullness. Any diminishment of its "otherness," any reduction of detail, any attempt at selectivity is to lose the experience altogether. For it is in the experience of otherness that the inbreaking of God's glory becomes possible.... "Seeing" the form, then, amounts to the capacity to receive the whole of a unique difference. That capacity depends on our willingness to be "formed" by the requirements of that which is

other.... "Seeing" is, paradoxically, an *act* of *recep-tivity* to that which is other.[20]

In the *act* of "seeing the form" of revelation, our praxis and reflection become con-formed to that revelation, for what is revealed "is not revelation and precept, but participation, *communio*."[21]

In Gutiérrez's terms, theological reflection on praxis must be undertaken "in the light of the Word," in the light of the divine praxis that already incorporates our own praxis as an act of reception and response. The *kerygma*, or content of rev-elation, is not externally or accidentally related to its partic-ular sociohistorical embodiment in the Word, in the body of Christ. From within, the Word of God itself illumines us; to perceive the content we must be able to perceive its form. "If we allow ourselves to be contemplated by God, and permit God to operate within us," writes Jon Sobrino, "we shall be able to contemplate God and the world in a unified way, and shall be able to love God and the world in a unified way."[22]

Yet it is precisely "the form" or, in Gutierrez's definition, "the Word" that is relativized in the modern turn to the sub-ject and deconstructed in the postmodern erasure of the sub-ject. Under the sway of a contemporary, Kantian gnosticism in which form becomes merely a pointer to the content that lies "behind" the form, we have become increasingly inca-pable of "seeing the form" as inseparable from the content of faith. Uncomfortable with the *necessarily* physical, bodily, and therefore particular character of revelation—in the Crucified and Risen body of Christ, in the *corpus verum* and *corpus mysticum*, in the *communio sanctorum*—we Christian theologians have too readily relativized that body in favor of some presumably more universalizable content that, since it is not intrinsically related to the form, could just as easily be expressed in other forms, could just as easily appear in dif-ferent clothing. Christ is thus severed from the particular form of his wounded body as it hangs on the Cross, appears to the disciples after the Resurrection, and is given historically in the Eucharist, the ecclesial community, the Church (itself, of course, a social *body*).

We are uncomfortable, especially, with the *wounds* on the body of Christ. We sever the wounded body of Christ from the *kerygma*, which is now free—we assume—to manifest itself in an almost limitless number of forms. Scandalized by the all-too-visible wounds on the *corpus mysticum*, we reject the *corpus verum* in favor of a presumably "purer" community, a "purer" faith. Thus the form becomes essentially irrelevant, as long as its content is affirmed, a content that is necessarily abstract inasmuch as "it" exists outside any determinate form; indeed, we often presume that, in order to salvage the content, we *must* excise it from any particular form. In order to salvage Jesus Christ, we must excise his message, what he "represents," from his wounded concrete, historical body; in order to salvage Christianity, we must excise "it" (whatever "it" is) from its wounded concrete, historical body.

The meaning of the *kerygma* is thus divorced from the wounded historical body in which that *kerygma* becomes really present in history, even if always also eschatologically. For if God is love, and if God is fully revealed in the person of Jesus Christ, then, as von Balthasar avers, "Jesus Christ is what he expresses." Or, in the words of Jon Sobrino, "the genuine Jesus appears both as the bearer of good news and that good news itself."[23] The content of the revelation is *fully* accessible only in and through the form in which it is expressed. This, indeed, is the scandal of the cross, namely, that "the ideal is only to be found in the real, not behind it."[24] It is, likewise, the scandal of the lived faith of the poor.

Von Balthasar unmasks the elitism underlying our inability, as professional theologians, to see the particular form of revelation as a unity of form and content, including the elitism of those of us who desire and claim to be in solidarity with the poor:

in relation to the central phenomenon of revelation we can by no means speak of "signs" which, according to their nature, point beyond themselves to something "signified." Jesus the Man, in his visibleness, is not a sign pointing beyond himself to an invisible "Christ of faith."...Not only everything sacramental and institutional about the Church, but Christ's whole humanity thus becomes all too clearly something for those "simple" Christians who need material crutches, while the advanced and the perfect can dispense with the symbol, whose spiritual core they have been able to reach.[25]

To suggest that it doesn't ultimately matter "what" one believes in, what the particular, concrete form of faith's content is, is to fall into a gnosticism that denies the reality of the body and historicity—and it is, conversely, to dismiss as naïve or infantile the lived religion of the poor, who refuse to thus "spiritualize" Christian revelation, to spiritualize the body of Christ for fear of its wounds. To argue that all forms of religious faith are ultimately reducible to some lowest common denominator of "core values"—and that all that matters is that we abide by these values—is to deny bodily, historical particularity as surely as the assertion of some common "humanity" on the part of white male Europeans denied the bodily, historical particularity of women and other races and cultures. We cannot have it both ways; we can't insist on the irreducible uniqueness of bodily, historical, particular existence and then deny the irreducible uniqueness of the body of Christ, the body on the Cross, in the Eucharist, in the Church—and, therefore, the truth-claims of that body.

For all the dominant U.S. culture's obsession with "the body," our reluctance to affirm the inseparability of the Christian message from its concrete, physical, bodily form in the Crucified and Risen Lord, in the Eucharist, in the materiality of popular Catholicism, and, yes, in the Church, is nothing less than an elitist gnosticism in postmodern guise. Whether the social body that is the Church, or the physical human body, we are repulsed by any body that is wounded, which is to say, we are repulsed by any real body. Referring to the Pauline notion of the body of Christ, Gutiérrez observes: "Readers often regard this theology of the church as simply a beautiful metaphor. However, we must, shocking though this idea may be, see through to the realism that characterizes the Pauline approach. He is speaking of the real body of Christ, which he looks upon as an extension of the incarnation."[26] "Many contemporary Christians," observes William Cavanaugh, "have shied away from the image of the church as the body of Christ, for naming the church as Christ's very body rings of the ecclesiastical triumphalism of past eras.... The danger does not lie, however, in the identification of the church with the body of Christ, but rather in the complete identification of the earthly body with the heavenly....the unfaithfulness of the church in the present age is based to some extent precisely on its failure to take itself seriously as the continuation of Christ's body in the world and to conform itself, body and soul, not to the world but to Christ (Romans 12:2)."[27]

And the character of the Church as a concrete, historical, social body, a *corpus verum*, has important implications for the Christian theologian. "I begin from the conviction," insists Gutiérrez, "that the theological task is a vocation that arises and is exercised in the heart of the ecclesial community. Indeed, its starting point is the gift of faith in which we welcome the truth of the Word of God, and its contributions are at the service of the evangelizing mission of the church. This ecclesial location gives theology its raison d'être, determines its scope, nurtures it with the sources of revelation— Scripture and Tradition—enriches it with the recognition of the charism of the magisterium and dialogue with the magisterium, and puts it in contact with other ecclesial functions."[28] Gutiérrez notes that the Church's visibility as a distinct social body is a crucial element in its ability to stand in defense of the poor in history.[29]

Our Western preoccupation with "the body" as an abstract ideal masks an underlying depreciation of wounded bodies: the wounded, if glorified, body of Christ as well as the wounded bodies of the poor. Gutiérrez notes that:

> some Christian milieus, usually in affluent countries, have promoted a reevaluation and "celebration" of the human body in cultural expressions—for example, some modern dances and other bodily forms of expression that are used in eucharistic celebrations.... Whatever the merits of this claim, I want to note here that the concern for the corporeal in Latin American spiritual experiences has come about in quite a different way.... It is not "*my* body," but the "body of the poor person"—the weak and languishing body of the poor—that has made the material a part of a spiritual outlook.[30]

The failure to see the form, to see the body of Christ *as it is*, ultimately prevents us from truly appreciating, truly taking seriously the lived religion of the poor, which is anything but gnostic. The people about whom Gutiérrez speaks do not flee from the wounded bodies in their midst to the illusory security of abstract, ideal bodies; they are not concerned with abstract ideals but with real persons. They know that "the ideal is only to be found in the real, not behind it."[31]

The Way, The Truth and the Life: The Form as Normative

Ultimately, of course, our inability to appreciate the character of lived religion and, specifically, lived Christianity as a praxis of reception-response to a gift whose very particularity, historicity, and physicality prevent us from extracting the gift's content from its form results in an inability to affirm the *normativity* of that form. Quite simply, the question of truth is reduced to a question of either meaning or usefulness: Is the faith of the poor meaningful for them? Does it work for them? Does it liberate? In my own work in the Latino community over the years, however, what the people have reminded me over and over again (though I haven't always been able or ready to listen) is that, for them, the fundamental question is, quite simply, "Is it *true*?"—not in an abstract, propositional sense, but in the sense of a reality that makes ultimate claims on our whole lives, a reality which defines us, gives us our identity and mission. When we are encountered by Christ, contends Gutiérrez, "we discover where the Lord lives and what the mission is that has been entrusted to us."[32] Thus, for the poor, liberation depends precisely on the truth, the reality, of the body of Christ and its claims. If those claims are true, if Jesus Christ was crucified and raised from the dead, if *La Morenita* did appear to Juan Diego, then everything else will follow from that truth, because it is the truth itself that saves and liberates us by con-forming us to itself, by drawing us into a participation in its own particular form, its own life. Our very identity is not "achieved" but is given us by that truth, by the Word, which itself overpowers us.

For the marginalized in society (and, I would argue, for the majority of people outside the ambit of modern Western culture), the most fundamental question is not, "Will it liberate?" or "Do I find it meaningful?" but "Is it true?" or "Is it real?" (though not in a modern conceptualist way that contrasts the symbolic and the real). And yet this is the very question that, in the dominant U.S. culture, we are reluctant to ask or, perhaps, are incapable of asking.

Does popular Catholicism liberate? Or does Guadalupe liberate? Does lived religion save us? Or does Jesus save us? Or does it matter? "Be the problems of the 'truth' of Christ what they may," writes Sobrino, "his credibility is assured as far as the poor are concerned, for he maintained his nearness

to them to the end. In this sense the cross of Jesus is seen as
the paramount symbol of Jesus' approach to the poor, and
hence the guarantee of his indisputable credibility."[33]
Because Jesus accompanies us, he is real, and because he is
real, he liberates. And the Cross is the guarantee that he
does, in fact, remain with us, that he does, in fact, walk with
us even today:

> A vague, undifferentiated faith in God is not
> enough to generate hope. Not even the admission
> that God is mighty, or that God has made promis-
> es, will do this. Something else besides the gener-
> ic or abstract attributes of the divinity is necessary
> in order to generate hope. This distinct element—
> which, furthermore, is the fundamental character-
> istic of the Christian God—is something the poor
> have discovered viscerally, and in reality itself:
> the nearness of God. God instills hope because
> God is credible, and God is credible because God
> is close to the poor.... Therefore when the poor
> hear and understand that God delivers up the
> Son, and that God is crucified—something that to
> the mind of the nonpoor will always be either a
> scandal or a pure anthropomorphism—then, par-
> adoxically, their hope becomes real. The poor
> have no problems with God. The classic question
> of theodicy—the "problem of God," the atheism
> of protest—so reasonably posed by the nonpoor,
> is no problem at all for the poor (who in good
> logic ought of course to be the ones to pose it).[34]

The Cross, which for the nonpoor is a sign of God's absence,
is, for the poor, the assurance of God's presence—not just
any god, not just a "vague" or "generic" god, but the God of
Jesus Christ, the God who accompanies us today.

I wonder, therefore, whether our fear of the truth-question
in favor of an essentially instrumental (as long as it "works"
for them...) and abstract ("love," "justice," "freedom")

notion of religious faith does not mask a patronizing refusal to take seriously, to respect the sacramental realism of the faith of the poor. What I mean to ask is whether a theology that, in the way in which these terms are understood in most modern and postmodern Western theology, takes "human experience" or even "praxis" as its methodological starting point can ultimately do justice to the faith of the poor. This is a faith that—contrary to all modern (and, I would argue, postmodern theologies)—does not take the autonomous, self-constituting human subject *per se* as its starting point at all but rather affirms, at great personal cost, a transcendent reality to which the human subject *responds* and in which he/she *participates* in the act of faith, or praxis of faith. A theologian, like myself, may be inspired by the Good Friday *Via Crucis* as a source of identity, empowerment, and counter-cultural resistance among U.S. Hispanics (indeed, I have written along these very lines). Yet, for the people themselves, the source of their strength and liberation is not the *Via Crucis* itself, not the values "behind" this religious ritual, but the God of Jesus Christ, the God whose Son suffered torture and crucifixion for us, and so continues today to suffer torture and crucifixion with us. For the *abuelitas*, what empowers and liberates is not the *experience*, not the ritual or the performance or the symbols, not the meaning behind the symbols, but *God*, and not just any god but *this* God, the God whose Son conquers death by dying on the Cross, the God who dies accompanied by his sorrowful mother. "To profess 'this Jesus,' to acknowledge 'Jesus the Christ,'" argues Gutiérrez, "is to express a conviction. It is not simply putting a name and a title together; it is an authentic confession of faith. It is the assertion of an identity: the Jesus of history, the son of Mary, the carpenter of Nazareth, the preacher of Galilee, the crucified, *is* the Only Begotten of God, the Christ, the Son of God."[35] "If we believe in Jesus as the Son," avers Sobrino, "it is because in him the truth and love of the mystery of God have been shown in an unrepeatable form, and been shown in a way that is totally convincing to a crucified people who have no problem in accepting Jesus' unrepeatable relationship with God so that they can confess him to be in truth the Son of God."[36]

If our praxis is liberating, it is only because it affirms something that is true. As Sobrino insists: "The resurrection of the one who was crucified is *true* [emphasis in the original]. Let it be foolishness, as it was for the Corinthians. But without this foolishness, because it is true—or without this truth, because it is foolish—the resurrection of Jesus will only be one more symbol of hope in survival after death that human beings have designed in their religions or philosophies. It will not be the Christian symbol of hope."[37] For the poor, the Resurrection is not merely the assurance of life *after* death; it is, above all, the assurance of life *before* death.[38] Because Jesus lives, we can dare to live. Either Jesus Christ lived, died, and conquered death for us, or he did not. Either he is the Way, the Truth, and the Life, or he is not. Either he accompanies us in our struggles today, or he does not.

The luxury of avoiding the question of truth is one accorded us theologians in the comfort of our offices, libraries, and homes; it is not a luxury available to a mother watching her child dying of hunger, or burying a child who was just caught in gang crossfire. Only our comfort, security, and affluence allow us to avoid questions of truth; there are no poststructuralists in foxholes, or in *barrios*—at least, I haven't found any yet. It is our ease of life that allows us to wait around until all the data are in before ever having to answer the question, "Is it true?" Not just in a disinterested way, but as a question whose answer makes ultimate demands on our lives.

Like Peter, who, after Jesus was arrested and taken to Caiaphas, followed Jesus "at a distance" and "sat with the guards to see the end" of Jesus' interrogation before Caiaphas (Matthew 26:58), I can too easily become accustomed to observing the interrogation of Jesus from a distance, waiting until all the data are in, until the exegetes, sociologists, literary critics, and post-colonial theorists have rendered their verdicts, before daring to render mine. Too often I remain content merely to observe from a distance as Jesus is put on trial and his testimony is dissected and deconstructed. Until, that is, I find myself confronted by the Cross; until I am confronted by the poor, in whom Christ continues to be crucified today.

Christ on the Cross does not have the luxury of avoiding the truth question until all the evidence is in. Indeed, *against* all the available evidence, he remains resolute in his faith: *"My God, my God,* why have you abandoned me?" Confronting death daily, the poor do not have the luxury of postponing an answer to the truth-question until all the evidence is in. A dying person does not have the luxury of observing Jesus' trial from a distance; he or she is faced squarely with a decision between belief and despair; not just belief in general, or in the abstract, but belief in either *this* or *that*, belief in either Jesus or Caiaphas. And, for the dying person, the difference between the "this" and the "that" is precisely what matters most; it is *all* that matters. To the hungry person, the truth of Christ's claims about himself is much more than an academic issue, to be debated and deconstructed by exegetes and theologians. If I take that hungry person seriously, then, so too must I be willing to render a verdict on those claims. Am I willing to stake my own life on those truth-claims? If I take the faith of the *abuelita* seriously, that is, if I truly respect *her*, I must eventually render *my own* verdict on her statement, "se quedó" (she stayed)—whether that verdict is positive or negative. The *abuelita* has certainly rendered *her* verdict. Will I engage that verdict, "se quedó," or will I ignore it, pretending that, after all, it doesn't matter whether the *abuelita's* verdict is correct or just naïve? To refuse to render my own verdict while, at the same time, re-interpreting hers in order to make it more "theologically acceptable," in order to "get behind" the

appearance to understand "what it really means," even if
with the best of intentions, is in fact to patronize her: "Isn't it
quaint how she really believes all those things even though,
as all of us theologians know, whether all that stuff is actually true is not really the important thing." (Hence, also the
importance of *critical* reflection as itself a necessary aspect of
the option for the poor, a necessary dimension of solidarity
with and respect for the poor.)

As embodied in U.S. Latino/a popular Catholicism, the
faith of the poor demands from us that we stake our own
existence on a reality, a truth that is not reducible to abstract
notions of love, justice, or freedom, but that irrupts in our
world in the form of the Cross, thereby subverting and over-
turning our own conceptions of love, justice, and freedom. It
demands, moreover, that we understand the *act* of receiving
a gift, or giving thanks, as indeed an *act*, as *praxis*. Such a
contemplative faith-stance becomes increasingly difficult,
however, in a society in which we are taught from childhood
that to be fully human we must be able and willing to grab,
to grasp, to acquire. We are indeed a contra-ceptive culture,
a culture obsessed with "doing" and averse to "receiving"—
as if the two were mutually exclusive.[39]

Yet this is not at all the understanding of freedom embodied in Latino popular Catholicism, where freedom involves
the capacity for receptivity, a capacity for responding to an
Other. The ability to receive is precisely what empowers one
to act. *Because* we are indeed accompanied by the Crucified
and Risen Christ, we have the courage to go on. Thus, for the
poor themselves, the question of truth is essential. Unless
Jesus Christ is the definitive form of God's love, then Jesus
Christ is but one among many possible forms of "love,"
which is then reduced to an abstract concept to be "clothed"
in interchangeable forms. Jesus, then, is not the one who
empowers us by accompanying us in our struggles. He
becomes, instead, merely a role model, an example to be
emulated—one among many others.

For the poor, whether or not Jesus Christ was truly raised from the dead is not an issue of secondary importance, ultimately reducible to some general affirmation of the "goodness of life"; whether or not Our Lady of Guadalupe actually appeared to Juan Diego is not an issue of secondary importance, ultimately reducible to some general affirmation of God's love for the poor; whether or not the dead are raised is not an issue of secondary importance, ultimately reducible to some general affirmation of the indestructibility of life, or a belief that our ancestors live on in our memories—though, of course, all that is true. But it is true *because* Jesus Christ was raised from the dead.

Moreover, to affirm the centrality of the Word as a unity of form and content, or sign and signified, is by no means to preclude pluralism; on the contrary, this is itself demanded by the truth of the Cross. Authentic pluralism and dialogue preclude either an abstract universalism or an abstract relativism, both of which deny the reality of *the form*, the reality of the particular as itself a precondition for pluralism and dialogue; both an abstract universalism and an abstract relativism represent fundamentally gnostic denials of the necessarily material character of revelation. Universalism and relativism are equally abstract, ahistorical denials of the sacramental principle, the assertion that the universal is necessarily mediated by the particular. Authentic dialogue *presupposes* that each participant makes normative truth-claims. Where religion is incapable of making normative truth-claims, religious faith will be reduced to a matter of personal taste. (And there is no point in discussing matters of personal taste: "I'm OK, you're OK.")

Insofar as, for Gustavo Gutiérrez, the preferential option for the poor calls us to read the gospel through the eyes of the poor, it subverts all our attempts to deconstruct that Gospel, to spiritualize or privatize it, to reduce it to a literary text, to reduce it to a helpful but ultimately non-essential guide for praxis, to reduce it to a matter of personal taste.

The preferential option for the poor thus calls us to "see the form," to apprehend and embrace the Crucified and Risen Christ revealed in history, in the Eucharist, in the visible Church, and in the Church's Scriptures, as the one who invites us to participate in his life. To participate in Christ's life is to do so wholeheartedly and single-mindedly. The demands He makes of us are absolute, that is, they call for a commitment of our *whole* life, in its full integrity. And we will only respond to that demand if we can embrace it as in fact true—not just meaningful, helpful, or empowering, but *true*—and if we can do so with the sense of urgency of those persons in our midst who confront death on a daily basis.

As Gutiérrez reminds us, Jesus asks his disciples and asks us: "Who do *you* say that I am? You; not the others. …what is asked refers to an objective reality, something exterior to the disciples… The question pulls us out of our subjective world and, 'turning us inside out,' locates the point of reference of our faith, and of our life, beyond ourselves, in the person of Jesus."[40] And the question, "Who do you say that I am?" demands not a theoretical answer but an integral answer; we answer that question with our whole lives.[41] As theologians, we might prefer the more abstract question, "Who do *people* say that I am? Who do *the crowds* say that I am?" But the Crucified and Risen Lord confronts each of us with the much more demanding question, "Who do *you* say that I am?"

Ultimately, the lived religion of the poor calls me, as a Catholic theologian, to conversion. If I want to understand popular Catholicism, I must allow myself to be transformed by the same God who accompanies the community on the *Via Crucis*, by his Mother, who stayed. For the poor themselves have no interest in "popular Catholicism"; most have never even heard the term. It is not "popular Catholicism" that they look to for hope; they look to the Crucified; they look to his Mother; they look to the saints. Can I, as a professional theologian, allow myself to be illumined by that light? "It is not the same thing merely to treat things scientifically and doctrinally," observes Sobrino, "as really to shed light on them. It is not the same thing to speak of many things as to allow things to speak for themselves."[42] But, of course, that presupposes that those "things" really do exist and are not merely social, cultural, or literary constructions or conventions. "Theology," argues Sobrino, "must allow God to speak."[43]

If taken seriously, then, the faith of the people overturns contemporary theological assumptions, not by proposing dramatically new theological truths, but by making present on the margins of our society and Church centuries-old, long-forgotten truths—indeed, by refusing to surrender the very question of truth itself. With Jon Sobrino, the faith of the people challenges us to ask:

> Is there anything that is ultimate and incapable of being manipulated, anything that makes an ultimate demand on human beings in the form of promise and fulfillment? Is there anything that will prevent us from relativizing everything, reducing everything to a lowest common denominator in terms of value, although perhaps without our knowing why we should not make such a reduction? Is there anything that makes a total demand on us—anything to remind us that despite the ideals of a consumer society, despite the growing preoccupation with material security and a life of self-centeredness, as we find for example in many places in the First World, there is after all a "something else," and a "someone else," and not just as a factual datum, but as a "something" and a "someone" in terms of which we either succeed or fail in our own self-fulfillment?[44]

Latino popular Catholicism embodies a "dangerous memory of suffering" that I dare not confront because it forces me to do what years of studying and writing about theological method, hermeneutics, and epistemology have made it possible for me to avoid doing, namely, answer the questions Sobrino poses. In short, the faith of the Latino community calls for a new *ressourcement*, one born not in the *aulas* of Le Saulchoir and Fourviére but in the *barrios* of New York City, Chicago, and Los Angeles, in the *favelas* of Sao Paulo and Rio, and in the *barriadas* of Lima and Mexico City. The faith of the people calls for a *ressourcement from the margins*, a retrieval of the wounded, yet glorified body of Christ as the locus of theology. It is a faith that, with Georges Bernanos, reminds us that "our church is the church of the saints" and that "we must seek the true cause of our misfortunes in the disincarnation of the Word."[45] The late Henri Nouwen already noted this a number of years ago when, reflecting on his experience working alongside Gustavo Gutiérrez in the slums outside Lima, Nouwen observed:

> As one who has been exposed to many styles of theological liberalism, I am struck by the orthodoxy of this Christ-centered spirituality.... The Christians of Latin America, as Gustavo himself once pointed out to me, came to a realization of the social dimensions of their faith without going through a modernistic phase. He used Archbishop Romero as a striking example. Through his direct contact with the suffering people, that traditional churchman became a social critic without ever rejecting, or even criticizing, his traditional past. In fact, Archbishop Romero's traditional understanding of God's presence in history was the basis and source of his courageous protest against the exploitation and oppression of the people of El Salvador.[46]

A Latino *ressourcement* would retrieve the sacramental understanding of the unity of form and content, sign and signified, as itself a "dangerous memory" that calls for and makes possible "courageous protest." In so doing, the faith of the poor will eventually force us all to take a stand, to declare: "*This* I believe; on *this* I am willing to stake my life." Then and only then will we be liberated, freed to commit ourselves wholeheartedly to struggle alongside the God who stays with the victims of history, the God whose nearness inspires in us a hope against hope. Insofar as our own praxis is conformed to God's cruciform praxis in history, we can become participants in the historical struggle for liberation:

> Train us, Lord, to fling ourselves upon the impossible, for behind the impossible is your grace and your presence; we cannot fall into emptiness. The future is an enigma, our road is covered by mist, but we want to go on giving ourselves, because you continue hoping amid the night and weeping tears through a thousand human eyes.[47]

Notes

1. See Orlando O. Espín, *The Faith of the People: Theological Reflections on Popular Catholicism* (Maryknoll, NY: Orbis Books, 1997).

2. Peter Casarella, "Questioning the Primacy of Method: On Sokolowski's *Eucharistic Presence*," *Communio* 22 (1995): 670-671.

3. Ibid., 669.

4. Ibid., 675.

5. Ibid., 700.

6. Thomas Merton, *Conjectures of a Guilty Bystander* (Garden City, NY: Doubleday Image, 1968), 265.

7. Gustavo Gutiérrez, *A Theology of Liberation: History, Politics, and Salvation* (Maryknoll, NY: Orbis Books, 1988), 11.

8. Gustavo Gutiérrez, *The Density of the Present: Selected Writings* (Maryknoll, NY: Orbis Books, 1999), 141.

9. Gustavo Gutiérrez, *We Drink from Our Own Wells: The Spiritual Journey of a People* (Maryknoll, NY: Orbis Books, 1984), 109-112.

10. Gustavo Gutiérrez, *On Job: God-Talk and the Suffering of the Innocent* (Maryknoll, NY: Orbis Books, 1987), xiii.

11. Gutiérrez, *We Drink from Our Own Wells*, 96.

12. Gutiérrez, *The Truth Shall Make You Free: Confrontations* (Maryknoll, NY: Orbis Books, 1990), 101.

13. James B. Nickoloff, introduction to *Gustavo Gutiérrez: Essential Writings*, ed. James B. Nickoloff (Maryknoll, NY: Orbis Books, 1996), 9.

14. Gutiérrez, *On Job*, 89.

15. Jon Sobrino, *Spirituality of Liberation: Toward Political Holiness* (Maryknoll, NY: Orbis Books, 1988), 56-58.

16. Nickoloff, "Introduction," 18.

17. Gutiérrez, *On Job*, xiii.

18. Roberto S. Goizueta, *Caminemos con Jesús: Toward a Hispanic/Latino Theology of Accompaniment* (Maryknoll, NY: Orbis Books, 1995).

19. Hans Urs von Balthasar, *Seeing the Form*, vol. 1 of *The Glory of the Lord* (San Francisco: Ignatius Press, 1982), 151.

20. Alejandro García-Rivera, *The Community of the Beautiful: A Theological Aesthetics* (Collegeville, MN: The Liturgical Press, 1999), 88-89.

21. Hans Urs von Balthasar, *Truth is Symphonic: Aspects of Christian Pluralism* (San Francisco: Ignatius Press, 1987), 38.

22. Sobrino, 69.

23. Ibid., 170.

24. Von Balthasar, *Truth is Symphonic*, 76.

25. Von Balthasar, *Seeing the Form*, 437-438.

26. Gutiérrez, *We Drink from Our Own Wells*, 69.

27. William T. Cavanaugh, *Torture and Eucharist: Theology, Politics, and the Body of Christ* (Oxford: Blackwell, 1998), 233.

28. Nickoloff, ed., *Gustavo Gutiérrez*, 270.

29. Gutiérrez, *A Theology of Liberation*, 206, n. 18.

30. Gutiérrez, *We Drink from Our Own Wells*, 102-103.

31. Von Balthasar, *Truth is Symphonic*, 76.

32. Gutiérrez, *We Drink from Our Own Wells*, 38.

33. Sobrino, 171.

34. Ibid., 166-167.

35. Gutiérrez, *We Drink from Our Own Wells*, 46.

36. Jon Sobrino, *Jesus in Latin America* (Maryknoll, NY: Orbis Books, 1987), 165.

37. Ibid., 158.

38. I am indebted to Professor Otto Maduro for this insight.

39. A provocative analysis of modern "contra-ceptive" culture is set forth in Dennis Martin, *Give and Take in the Grail-Quest, Gawain, and the Roman Missal: Why Perceval Just Doesn't Get It*, unpublished manuscript.

40. Gutiérrez, *We Drink from Our Own Wells*, 48.

41. Ibid., 51.

42. Sobrino, *Spirituality of Liberation*, 70.

43. Ibid., 71.

44. Ibid., 105.

45. Georges Bernanos, quoted in Jean-Francois Six, *Light of the Night: The Last Eighteen Months in the Life of Thérèse of Lisieux* (Notre Dame, IN: University of Notre Dame Press, 1998), 175-176.

46. Henri Nouwen, foreword to Gutiérrez, *We Drink from Our Own Wells*, xviii.

47. Luis Espinal, quoted in Gutiérrez, *On Job*, 91-92.

Lived Research on Lived Religion

Fredric M. Roberts
*Director, Metropolitan Detroit and Lansing
Congregation Study Project &
Associate Professor of Anthropology
at Michigan State University*

I would like to address the theme of "Lived Christianity" by discussing the basic tenets and approach of some social science research my colleagues and I have been conducting with the support of the Lilly Endowment, what we call the Metropolitan Detroit and Lansing Congregation Study Project (MDLCSP).[1] As the project has evolved over the last one and a half years, I have seen it develop a logic and life of its own. So here my topic will be "Lived Research on Lived Religion." In particular, I want to discuss the challenges and complexities of understanding lived religion in the context of a multidisciplinary, social scientific study of American mainline Christian congregations.

Defining Lived Religion

A number of very distinguished scholars have provided a variety of sophisticated definitions of lived religion.[2] For purposes of this paper, however, I will be defining lived religion quite simply and then illustrating how complex it is to study such an apparently simple phenomenon. Here I define lived religion, specifically lived Christianity, as the types of knowledge, beliefs, practices, experiences, and feelings that

38

members of Christian congregations bring to their religious lives. My emphasis is on the varied sources and resources different individuals *bring* to religious life, because an individual's knowledge, beliefs, practices, experiences, and feelings can originate both in the realm of religion and outside it. Even when the sources and resources are religious, they are not necessarily Christian. Congregation members may draw from Judaism, Islam, Buddhism, New Age spirituality, etc. in constructing their own belief systems and practices.

There are at least three dimensions to lived Christianity as I have defined it. First there are the types of knowledge, practices, beliefs, experiences, and feelings individuals bring to the *religious elements of congregational life*. In some cases, those religious dimensions can be obvious and pervasive— as at an intense Bible study. In other situations, they may seem obscure or almost nonexistent—as at a trustees' discussion of how to deal with a leaky roof. Usually, however, the border between the sacred and the profane is crossed so often that an observer feels like a spectator trying to follow the ball at a particularly lively tennis match.

Second, there is lived Christianity *beyond the boundaries of the congregation*. Only a small portion of a congregation member's life is lived in the congregation itself. What is the character of an individual's religious life in the family or at work? To what extent does life in the congregation influence those key arenas and vice versa? What role do outside religious groups (e.g., Bible studies at a church of a different denomination or involvement in Promise Keepers) play in someone's religious life? Again, we are faced with charting a sometimes bewildering series of border crossings, as knowledge, practices, beliefs, experiences, and feelings flow back and forth from one facet of an individual's religious life to another.

Finally, there is the *historical dimension of lived Christianity*. The sources and resources that an individual brings to his or her contemporary religious life (inside or outside the congregation) must also be understood as the product of a long and complex development over time. Once again border crossings are more the rule than the exception, as a person routinely draws upon resources from many stages of his or her life in facing contemporary religious challenges. To understand a person's lived religion today, a researcher must have some understanding of that person's spiritual life history.

Knowledge Encounters

Let me now describe the origin of our research project, in order to explain why I have put knowledge first in my definition of lived religion.[3] The MDLCSP began as a collaborative effort by Michael McCallion, Director of Pastoral Resources of the Roman Catholic Archdiocese of Detroit, and myself. Previously, we had separately carried out extensive field research on different facets of the implementation of the post-Vatican II liturgical renewal in the American Catholic Church.[4]

McCallion and I had noticed how common it was for religious leaders—ordained and lay, professional and nonprofessional—to be met with less than enthusiastic responses from many members in a congregation when they come to a church with a new idea (e.g., on how to change worship or how to study the Bible or how to stimulate church growth). All too frequently these religious leaders feel rejected or angry when they meet with resistance. They are tempted to accuse the people in the pews of being ignorant, uneducated, unenlightened ("If they only understood me or knew what I know, they would agree with me") or to argue that the people in the pews are afraid of change.

Our previous research suggested that, in fact, the situation is far more complex. Religious leaders frequently level these types of charges when they actually know very little about what is going on in the minds of the people in the pew. What is frequently occurring are what we term knowledge encounters.[5] By knowledge encounters, we mean that people in the pews are apt to be evaluating these suggested changes on the basis of their own alternative and often-competing forms of belief and knowledge.

Today a major challenge for religious leaders is to find out what people really do believe and why, so the leaders can deal sensitively and constructively with opposition to their proposals. This isn't a simple task. Perhaps more than at any other time in our history Americans today are faced with an incredible variety of sources of knowledge, information, and influence about religion. These range from what they learned from their parents, or school and church as children, to what their spouses (who often come from different church backgrounds) believe, to the impact of their work life, to the influence of their own children. The sources include the articles on religion they read in newspapers and magazines, as well as the television shows and movies they watch (from Public Broadcasting System documentaries to "Oprah" to "Touched by an Angel" and from *The Ten Commandments* to *Jesus Christ Superstar* to *Babette's Feast* to *The Apostle*). Increasingly, the sources include what people find as they surf the Internet. In addition, there is the powerful impact of the life crises many people have had to face at various stages of their lives.

Our project aims at finding answers to two key questions: In the light of this abundance of competing forms and sources of religious knowledge, what do people really believe? What criteria do people use to decide what they will and will not believe on key issues of religious faith and practice? Our comparative research in congregations in the metropolitan Detroit and Lansing areas will allow us to see how the answers to those questions are affected by such factors as gender, social class, ethnicity, generation, denomination, congregation size and history, forms of pastoral and lay leadership, etc.

I should emphasize that this is an applied project, to help

religious leaders at every level. The Lilly Endowment agreed to fund this project because McCallion and I were able to convince Endowment officials that we were not "typical" academics whose main goal was to publish in journals read only by other academics. We expect, instead, to make presentations concerning our findings and to provide workshops at seminaries, at national and regional denominational meetings, and at individual congregations and parishes. Our writings will target pastoral types of journals and magazines, as well as academic venues.

Lived Research

Having provided you with a sense of what I mean by lived Christianity and by knowledge encounters, let me turn to the issue of lived research. It is crucial to recognize the varied sources and resources that congregation members bring to their religious lives. It is equally important to acknowledge that researchers bring to studies of Christian congregations their own types of knowledge, beliefs, practices, experiences, and feelings, and that these powerfully influence the outcome of their study. I want in this case to underscore "experiences and feelings" and emphasize that I am referring not only to differences in theoretical orientations, though they are obviously important. I want to stress that when researching a topic as emotionally charged and intimate as religion, the whole researcher is engaged in the study. This is particularly true for our project, where the main techniques of study are participant observation and interviews.

The types of questions we are exploring can't be answered in any depth by looking at how people respond to multiple choice questions on a survey. People will usually express themselves openly on our types of questions when a trust is developed between the researcher and the faith community. It is also necessary for researchers to go beyond what people say about their beliefs and values to observing how people actually behave as they participate in the daily life of the church. That is why we become, in essence, new members of the congregations, participant observers in a wide variety of activities.

There are four of us conducting the research over a period of almost three years. "Inside-outsider" most accurately describes our role as researchers in those churches. As participant observers, we seek to be as inside the community as possible, both in terms of access to people and events and in terms of gaining a sense of what it is like to be a member of that congregation. But as researchers, we are always also outsiders. People know that, however intense our present involvement, we are not there for the long run. More important, our primary role as observers/researchers is very apparent in the form of our ever-present open notebooks.

Although we are primarily observers, the impact of what we as researchers bring along with us to our lived study of lived Christianity is particularly evident in this project because we have worked closely as a team. The two sociologists and two anthropologists on the staff meet weekly or biweekly, to discuss our recent experiences. In our discussions, it is often very evident how our different personal backgrounds influence our research. In some cases these are differences in theoretical orientation. We differ from each other on such fundamental issues as how "real" we consider the spiritual experiences our subjects report. We differ from each other in our areas of religious expertise—from embodied religious knowledge to knowledge of biblical hermeneutics. We differ from each other in what aspects of an event or interview we most carefully observe and remember.

In terms of our personal "feelings and emotions," these individual differences are equally significant. Sitting in discussions at Protestant congregations when scathing comments are being made about the Catholic Church by ex-Catholics and others can pose quite a challenge to the two practicing Catholics on the team. One of my project colleagues, Randal Hepner, had been intensely involved in controversies with Protestant fundamentalists at an earlier stage of his life. It is hard for him not to revert to the former combatant role, or what he might term his instructive mode, when someone in a Bible study begins to espouse what sounds like a fundamentalist position. That urge to leap into an interesting or lively discussion is particularly strong for me when the talk touches on issues that are personally important, for example, some aspect of being a father or a husband that happens to be on my mind at that time. In practice, the border between participant and observer is not all that clear-cut or easy to maintain in lived research.

This is especially true when you are working in your own society, where you are not perceived as being radically different from those you are studying, and people can assume you have relevant opinions on the issues that matter to them. Also, fieldwork involves reciprocity. When people tell you about their lives, they expect to find out something about yours. Just as subjects are constantly making decisions about what to reveal and what not to reveal to a researcher, so we, as researchers, are faced with the same challenge. When asked to give a witness as a member of a retreat team, for example, I have to be very careful about what I can say about myself. I need to respond openly, but not become the center of attention nor say something that could offend the people with whom I am working.

There is one other major way in which this is lived research. This study has taken on its own life, evolving over time. A major step in the evolution of the project came while it was still a proposal. McCallion and I originally planned a relatively modest study focusing almost exclusively on a small number of Catholic parishes and submitted a preliminary proposal on that scale to the Lilly Endowment. When Lilly Endowment officials, apparently intrigued by our knowledge encounter approach, asked if we would be willing to expand our research on knowledge encounters to include mainline Protestants, indeed to have a Protestant majority (eight mainline Protestant congregations and five Catholic parishes), we gulped, but leaped at the offer.

It was a kind of dream come true to be provided with the resources to have a team of scholars work for several years on our study. But you have to be careful about what you wish for. Initially, we were daunted by our innocence about matters Protestant. It wasn't until later that we occasionally felt overwhelmed by the sheer scale of the project.

Denominational and Pastoral Staff Interviews

We planned to study six congregations in the first year of field research and seven in the second. Since we assumed that we had a pretty good feel for the Catholic scene, we decided that it was better to tackle the unknown challenges of mainline American Protestantism first, choosing five Protestant congregations and only one Catholic parish for our initial sample. From the perspective of this presentation, it's not really important to describe the details of how and why we chose particular congregations (i.e., the intricacies of our sampling criteria). Rather, I want to focus on one facet of our experience in picking the congregations, since it has had a major influence on the evolution of our project. As a way of learning about the Protestant denominations, as well as helping us in choosing our research sites, we conducted interviews with regional officials and experts from nine mainline Protestant denominations. Interviews always began with a description of the project and then moved to questions on both the personal background of the representative or expert (i.e., a brief life history) and on the denomination's distinctive features, current challenges and controversies, most influential figures, ideas, and institutions (particularly related to worship) on the national and regional levels. These subsequent questions clarified for the interviewee the types of issues that were central to our research and specifically what we meant by "knowledge encounters." We then felt more comfortable in explaining the types of congregations we were looking for and in asking for suggestions.

In retrospect, what is very striking to me was a major source of knowledge that denomination people frequently drew upon in answering our questions—church consultants and church consultant organizations. Names like Loren Mead, Lyle Schaller, and the Alban Institute were repeated like some sort of mantra. These were not names with which I was familiar. When I returned to campus and checked our university's library for Loren Mead, Lyle Schaller, and Alban Institute; I found almost nothing.[6] This happened frequently as I checked up on references to other authors and book titles that I was picking up in my interviews. On the other hand, the names of academics who seemed to me to be authorities on the contemporary American religious scene, e.g., Nancy Ammerman, Robert Orsi, R. Stephen Warner, or Robert Wuthnow, seldom if ever came up in the interviews.[7]

Aside from displaying my own embarrassing lack of knowledge and suggesting the apparent gap between the academic and church professional literatures, there are two points to be made about this experience. First, we had been at pains to assure Lilly Endowment officials and then these denomination people that the project's goals were practical and applied—helping religious leaders cope with the complex problems that knowledge encounters posed for them when they are trying to implement change in churches. But we found it much less difficult than we expected to convince church leaders of our usefulness. Apparently, these church consultants, who draw upon concepts and data from the social sciences, command a very high level of respect. Denominational leaders seemed to see us as a subspecies of consultant. This was probably a major reason why they were willing to sit down and talk with us when we called them—often out of the blue—to ask for an appointment. As important, the existence of the widely accepted role of church consultant provided us with what was an appropriate and acceptable role when we approached both pastors and their congregations to receive permission to begin research in their churches.

As with the denomination representatives, in virtually every case the pastors we called were responsive to our requests for interviews, as well as generous in the time they spent in our first meetings. Our initial interviews with pastors, which covered both their personal life histories and their views of the key characteristics of their own churches, served as our introduction to the pastors and the congregation, as well as the pastors' introduction to us and our project.

For me one of the most complex elements of this lived research has been my personal relationship with pastors and other members of the pastoral staff. It is hard not to develop strong feelings about them and very easy to form close attachments. After all, we have a deep-seated interest in common, a preoccupation with the congregation, its problems, and challenges. Few people spend as much time in the church building and are as likely to be at the same wide variety of congregation meetings and events as the pastoral staff and the researcher.

Here my insider-outsider status certainly played a role. Pastoral staff members and I do have intense discussions on how to solve the problems of the larger Church. However, most of the concerns that absorb both the pastoral staff and me are theological, spiritual, and management issues as they are embodied in the specific problems of specific people at a specific time and place. As an insider, I increasingly know the backgrounds of the people involved and the history of an issue as it has played itself out in a particular congregation. Yet I remain an outsider, a non-player who can offer a sympathetic ear and a perspective informed by a different type of expertise.

In reality, all field studies are dialogues between the researcher and those he or she studies—with each side asking and answering questions. My relationships with pastors and pastoral staffs involve professionals on both sides who deal with often intimate, confidential information. Each side has important ethical standards to follow in order to safeguard those confidences. Our conversations, while quite valuable to both sides, can be difficult to negotiate with integrity, an example of just how complex the lived study of lived religion can be.

Participant Observation

If lived research on pastors and pastoral staff entails great complexities, moving beyond that to the rest of the congregation involves in some ways even more daunting challenges. The focus of this project was originally worship, the area in which McCallion and I had extensive research experience. It is easy to say that you will study worship as lived religion—as I have defined it in terms of the sources and resources people bring to worship and the knowledge encounters that sometimes occur when leaders propose changes in that worship. It is quite another to actually carry out this research when the subjects are not a small number of easily identifiable and public figures (e.g., pastors and pastoral staff), but the congregation as a whole, or at least significant segments of it. It is difficult when the church has only 130 members and a real challenge when it has several thousand.

Where do you begin? Obviously, you can attend all the worship services at a church, making careful and detailed observations. That is a first step. However, you don't find much about what people bring to worship, much less how they experience it, by simply watching them. Indeed, mere observation of worship can lead to extremely misleading conclusions. For example, it is common for dedicated church people to fulminate against those who sit in the rear of the sanctuary, assuming that those in the back are somehow less involved in worship.[8] For example, in one church a woman very active on the worship commission often could be heard making snide comments about the people in the back pews. However, in that same church one of the most active volunteers sits in a rear pew. Why? Such a simple decision—where to sit—and yet behind it is a very long and moving story. In brief, this woman had left her family's denomination when she married many years before. She had agreed to worship at her new husband's church, though she never found it spiritually very satisfying, and her husband wasn't particularly active in that congregation. Decades later her husband was suffering from a terminal illness. On an impulse, the woman stopped in at her present church. That congregation belongs to her childhood denomination and was on the route between her house and the nursing home where her husband was spending his last days.

> Well, when [my husband] was ill, I felt God was very close to me and I think He was close to me when the car turned into this parking [lot], and I walked in. He was close to me when I sat down, and I happened to sit right next to [Jane in that back pew]....
>
> And, she wouldn't let me get out of that pew without saying who she was, and I told her, "I have to be going. I have to be down to the nursing home...," and she said, "Come back!"
>
> I was down at the post office and [ran into Jane again], and she said, "Would you like to join a circle?" And I said, "Well, what do your circles do, cause I belonged to a circle when I was a kid, and we did missions." She said, "Well, we study the Bible. We do some mission work." And I thought that sounds familiar. She said, "Different ones do different stuff. Some of them go to the art museums. Some of them do plays." She said, "Well, which one would you like to join?" I said, "I'd like to join one that studies the Bible. There's no point in doing all this other stuff. You can do that with your bridge club." So she said, "That's the one I belong to."[9]

The rest, as they say, is history. She sits in the back because of that very dear memory of the first time she stopped in at the church. However, she also sits there because she is a church shepherd. Sitting in the back allows her to get out of the sanctuary fast and wait in the narthex to greet the members of her flock.

Another woman always sits toward the front of her church. What is striking about her is not where she is sitting but something that she is very careful to keep to herself. In a church with a fairly staid liturgy, she is sometimes speaking in tongues—but very, very carefully, to herself.

> Interviewee: During a time of prayer [at church], sometimes it comes over me, and I will go off in my head or quietly.
>
> Interviewer: In different tongues?
>
> Interviewee: Yeah.
>
> Interviewer: Do you ever share that,...? You seem to be a very private person.
>
> Interviewee: Well, I share when there is opportunity. I just don't go, "Hey, I want to share this with you." They'll say, "Well, stay away from me. You're ready for the funny farm." There are times...I have shared it, yeah.[10]

How did she come to be doing this? That story is too complex to even begin to tell here, though I might suggest that it is indicative of one very important facet of mainline congregations. They contain many people who feel more socially comfortable in those respectable sanctuaries, though they are more religiously and spiritually in tune with churches outside the mainline.

How did I find out what was behind the seating decisions of these two women, what they brought with them to worship? People don't usually talk about worship, and certainly not the intimate details of what they bring with them to worship, at worship. You can't even necessarily tell how members of the congregation react to a particular service (e.g., the sermon preached and the music sung or played), much less why they felt that way, just by watching them during that specific worship event. Certainly, I have learned not to use my own reactions as a guide to how others felt. Time after time, I have discovered that sermons that deeply moved me were boring to others. Services that seemed so dull to me that it was hard to keep from yawning were inspiring to those sitting next to me.

My favorite cautionary tale on this subject was told by McCallion, the project's Associate Director. In addition to a Ph.D. in Sociology, McCallion holds a M.A. in Theology/Liturgy from the University of Notre Dame. He certainly has a firm grasp of professional standards for evaluating homilies. On St. Patrick's Day, McCallion went to Mass at one of the Catholic churches in the study and heard what he considered to be an excellent homily given by a visiting priest. Later that St. Patrick's Day, McCallion, as a dedicated researcher, was conducting participant observation at an Irish-American bar. He happened to encounter a parishioner and inquired about her reaction to the homily. He was shocked to hear her trash it. Ever the researcher, McCallion pressed on to find out what she didn't like about the homily. Eventually it came down to the fact that it was St. Patrick's Day, and the priest was not Irish. McCallion reminded her that the priest had told them he was part Irish. Sneering, the parishioner put her thumb and forefinger close together and commented, "Just this much Irish." Even at the University of Notre Dame, that was not included in the criteria McCallion had learned in courses on homiletics.

Of course, aside from frequenting bars on St. Patrick's Day, one way to gain such information is to remain during fellowship hour after services and listen in as people mill around drinking coffee and munching donuts. But at fellowship hours there is usually the risk of being overheard, so people tend to be guarded in their comments. Besides, most conversations there are short and pretty superficial. People generally are on their way to someplace else, picking up children from Sunday School or going to brunch or the golf course.

The first step in getting the type of in-depth information about lived Christianity that is represented by the background to the seating decisions of those two women involves the time consuming task of attending the numerous and varied activities of a lively church. At the simplest level, by sitting in on meetings of church councils, outreach, Christian education committees, Bible studies, circles, retreat teams, small faith groups, I become acquainted with the more active people of the church. Faces at worship, as well as other events, begin to have names attached to them.

In this first stage, a church's picture directory is an indispensable tool. When I return from a meeting, I look up the participants at the events in the directory and check the pictures for their spouses and children. I've also learned to check in the directory for how many other families there are in the church with the same surnames as those participants. Although it varies from church to church, kinship can play an incredibly important role in a congregation. I was amused to have the same bit of folk wisdom repeated to me in U.S. congregations that I had been told many years ago in the small village in Finland that was the site of my first fieldwork. "Watch out what you say about anyone here, you may be talking to a relative!"

As important as my getting to know people at the events is their opportunity to observe me. In most churches, news of the researcher showing up at one meeting can get spread to a whole family or friendship network, making entrance into new groups and events progressively easier.

If, over time, it gets easier to enter into new groups in a church, the fact that this is lived research means that there are always some key elements influencing how comfortable I am in walking into a particular meeting or event: my age and gender. When I did my first field research in a rural Finnish village, I was twenty-eight years old. I could participate in a wide variety of athletic competitions, from track to orienteering to cross-country skiing (common social events among males), as well as be a kind of surrogate son to a number of older men and women.[11] I am now nearly twice that age, and I am acutely aware that I fit in better and have better rapport with the retirees at a church than with the young marrieds, much less with the young singles. I studied two different men's retreat teams at one church. It's not surprising that I had greater access to the group that included some men of my age, with empty nests at home, than to the group where much of the talk was of the trials and tribulations of raising young children.

If age has altered the obstacles to fieldwork, gender has remained a challenge. As I was the only male who ever regularly attended the Women's Agricultural Society and the Missionary Sewing Circle in my Finnish village, I am probably one of the few men to visit the women's circles and retreat meetings in my American churches. A meeting of a woman's retreat team stands out for me as perhaps the only time as an anthropologist that I felt like a fly on the wall. The women spent several hours speaking of some incredibly intimate details of their lives while barely acknowledging my existence, seldom even making eye contact.

Even long-term pastors have told me they have never attended meetings of the women's circles in their churches (though they know the circles are centers of power and influence), and one pastor was particularly concerned about what sort of Bible study really went on in the circles. When I first introduced my colleague, Angela Martin, to an almost exclusively female Bible study at one church, she was struck by the fact that some women assumed she was my wife. There is quite a difference in our ages, and I had clearly stated that Martin was one of the project researchers. Martin soon gained far better rapport with the Bible study participants than I ever could.

Whatever challenges these meetings and events may present, they are where people often reveal something of the complexity of their religious lives, certainly in terms of what they bring to congregation life. During prayer and study, the life crises that participants are facing often come out and lead to discussions among people about how well or poorly they are coping with these crises.[12] Also, it is at Bible studies, women's circle meetings, and small faith groups that people talk about what had happened in worship the week before. For example, they discuss what they thought about the pastor for the first time delivering his sermon from the central aisle instead of from behind the pulpit, or the new music director's hymn selection.[13]

In fact, these types of events are such incredibly rich sources of information about the lived religion of the pastoral staff and congregation members that the project developed a protocol for taking almost verbatim notes of what was said by all the participants. As I explain to participants, these notes allow me to include their own collective voices, not just my summary of what I thought they had said. They have the chance to speak for themselves. When we report back to them about their church, they should be able to hear themselves as a group in our descriptions. It should sound to them like their own congregation.

Also, as I type up those handwritten verbatim notes, it is very much like reliving the event, my own version of instant replay. I usually get a general sense of an individual from being in an event with that person. However, as I hear someone's words again while typing my notes, I start to get a feel for the specifics. I can focus not only what was said but also how it was said. I can pay careful attention to the kinds of sources an individual drew upon in making these comments and reflections.

These verbatim notes all get entered into a qualitative research computer database that, after coding, allows us to call up what a particular individual has said in any of the events that we have attended. It is thus possible to get a sense over time of the various facets of an individual—as he or she moves from a faith sharing group to a finance council meeting or provides a series of updates on an ongoing life crisis.

This database also allows us to call up all the mentions of a particular church issue in a variety of settings, for example a debate over a worship change—introducing banners into the sanctuary or moving from grape juice to wine at communion. This can provide the material for an in-depth case study. Alternatively, we can search the database for the sources that were mentioned as justifying positions taken in the debates at the church councils on a variety of key issues facing the congregation during the year it was under study. This can give valuable information about the religious dimensions of the decision-making process. For example, how often and when were biblical sources quoted as opposed to principles of business management?

Core Members and Spiritual Life History

After months of this type of intensive lived research, it was clear that the spiritual lives, the lived religion, of those individuals whom we repeatedly met at a wide variety of church activities often were not only quite complex, but the product of long and sometimes surprising stages of development. While suggestive sketches of those individual lives could be pieced together from the fragments we heard told in various church contexts, it was clearly important to explore those stories in a more systematic and in-depth manner. We needed to ask about an individual's lived religion in the three dimensions I described earlier—(1) the types of knowledge, practices, beliefs, experiences, and feelings he or she brought to the religious elements of congregational life, (2) his or her lived religion beyond the boundaries of congregational life, and (3) the evolution of an individual's lived religion over time. We decided to develop a Spiritual Life History Interview. After a number of pretests, we produced an eleven-page, detailed set of open-ended questions that led individuals to think back on the various stages of their lives and to describe the major influences on their religious or spiritual lives during each of those periods. We also asked them to reflect on their contemporary experiences, focusing on their involvement with and perception of their present congregation.

One reason for such a highly structured interview was that it allows us to use our qualitative database to rigorously compare the spiritual life histories of different individuals. Another is that we were speaking with people who were far more varied than the pastors and pastoral staff in their ability to tell of their life journeys at the drop of a hat. Although all interviewees were asked the same questions in the same order, the length of the interviews varied greatly, from approximately 1 to 6 hours.

For practical and theoretical reasons, we decided to administer these Spiritual Life History Interviews to a sample of what we called core members of the church. The principal researcher at the church drew up a preliminary list of core members that was then commented on, deleted from, and added to by the congregation's pastor on the basis of the following criteria: "If a significant change were to be proposed for your church, would the individual play a role for or against and would the person have any significant impact? In making this decision, we're not asking you to evaluate whether an individual is a good or bad core person."

From church to church, cores differed greatly in number, ranging from fifteen to eighty-seven. Although the overall size of a church obviously has an effect, the size of the core was not simply a function of congregation size. The church with the largest core, eighty-seven, had only 301 in its worshiping community, while one church with 501 in the worshiping community had only twenty-seven in its core. Is the core strongly influenced by the different ways the pastors understood the criteria? Perhaps, but our other observations of the community dynamics of each congregation suggest that the size of the core in proportion to its worshiping community may also reflect types of leadership styles, and may, in fact, be one significant indicator of a healthy congregation.

Core congregation members are the central people we studied to learn about knowledge encounters and to observe reactions to change. In terms of church growth, a subject that preoccupies most of our congregations, the core members are the key. They are the people prospective new members are most likely to meet. Also, when peripheral members find themselves potentially becoming interested in heavier involvement (e.g., because of a life crisis), the core members are the people (aside from the staff) to whom they are most likely to turn.

Given the expense of transcribing interviews, we had to limit ourselves in the initial round of research to sixty-five Spiritual Life Histories spread over the first six congregations in rough proportion to the size of their core groups. The sample to be interviewed in the core of each church was randomly selected to match the overall demographics of the core in terms of age and gender.

As our first set of sixty-five Spiritual Life Histories has not yet been fully transcribed, I can only make some very tentative observations. As I mentioned earlier, even with an elaborate and intricate question protocol, the interviews varied greatly in length. However, I should add that the duration of interviews did not necessarily correlate with the interviewee's age. To some extent, it reflects their different life experiences, the varying intensities of their religious or spiritual lives. It also reflects their different narrative styles or abilities. Pelto and Pelto have pointed out that while life history narratives can be extraordinarily valuable documents, they tend to be "collected from a small number of persons with whom the anthropologist has especially good rapport" and "who are unusually eloquent and sensitive in their presentation of personal and cultural data. Thus, in most cases, life histories represent the lives of exceptional rather than representative or average persons in the community."[14] Our Spiritual Life History interviewees were rigorously chosen from among the core members of each church in order to avoid such a sampling bias.[15]

There is probably no more intense lived research experience on lived religion than doing Spiritual Life History Interviews. In some cases, people were repeating stories they had told often before. However, in other cases, a question seemed to momentarily startle the interviewee, stirring up some long suppressed memories or drawing the interviewee into the remote storage facility of his or her mind.

What truly struck me, particularly in the affluent suburban churches, was how often the Spiritual Life History Interviews took us beneath the prosperous surfaces, and into worlds full of tragedy—murders, rapes, drug abuse, alcoholism, suicides. I think, for example, of one woman's heartbreaking struggle dealing with a daughter's drug abuse. I was particularly startled by how grateful she was to the members of what might appear to be a rather straitlaced and "respectable" congregation.

> Prior to all of that experience, I would have thought that the people of the church would have really just said, "You know, if you had been a better parent, then you wouldn't be in this position, and, you know, I saw this coming. You did this wrong and that wrong and this wrong." And that isn't at all what happened. In fact, when [my daughter] was running away, one of the other families in our congregation...have a police radio or something like that at home that they listen to sometimes.
>
> And they heard [my daughter's] name, because every time we did report her as a runaway, and so they'd have her name and her description and

everything. And so they went through the minister to ask if it was, you know, did we need anything, could they help in any way, and they were
very kind, you know. And the ministers were
kind as well, and very caring, but not intrusive
either, you know…. And so, as a result of that, I
stayed in the church and at a very bad time in my
life, when I think I would have left. I think I
would have just been too embarrassed to stick
around. And it was the best thing I think I've ever
done for my faith and for my faith in the congregation, and the church as a family. That nobody,
nobody was interested in pointing fingers of
blame or anything like that. It was very supportive and has continued to be so….[16]

Among some social scientists, there is a tendency to view
religion as an illusion, an escape from the grim realities of
life. In the privacy of the Spiritual Life History Interview, as
so often in small group discussions in churches, what struck
me, instead, was how the core church members grappled
seriously and realistically with the tragedies of life.

Survey of Worshiping Communities

Although it was necessary to limit the very time-consuming
and intimate Spiritual Life History Interviews to a sample of
the congregations' core members, it was vital to find out
more about the lived religion of non-core congregation
members who were part of the worshiping communities. We
defined the worshiping community as congregation members who on average attend services twice a month during
the school year. We wanted to know the degree of consensus
or difference in terms of key issues of lived religion among a
church's pastoral staff, its core members, and its worshiping
community.

Time after time, I have heard endless discussions at church
councils of why is it always the same small group of people
who do all the work in a church. How, they asked them-

selves over and over, can the other eighty percent of church members be transformed into active participants in congregational life? Obviously, data on the lived religion of the worshiping community would be of immense interest to the leadership of these churches.

How could we collect this data? How do we get a significant portion of the worshiping community to answer questions that paralleled those in the Spiritual Life History Interview? Finding a satisfactory answer to such a daunting challenge was truly a crucial part of our research project. Indeed, it was a demanding task that required several months and countless hours of discussion and debate over an incredible range of issues, from the highly theoretical to the absolutely mundane. We decided to survey the entire worshiping community in each church. But, what topics had priority? What question format was most appropriate for which topic? How should each question and alternative answer be worded so as to be clear and understandable to a group of respondents with a wide range of educational and cultural backgrounds? How could the survey be physically laid out so that it was most user friendly and visually attractive?

It is amusing now to look at my first annual report to Lilly Endowment. I wrote then that "…we will administer a brief questionnaire…at each of the six congregations."[17] Although we were ruthless in editing it, the "brief questionnaire" eventually ended up twenty pages long. Yet our response rate from the churches was spectacular. Of the 1822 surveys mailed out to the members of the worshiping communities of the six churches, 1065 were satisfactorily completed and returned. This is an overall return rate of fifty-eight percent, with individual congregation return rates varying from a low of forty-four percent to a high of seventy-six percent. Furthermore, the text responses to the surveys, where people were asked to respond to an open ended question or where they were given the option of checking "Other" as a response to a question and then invited to "Please describe," were overwhelming. There were 261 pages worth of such responses.

Since the data from the survey are still being entered and coded, I can't yet report on our results. However, I can share an example of the sort of questions we included.[18]

> *Recall a major illness or accident or other life crisis recently experienced by you or a family member. Did religion or spirituality play any role in how you or your family responded to it?*

> ____ YES   ____ NO

> *Please briefly describe the type of life crisis:*

> *Please put a check next to items below that were* **important in dealing with the crisis.** *If religion or spirituality* **did not** *play a role (that is, you answered "NO" above), please skip to Sources of Information and Advice below.*

____ Prayers offered by the congregation

____ Prayers by you for support or resolution of the crisis

____ Pastor's visits and/or counseling

____ Visits and counseling by congregation members

____ Cards and calls from congregation members

____ Material support (such as food, clothing, money) from the congregation or members of the congregation

____ Going to a retreat or encounter

___ Counseling by a church professional other than a pastor

___ Reading the Bible

___ Hearing the voice of God inside of you

___ Experiencing a feeling of reassurance or peace

___ Receiving a visit from an angel or type of messenger from God (someone who, it later turned out, could not be identified or explained in any other way)

___ A visit by a hospital chaplain

___ Religious or spiritual counseling by medical staff

___ Being visited by a deceased relative or friend

___ Being visited by Jesus

___ Being visited by Mary, the Mother of God

___ Being visited by a saint

___ Other—please describe:

Conclusion

By now I hope that I have succeeded in showing just how complex lived research on lived religion can be. In conclusion, I want to return to one of our particular concerns with lived religion—sources of knowledge. While we were originally interested in the sources of religious knowledge the people in the pews bring to knowledge encounters, I have earlier mentioned one very striking source of knowledge for church professionals: church consultants and church consulting organizations, like the Alban Institute. I want briefly to describe their impact on our research on the congregational level, and suggest some challenges that the pervasive influence of these consultants offer to academic scholars in theology and religious studies, as well as in the social sciences.[19]

As with denomination representatives and experts, how we were received by the pastors and subsequently presented to the church councils was, I think, heavily influenced by congregation leaders' familiarity with church consultants and consultant organizations. Pastors often had personal libraries well stocked with material written by some of the leading gurus and regularly went to workshops offered by them or consultant organizations. It was not unusual for the churches to have been led through a master planning process by a church consultant. In some cases, the pastors themselves occasionally worked as consultants, e.g., brought in to deal with a type of conflict with which they had extensive experience. Especially in the middle class churches, where there were a large number of professionals in the lay leadership, consultants were an accepted part of their everyday world.

When we went to the church councils of the second set of congregations this winter, seeking the councils' permission to conduct research in them, we had a list of the types of data we would give them. We emphasized that their churches would have more information about themselves than the vast majority of churches in this country, and this type of information would probably cost them thousands of dollars if it were collected by consultants.

There were, however, some serious downsides to being associated with church consultants. Above all, by the nature of their profession, consultants need to have a set of clear cut, alternative diagnoses ready for the problems they are brought in to solve. They need ready made solutions for those problems and challenges (often in the form of exam-

ples of how other churches have coped with them successfully), or at least straightforward processes for producing
solutions in a relatively short time.

 With that sort of consultant model in their minds, it is not
surprising that people in churches often were startled to find
that we needed to spend so much time with their congregation. Even though I had said I would be participating in all
facets of their congregation life for a period of at least a year,
repeatedly people seemed amazed to find me still there after
a few months. I don't know if they were disappointed, but I
found it hard not to be able to give quick, definitive answers
or advice when pastors or other church members wanted to
know what I thought about this or that facet of the church,
sometimes only a month or two after beginning research in
the congregation. Even today, when I have spent over a year
in some of the churches, I feel like there is still much that I
don't know about them.

 In fact, one difficulty in my relationships with pastors is to
avoid making critical comments about some of the too clear-
cut and overly confident consultant "truisms" that I hear
them repeat in meetings. One pastor returned from a conference given by a megachurch and told a group of congregation members:

> At times it was disturbing, where the church will
> be in the future. The first speaker said that three-
> quarters of mainline [Protestant] congregations
> will be out of business [in the next 25 years]....
> The world is changing. The postmodern genera-
> tion. In that generation, there are no absolutes,
> like for us oldsters. We knew right from wrong.
> That's not the case with the younger generation.
> It's pick and choose.... We have to change or be
> like dinosaurs in a new environment.

The message from the conference was clear—change rapidly
and in the directions the megachurch consultants were sug-

gesting (and selling in terms of publications, etc.) or your church will be among those slated for extinction. The frightening statistical projection about the drastic decline of mainline Protestant congregations was repeated at virtually every public occasion at the church as part of a call for urgent action. I kept thinking to myself that one major lesson I had learned in my congregational studies was the incredibly inaccurate and inadequate state of church statistics. There are lies, damn lies, and church statistics.

It also became clear to me that one of the dynamics going on was that pastors were tempted to take a generalization or typology learned from the consultant literature or a workshop and apply it to their own situation, regardless of how well it actually fit the specifics of their church's conditions. At worst, much time and effort were wasted and conflict generated; in other situations, the pastor simply appeared foolish or self-serving. For example, one minister very solemnly justified an important personnel decision by referring to the literature on stages of a pastor's ministry. Certainly, a number of key members of the congregation clearly saw, as I did, that the decision simply reflected the long-standing personal preferences of the pastor, as well as the pursuit of his self-interest and ambitions.

What I am saying should not be construed as an attack on church consultants. First, my own knowledge of them is mostly hearsay, how pastors and other church leaders have described what they have read and the types of advice they have been given. I now have one of my research associates working half time to survey the vast and varied church consultant literature on subjects germane to our own research. Second, while I have certainly heard some critical comments made about consultants, it is also clear that there are church professionals whose judgment I respect that hold a number of consultants in high esteem.

The church consultant industry is filling what seems to be an absolutely essential need in the mainline churches, providing concrete, accessible, easily applicable nuts and bolts advice and suggestions for dealing with the incredibly complex challenges and crises that such congregations routinely face today. Since beginning work on this project in August 1997, I have come to believe that if there is one constant in congregational life today, it is change. One of the main criteria we used to select the churches for our sample was that they were healthy, stable congregations. In some cases, those churches were more than healthy and stable; they were thriving. Yet, in virtually every case, in the period of only one year, our congregations have faced some serious and usually unexpected problem. Key personnel (paid and volunteer) have been lured away, burned out, discouraged, alienated, or pushed out, and smoothly running programs have become centers of bitter controversy or simply gone moribund.

The more I study congregations, the less surprised I am by this state of affairs. I believe there are few institutions in American life that are more complex than the congregation, especially given the modest size and budgets of many. Consider the following characteristics of congregations. They are truly full-service institutions, dealing with the joys and sorrows of the major life events from birth to death. They can be centers for education, music, sports, fellowship, counseling, outreach, as well as spirituality, prayer, and worship. They are multigenerational. Where else but on a Sunday morning at a church can you find people of every age regularly gathered together, and sometimes even closely interacting with each other? They are not only one of the few institutions in the U.S. where a whole family may be actively involved, but also where kinship ties can play a major role, for good or ill.

Congregations require the services of both paid professionals and volunteers to survive, much less flourish. Those professionals run the gamut from full-time to part-time, from the highly credentialed to the uncredentialed (with level of credentials not necessarily correlating with competence). The volunteers range from the very occasional to the absolutely dedicated and from those currently at their peak of active involvement to what I call the distinguished alumni. In many cases, considering the salaries they are paid, the borderline between paid professional and dedicated volunteer is difficult to establish. I could go on and on, and, in fact, we have been developing what we call the complex or hybrid model of congregations. (One of the pastors we work with prefers to call it the chaos model.)

These institutions that are such central elements in the lived religion of many Americans today are not simple places facing simple issues. Obviously, the congregations often need the help of church consultants. However, I believe that scholars of American religion also are sources of knowledge that are potentially of great value to congregations and their members. This is not a strident call to a total dedication to relevance, like the one that had such a disastrous impact on colleges and universities in the 1960s. The glory of academia is that scholars are able to pursue subjects and approaches that appear "irrelevant" to the rest of the world. Rather, I suspect that much of what we, as scholars of religion, already do has relevance to the lived religion of congregations. The challenge is how to make that knowledge accessible, applicable, and useful to congregations. My team and I are now struggling with that challenge in the context of our project. Other scholars may, for example, choose to review the church consultant literature seriously and critically to see how well the accepted "truisms" resonate with the academic literature in theology and religious studies or how well the data on which consultants base their advice stand up to scholarly standards for research.

I assume one of the reasons for choosing the topic of this conference is your recognition that scholars in theology and religious studies must take lived religion seriously. I hope this essay has demonstrated that such research can lead scholars deep into the intimate realms of individual and congregational lives. To be allowed access as a scholar to those often-vulnerable areas of religious life, in my view, is also to assume grave responsibilities. Those of us who study lived religion should, I believe, seriously consider whether we have a moral obligation to seek ways for our work to have a positive impact on that lived religion. I, for one, am convinced that we do.

Notes

1. In addition to Roberts (the Project Director and Principal Investigator), the research staff includes Michael McCallion (Associate Project Director), Randal Hepner, and Angela Martin. All research staff members are affiliated with the Department of Anthropology of Michigan State University. Roberts is deeply indebted to the rest of the staff for the many fine contributions they have made to the project and this paper.

2. For an excellent source on the study of lived religion, see David D. Hall, ed., *Lived Religion in America: Toward a History of Practice* (Princeton: Princeton University Press, 1997).

3. This discussion draws extensively upon the proposal submitted by Roberts and McCallion to Lilly Endowment and presentations made to church councils by project staff when seeking permission to conduct research in those congregations.

4. See Michael McCallion, "The Implementation of the Rite of Christian Initiation of Adults in City and Urban Parishes of the Archdiocese of Detroit" (Ph.D. diss., Wayne State University, 1996); Michael McCallion, David R. Maines, and Steven E. Wolfel, "Policy as Practice: First Holy Communion as a Contested Situation," *The Journal of Contemporary Ethnography* 23, no. 3: 300-326; Fredric M. Roberts, "Conversations among Liturgists," *Liturgy Digest* 2, no. 2 (Spring/ Summer 1995): 36-124; Fredric M. Roberts, "American Catholic Worship: An Anthropological View from the Sidelines," *New Theology Review* 10, no. 1 (February 1997): 6-21; Fredric M. Roberts, "Are Anthropological Crises Contagious? Reflexivity, Representation, Alienation and Rites of Penance" in *Reconciling Embrace: Foundations for the Future of Sacramental Reconciliation*, ed. Robert J. Kennedy (Chicago: Liturgy Training Publication, 1997), 45-59.

5. The term knowledge encounter was borrowed from the title of a workshop, "Knowledge Encounters: Ideas and Practices in

Development Sites," held at the Harvard Institute for International Development. Anne Ferguson, a colleague of Roberts at the Department of Anthropology of Michigan State University, was invited to present a paper at the workshop. Ferguson showed the invitation letter to Roberts. Pauline Peters to Anne Ferguson, East Lansing, Michigan, 22 May 1995.

6. The Michigan State University Library did have four works by Schaller in its collection, but they were all published in the 1960s. Schaller has published numerous books since that time (at least fifteen in the 1990s alone).

7. It is worth noting, however, that Ammerman and Warner are both contributors to a recent volume whose main target audience consists of clergy and seminarians—Nancy T. Ammerman, Jackson W. Carroll, Carl S. Dudley, and William McKinney, eds., *Studying Congregations: A New Handbook* (Nashville: Abingdon Press, 1998). See the "Introduction" to that volume for a brief list of major church consultant organizations.

8. For an illuminating example, see Roberts, "Conversations with Liturgists," 57-58.

9. Spiritual Life History Interview conducted by Fredric M. Roberts, June 1998. Transcript, Metropolitan Detroit and Lansing Congregation Study Project, East Lansing, MI. Names and the exact date of the interview have been altered or eliminated in this quotation and citation to conceal the identity of the interviewee and the congregation.

10. Spiritual Life History Interview conducted by Fredric M. Roberts, May 1998. Transcript, Metropolitan Detroit and Lansing Congregation Study Project, East Lansing, MI. Names and the exact date of the interview have been eliminated in this quotation and citation to conceal the identity of the interviewee and the congregation.

11. Fredric M. Roberts, "Under the North Star: Notions of Self and Community in a Finnish Village" (Ph.D. diss., City University of New York, 1982).

12. See Daniel A. Olson, "Making Disciples in a Liberal Church" in *"I Come Away Stronger": How Small Groups are Shaping American Religion,* ed. Robert Wuthnow (Grand Rapids, MI: William B. Eerdmans Publishing Company, 1994), 131.

13. For an example from another study, see J. Bradley Wigger, "Gracious Words: A Presbyterian Bible Study" in Wuthnow, *"I Come Away Stronger,"* 41.

14. Pertti Pelto and Gretel Pelto, *Anthropological Research: The*

Structure of Inquiry, 2d ed. (New York: Cambridge University Press, 1978), 75.

15. Recently, Wuthnow has also stressed the importance of life history interviews for understanding the spirituality of "ordinary" individuals. Wuthnow conducted a national study including 200 interviews with persons from a variety of Christian backgrounds, as well as from Jewish, Muslim, Hindu, and eclectic faith traditions. Those interviewees may, in fact, be ordinary, but they are certainly not representative of a well-defined population, such as the core members of a particular congregation. Robert Wuthnow, *Growing Up Religious: Christians and Jews and Their Journeys of Faith* (Boston: Beacon Press, 1999), xi-xiii; xxxii.

16. Spiritual Life History Interview conducted by Fredric M. Roberts, November 1998. Transcript, Metropolitan Detroit and Lansing Congregation Study Project, East Lansing, MI. Names and the exact date of the interview have been eliminated in this quotation and citation to conceal the identity of the interviewee and the congregation.

17. Fredric M. Roberts, "Annual Report to Lilly Endowment on Grant # 1997-0289: The Study of Conflicts in Congregations, 1997-1998" (East Lansing, MI: Michigan State University, 1997), 7.

18. "Metropolitan Detroit Congregation Study Project: Survey Questionnaire" (East Lansing, MI: Michigan State University, 1999), 18.

19. In his 1998 Presidential Lecture to the Religious Research Association, Carl S. Dudley addressed a number of the issues discussed in my conclusion. For example, he commented that: "*At the moment there exists an industry of mediators and translators who broker the research generated by members of RRA/SSSR* [Religious Research Association/Society for the Scientific Study of Religion]. Some of these interpreters are sophisticated, and [others] appear shallow in appreciating research; some have remarkable insights, and others specialize in Delphic aphorisms about social dynamics. With all the effort that members of our societies have invested in disciplined research, I am surprised that so little work is directed to studies of the changes introduced by consultants, interpreters, and spokespersons who translate your work into the vernacular of religious leaders. Some are excellent, some are shoddy, and some are dangerous, and I share your concern that you will be quoted out of context or used for inappropriate purposes." Carl S. Dudley, "Significant Research: When Information Has Impact," *Review of Religious Research* 40, no. 4 (June 1999): 393-406. Because Dudley's

address was only published in June 1999, I was unable to include it as an integral part of my text.

Part II
CLIMBING ONTO SHOULDERS:
RETRIEVING TRADITIONS

The Inculturation of Christianity in Asia: From Francis Xavier to Matteo Ricci

Ronald Modras
Professor of Historical Theology
Saint Louis University

The vast differences between today and the late sixteenth century make it appear unlikely that someone from that era could serve as an exemplar of lived Christianity for our own. We travel halfway around the globe in a day instead of a year. English, not Latin, is the international language. Enlightenment ideals have secularized the national cultures of what was once Christendom. And if wars of religion are not yet obsolete, at least Christians have begun talking to one another and to people of other faiths in ecumenical and interreligious dialogues. So what does anyone from the pre-modern, late Renaissance, early Baroque period have to say to us, in an age increasingly described as postmodern? A great deal, if that man is Matteo Ricci, one of the most remarkable human beings to live at any time, in any culture, and of any religious conviction.

Matteo Ricci (1552-1610) is the man who coined the name Confucius to translate K'ung Fu-tzu ("Master Kung"), when he introduced China's greatest sage to the Western World. In his late thirties, this Italian Jesuit found himself studying the classical literature of China, much as he had studied Latin classics as a schoolboy. He mastered the language enough to do the first Western (Latin) translation of the Confucian *Analects* and to be the first Westerner to write and publish books in Chinese. Some of his writings even came to be included in a canon of Chinese classics.

More than an author, Ricci was also a pioneer. He won entrée into cities and circles where few or no outsiders had been welcomed before him. He brought Western mathematics and science to China and wrote the first detailed descriptions of Chinese life and culture for the West. In addition to titles like Renaissance man and humanist, he warrants the title "father of sinology." But because he was also and foremost a missionary, his contributions to secular cultural history often go unnoted. He introduced West to East and East to West. And in him the twain did meet.

Ricci had high regard for Confucius and used words like virtue, self-mastery, and even holiness to describe him. As one who studied Aristotle and Cicero, he classified Confucius as a philosopher, "the equal" of the pre-Christian philosophers of Greece and Rome and "superior to most of them." Ricci's journals reveal a similar admiration and respect for the Chinese people and their culture altogether, though he could be quite critical of their failings. Theirs was a civilization that pre-dated Christianity by centuries, based on an ethics derived, he wrote, "under the guidance of the light of reason."[1]

Ricci's reference to guidance by the light of reason may not seem important in itself. Its significance becomes apparent only later in his journals, where Ricci describes the ancient Chinese as worshiping one Supreme Being and teaching that every human action should hearken to the dictates of reason. "One can confidently hope that in the mercy of God, many of the ancient Chinese found salvation in the natural law, assisted as they must have been by that special help which, as the theologians teach, is denied to no one who does what he can toward salvation, according to the light of his conscience."[2]

Ricci faced the same culture shock that other sixteenth-century explorers and missionaries did on discovering lands and peoples previously unknown to Europe. But unlike many if not most of the earlier missionaries who followed Spanish and Portuguese explorers, Ricci had the advantages of a classical humanist education and encountered in China not a culture of hunters and gatherers but a civilization largely dominated by Confucian scholars, a class of humanists like himself, given to reading classic texts. The Chinese, he learned and then pointed out, had been printing and devouring books long before the invention of movable type in the West.

As a Jesuit and a priest, Ricci was confronted with the reality of millions of people who for thousands of years had lived and died without ever having had the chance to hear of Christianity or Jesus Christ. Were they all doomed? While it had been the long-held Christian conviction that there was no salvation without Christian faith and baptism, St. Thomas Aquinas had taught that God willed the salvation of all humankind. Medieval Europe was quite sure that the gospel had already been preached to the ends of the earth. Theologians in the Middle Ages speculated about the off-chance of a solitary child surviving in a wilderness without hearing about Jesus Christ. In such a peculiar situation, how could such a person be saved? By a special revelation, an illumination, or the preaching of an angel? According to the medieval mind, Jews and Muslims who refused to accept Christianity did so by their own choice and through their own fault. But this was palpably not the case with the peoples of the Far East, nor with the Native Americans the missionaries found in the New World. How could millions of people be faulted, let alone damned, for lacking a faith in a Savior they never heard of?

Catholic theologians had already begun facing the new realities and adjusting their theological opinions accordingly. Robert Bellarmine (1542-1621), Ricci's Jesuit contemporary teaching in Rome, suggested that God gives the light of faith to those who have not heard the gospel but know through natural knowledge of creation that God exists and judges human behavior. Francisco Suarez (1548-1619), another Jesuit theologian in Rome at the same time, taught that an *implicit faith* in Christ and an *implicit desire* for baptism sufficed for the salvation of peoples who believed in God and wanted to do God's will.[3]

Ricci could appeal to such thinking about natural law and conscience to buttress his confident hope in the mercy of God. The new thinking was of more than just theoretical interest for him. In his mission deep in the interior of China, Ricci found flesh and blood people for whom he had left family, friends, and native land. He cared about their salvation but he also cared about them as human beings. His journals reveal that, even without their conversion, he had come to regard any number of them as friends.

Ricci sailed to the East in the wake of St. Francis Xavier. I do not wish to be dismissive of Xavier's merits, but in more ways than one Ricci surpassed him, or perhaps better, stood on Xavier's shoulders. And we can best measure Ricci's own stature by pointing out how he did so. Ricci took up literally where Xavier left off, dying on a deserted island just off the coast of China, waiting for a ship to take him to the mainland. That was in 1552, the same year in which Matteo Ricci was born.

In the Wake of Francis Xavier

When Francis Xavier arrived in India in 1542, he found in Goa what he described as "a completely Christian city."[4] In the hands of the Portuguese for some thirty-two years, Goa already boasted a monastery, several churches, and an "ornate cathedral." There Xavier walked the streets ringing a bell and drawing the curious, mostly children, into a church, where he would teach them in Portuguese. (Contrary to the popular myth, Xavier was not a linguist.) Goa was a European enclave with a European culture. The natives who became Christian were expected to adopt European ways.

When, after several months, Xavier began to work among the Parava villages on the opposite coast of India, he found natives who spoke only Tamil, the principal language of south India. Xavier was accompanied by three young native Tamil-speakers who had come to Goa as boys and had learned Portuguese. With their help Xavier prepared a Tamil version of the Ten Commandments and the Apostles' Creed, with a brief commentary on each point. Neither Xavier nor his young helpers had sufficient command of each other's languages, and their translations proved to be poor. But that inadequacy does not take away from the significance of the deed. For the first time Christianity was being translated into the language of a non-Western culture. Though Xavier appears to have been unaware of the fact, he was crossing a cultural frontier.[5]

Xavier's letters from Portuguese colonies in India and then Indonesia, express his disdain for the religious practices of the local peoples. Though fond of his converts, he had little respect for their native cultures. In Japan Xavier first encountered the challenge of presenting the Christian faith to people with a high culture dissimilar from his own, and he accommodated. When he first appeared before the provincial warlord (*daimyo*) of Yamaguchi, Xavier wore his shabby black Jesuit habit. When he was granted another audience, Xavier appeared before him dressed splendidly in silk.[6]

As in India with the Tamil-speakers, Xavier once again had the creed and a variety of prayers translated into the local language. And he soon learned that translating the Christian message into Japanese could pose peculiar challenges. How, for example, should one translate the creedal statement that Jesus sits at the right hand of the Father, when in Japanese culture the place of honor was at the left? Even more troublesome was finding the proper word for God. Xavier finally chose simply to transliterate *Deus*, the Latin for God, into Japanese. For the Japanese this meant that the God of the Christians was named *Deusu*.

Time and again, when hard-pressed in an argument, Xavier noticed how the Japanese would appeal to the authority of the Chinese. Why had so great a nation not accepted *Deusu*? Xavier was sure that if China became Christian, Japan would follow suit. He would merely need to convert the Chinese emperor. Xavier returned to India, set his affairs in order, and set off for China. In late August, 1552, he arrived on the island of Sancian, at the mouth of the Pearl River, where for three months he waited patiently for permission to enter the mainland. Permission never came. He became ill, and on December 5, 1552, he died, hoping almost to the very end for an audience with the emperor. He had no idea of the distance to Beijing or of the audacity of his project. China was a closed society. In the late Ming period, with the exception of his wives and the palace eunuchs, virtually no one saw the emperor, not even the Chinese. The imperial palace was named the Forbidden City for good reason. That within one lifetime another Jesuit would enter those hallowed precincts speaks volumes for the genius of Matteo Ricci. But it speaks as well for the ingenuity and vision of another Jesuit, Alessandro Valignano. He saw in Ricci the qualities necessary for getting to Beijing and had the acumen to figure out how he was to get there.

The Vision of Alessandro Valignano

Alessandro Valignano (1539-1606) seems to have been born to leadership.[7] Shortly after his ordination to priesthood, even before he had completed his studies, he was made master of novices, a position he held only briefly, but precisely at the time in August 1571, when nineteen-year-old Matteo Ricci entered the Jesuit novitiate. The following year

Valignano was appointed rector of the College in Macerata, Ricci's hometown. During this time Valignano asked to be sent to work in the missions in India. He could not have expected that the Jesuit General would put him in charge of them.

The missions in the East Indies were simply a part of Portugal's colonial enterprise, an extension of its European culture on foreign soil. Converts were expected to assume not only a new faith but its European trappings as well, in effect cutting themselves off from their native culture and heritage. Such was also the case in the Spanish colonies in the Philippines and the New World as well. When converts were poor and illiterate, barely dressed or polygamous, weaning them from their native cultures was regarded as doing them a favor. Europeans viewed it as largesse and Valignano concurred with the common opinion: the colonists were bringing these indigenous peoples not only the true religion but also a superior culture. His thinking first began to change on his way to Japan, when he encountered Chinese and Japanese converts in Macao, a peninsula on China's southern coast. He set about trying to learn why all previous missionary efforts at getting into China had failed.

China was hermetically sealed. Not unlike Europeans, the Chinese thought of themselves as the center of the world. They called themselves the "Middle Kingdom" and, as the name indicates, regarded their neighbors as peripheral. Foreigners were for the most part barbarians with little to offer that China did not already have. Wary of spies and fearful of foreign invasion, the Chinese government restricted foreigners to the peninsula of Macao. Only twice a year and under strict supervision, foreigners residing in Macao were allowed to enter the mainland and travel the short distance to Canton to serve as middlemen for the lucrative silk trade with Japan.

In Macao Valignano was dismayed to see that the Jesuit missionaries had become no more than chaplains to the

Portuguese traders; they had given up any hope of getting to the mainland. And, as in India, whatever converts they did make had to learn about their new faith in Portuguese and to assume Portuguese dress and manners. In Japan Valignano needed only two years to convince him that the Japanese were not a people to be governed by foreigners. The only way Christianity could be established in Japan was to educate the native Japanese to run things themselves and in their own way. That could be done only by the missionaries earning the respect of the Japanese and learning their way of doing things. The Japanese, he would write, were so attached to their own ways that they would never accommodate themselves to foreigners. The western missionaries would have to accommodate to them.[8]

Toward the end of 1581, Valignano composed a short handbook of decorum for the guidance of Jesuit missionaries.[9] If the missionaries were not to make themselves look ridiculous in the eyes of the Japanese, they had to know how to interact appropriately within Japanese society. On the advice of knowledgeable Japanese, Valignano boldly decided that the proper rank of the missionaries corresponded to that of Zen Buddhist monks. They would all dress and act according to the Zen model of decorum that would be expected at a Buddhist temple. Valignano went into minute detail, describing how letters were to be written, how priests were to travel, how guests were to be received and entertained with the traditional tea ceremony. To this end all Jesuit mission houses were to be constructed in a Japanese style with parlors for receiving visitors according to ceremonial custom. Proper decorum determined everything, even the kind of tea one served one's guests. A *faux pas*, even if unintended, could mean both embarrassing oneself and insulting another.

Not surprisingly, Valignano had to defend some of his novel ideas to his fellow Jesuits, including the Jesuit General in Rome. If Christianity was to take root in Japan, he argued, it dared not appear inferior to Buddhism. The missionaries had to learn from their mistakes. By not adapting to Japanese customs, they had lost the respect of the Japanese and failed to make their converts feel at home.[10]

Accommodating to circumstances was a cardinal principle of Renaissance rhetoric. The first Jesuits were educated in that ethos and had built it into their initial vow at Montmartre. Ignatius wrote accommodation into the very *Constitutions* of the Society of Jesus.[11] So Valignano was only following in the Jesuit tradition and its Renaissance origins when he made cultural accommodation a principle of Jesuit missionary efforts in China and Japan. Converts should not be required to become strangers to their own people. Chinese and Japanese Christians, as he put it, should be able to "feel at home" in their new faith.

At Valignano's request, Michele Ruggieri, a young Neapolitan Jesuit, had been sent to Macao. His task—to do nothing else but study Chinese—was formidable. Spoken Chinese has five tones, each of which changes the meaning of the same sound, and instead of a phonetic alphabet, written Chinese has a different character or ideograph for every word. And if those were not troubles enough, the other Jesuit missionaries resented the hours Ruggieri spent studying Chinese ideographs when he could be doing something worthwhile, like ministering to the Portuguese. They assured him he was wasting his time. Chinese was impossible for a Westerner to learn, and he would never be allowed access to the mainland anyway.

Ruggieri proved his colleagues wrong. On three different occasions he accompanied the Portuguese merchants in their semi-annual embassies to Canton to buy silk. He was not a gifted linguist, but he had learned enough of the language and culture to impress some senior Chinese officials. They gave him permission to set up a chapel in Canton in the quarter for foreign embassies. They apparently saw Ruggieri as being different from the other Western barbarians. He knew, for example, how to behave appropriately and acknowledge their office with the customary profound bow or "kowtow." Most Europeans saw the kowtow as beneath their Christian dignity. For the Chinese, Ruggieri learned, it was simply good manners. But Ruggieri knew his limitations. He asked Valignano to send the more gifted Matteo Ricci, then still in India, to join him in the new enterprise. Valignano agreed.

An Italian Humanist in China

Ricci was thirty years old when he arrived in China, the product of a Jesuit humanist education.[12] At the Collegio Romano he studied the classical authors of antiquity and conversed with his colleagues in Latin. He also studied the art of memorizing, then regarded as the root of all eloquence. He learned the mnemonic device of creating dramatic images and then organizing them into "memory palaces."[13] Years later he would come to demonstrate his extraordinary memory skills by his ability to look at and then recall lists of four or five hundred Chinese ideographs.

For four years at the Collegio Romano, Ricci studied under Christopher Clavius (Klau), the mathematical genius responsible for our modern, Gregorian calendar. Under Clavius Ricci learned to construct sundials, clocks, and perpetual calendars. He learned the use of quadrants to measure altitudes and of astrolabes for calculating the motion of the planets and stars. Ricci remained in correspondence with Clavius the rest of his life.

Ricci and Ruggieri set up their first house on the Chinese mainland in the south, in Zhaoqing, not far from Canton. The rest of Ricci's life and career would be spent in a slow, circuitous journey north to Beijing. At the beginning of that career, Ricci applied himself to learning Mandarin, the language of China's literati and of Confucian classical literature. This he did only with the help of a Chinese Christian born in Macao, without the aid of dictionaries or grammars. In addi-

tion, at Valignano's request, he began to write up a comprehensive report on China—its people, customs, government,
and institutions. Though he would later correct a number of
his early opinions, Ricci's was the first serious, reasonably
accurate report about China to be written for the West.

Like the Jesuits in Japan, Ricci and Ruggieri attired themselves as *bonzes*, as Buddhist monks. The category of
Buddhist monk seemed at the time to be the most appropriate niche for them in Chinese society. The provincial governor confirmed their identity by having a plaque placed on
their mission house stating "Temple of the Flower of the
Saints." Though Ricci preferred to read this as a reference to
Jesus' Mother, Mary, the Chinese interpreted it to mean that
the Jesuit mission was a Buddhist temple. This had disadvantages, since it meant that the mandarins, as they came to
be called in the West, could visit at any time of the night or
day, as if the mission was an inn or public gathering place.
The advantage was that Ricci had the opportunity to meet
and converse freely with a segment of society he could not
have reached otherwise. Decorum forbade the mandarins to
visit the private residences of anyone not a member of their
class.[14]

Mandarins, in the broadest sense, were an intellectual elite
from whom were drawn the bureaucrats who governed
China in a kind of meritocracy. One entered their numbers
only by passing rigorous triennial examinations in the
Confucian classics. Ricci refers to these Confucian scholars in
his journals as the "sect of literati" and describes them as ruling the country and, more than any other class, respected for
their learning: "They do not believe in idol worship. In fact
they have no idols. They do, however, believe in one deity
who preserves and governs all things on earth."[15]

Unlike Xavier before them, Ricci and Ruggieri did not
preach in the streets. Their status as resident aliens was too
politically precarious to do so. Instead, they engaged in
lengthy conversations with the Confucian scholars who

came to their residence to meet the strangers from the West. Their Chinese visitors were curious to see their books and examples of Western art, so strikingly realistic because of its use of perspective. They also came to see the map that Ricci had produced, astounded at the existence of so many far-away lands it claimed to exist west of China. To his visitors' satisfaction, Ricci had prudently placed China in the center, as the Middle Kingdom deserved. And when the conversation turned from geography to matters philosophical, Ricci interjected information about the Westerners' Christian faith.

Ruggieri was reassigned by Valignano to return to Europe to engage in fundraising for the Chinese mission, and other Jesuits joined Ricci, who in 1589 relocated to Shaoshou, north of Canton. Here, in a residence utterly Chinese in architecture and appearance, Qu Rukuei entered Ricci's life. A Confucian scholar three years Ricci's senior, Qu was quite sure that Ricci's knowledge of science included alchemy. To learn Ricci's supposed secrets, Qu asked him to become his teacher, and Ricci agreed. In a formal dinner for his mandarin colleagues and friends, Qu made the ceremonial kowtow to Ricci and declared himself Ricci's disciple. He would be honor-bound to acknowledge Ricci as his master for the rest of his life.

Ricci was able to wean his new disciple from interest in alchemy and turn him to mathematics, which at that time was only rudimentary in China. He opened the world of Euclidean geometry to Qu and, when the opportunity arose, would relate something about Christianity. Qu proved an adept student. He took careful notes and astounded his teacher one day with a series of perceptive questions about the Christian faith, all deriving from a Confucian scholar's point of view. The exchange proved significant for both master and disciple. Qu eventually became a Christian, and Ricci learned the importance of relating Christianity to someone steeped in Confucian tradition. It was becoming clear to Ricci that for all segments of society, not only the mandarins,

China's dominant value system was Confucian. He began studying the Four Books that form the heart of Confucianism and translating them into Latin.

Qu spread the fame of his master throughout his network of colleagues and friends, many of whom also became Ricci's friends. All this time Ricci still shaved his head and wore the garb of a Buddhist monk. After a year of almost daily conversations with Qu and his friends, however, Ricci became convinced that dressing like a bonze was not the appropriate way to present himself (Buddhism was regarded with contempt by Confucian scholars at the time). Ricci conferred with Valignano, who agreed with his assessment. Christianity was more compatible with Confucianism than with Buddhism and their dress was causing the Chinese to mistake the missionaries as representing a Buddhist sect.

Ricci had already adopted Chinese diet, manners, and sleep patterns. Now he began to let his hair and beard grow. In 1594 he put aside the gray robe of the Buddhist monks and put on an ankle-length purple silk robe with loose flowing sleeves. On his feet he wore embroidered silk slippers and on his head a high square black hat not unlike a bishop's miter. He drew a line when it came to the practice of some mandarins who let their fingernails grow to considerable length, but he did carry a fan. And if he ever thought to ask himself what Ignatius and Francis Xavier would have said were they to see him in so splendid an attire, he could presume that they would understand. In good humanist fashion, he had accommodated himself to circumstances. He was not in Rome but in China, no longer Matteo Ricci but Li Madou.

Confucian Scholar

The following year, in 1595, Ricci and the Jesuit mission received permission from the government to move further north, to Nanchang. Here he began to meet scholars and high-ranking mandarins who had never known him in the garb of a Buddhist monk. With his now excellent Chinese, good manners, and familiarity with the Confucian classics, Ricci was accepted as one of their own kind. His circle of influential friends and admirers broadened, and the number of visitors to the mission multiplied, as did the invitations to dine. Dinners among the literati were quite formal occasions, conventionally short on food from a Western perspective, but long on ceremony and conversation. Ricci's Jesuit heritage put a high value on conversation, and he used the opportunities offered by the dinners to share ideas with his fellow scholars. Each from their respective Christian and Confucian perspectives, they talked philosophy, ethics, and religion.

Ethics lay at the heart of Confucian philosophy, organized according to the so-called Five Relationships (father-son, husband-wife, elder and younger brother, ruler-subject, and friendship).[16] Friendship, as one of the Five Relationships, would come up naturally enough in Ricci's conversations with the mandarins, and one of them encouraged Ricci to put down in writing Western thought on the subject. In late 1595 Ricci completed a treatise on friendship, the first effort altogether by a Westerner to conceive and write a work in Chinese ideographs. It consisted of seventy-six, in a later edition one hundred, maxims, written in the proverbial form found in the Confucian canon.[17] This collection of aphorisms garnered Ricci more respect than anything he had done up to that time. His prisms and clocks may have won him a name for cleverness, but the treatise on friendship won him a reputation for learning and virtue.

Ricci composed a second book in Chinese, a short treatise on the art of memory, which he presented as a gift to the provincial governor and his three sons. The young men would have to take the state examinations in the Confucian classics, and Ricci hoped that this book would earn him enough influence with the governor that the latter would help him get to Beijing, where he still hoped to convert the emperor. That ascent to Beijing would involve an initial failed attempt, two years in the old capital of Nanjing, unfriendly encounters with a highly influential eunuch of the imperial court, and finally a second, this time successful, trip to Beijing in 1601. The fact that the Jesuits were allowed to establish a residence in Beijing was due in no little part to the gifts Ricci presented to the emperor, among them a large chiming clock and a harpsichord. When the clock ran down, Ricci and a Jesuit companion were summoned to the imperial palace to teach the eunuchs how to wind it. The harpsichord would occasion the invitation to the Jesuits to teach the eunuchs how to play it. Ricci found himself writing the Chinese lyrics to eight songs.

Ricci's literary output would come to include *Twenty-Five Sayings*, a booklet on virtues drawn from the Greek Stoic philosopher Epictetus; a Chinese translation of the first six books of Euclid's *Elements of Geometry*; and *Ten Truths Contrary to Public Opinion*, a reference to a third-century BC Taoist classic. But the most important and original of Ricci's writings was unquestionably *The True Meaning of the Lord of Heaven*. Published in 1603, it was in every way a *tour de force*—the fruit of two decades of immersion in Chinese culture and an emblematic demonstration of Valignano's vision of cultural accommodation.

The True Meaning of the Lord of Heaven is framed as a dialogue between a Chinese and Western scholar. Though later critics would unfairly fault the book for omitting basic doctrines (and accuse the Jesuits of watering down the gospel), it was never intended to be a full exposition of Christian faith. Its purpose was propaedeutic. Quoting the Bible would obviously have been meaningless to Ricci's Chinese readers. The only authorities he could appeal to were the Confucian classics, which he cited frequently and interpreted as supporting Christian faith.

That Ricci needed to interpret, not merely cite, Confucian texts calls for some comment. Confucianism during the Sung dynasty (960-1279 AD) had come under the influence of Buddhism, particularly its monism by which God was taken to be an impersonal substance united with and uniting all things. The upshot was a development into what has come to be called Neo-Confucianism. Ricci set about attempting to show that the personal God of Christianity, not the impersonal monism of Buddhism, was more fully in accord with Confucian origins.[18] Not surprisingly, both Buddhists and Neo-Confucians challenged Ricci's interpretation. But, more significantly, there were also leading Confucian scholars who agreed with him, and still others who, while not agreeing, accepted his interpretation as tenable and worthy of consideration.

The True Meaning of the Lord of Heaven argues for three fundamental principles of natural law, which Ricci saw as common to both Christianity and original Confucianism: the existence of a personal God, the immortality of the soul, and eternal reward or punishment. The influence of Thomas Aquinas is apparent throughout, as Ricci argued from reason against such Buddhist notions as nirvana and reincarnation. Ricci evinced little sympathy for Buddhism, which he took to be rife with superstition and idolatry. He regarded it as competing with Christianity and incompatible with it. More positively, his aim was to demonstrate that one did not have to give up Confucian culture in order to become Christian. On the contrary, Ricci argued, Christianity completed the philosophical ethics of China's sages. To demonstrate that, however, Ricci also needed to address questions of Confucian practice.

In the abstract, the virtue of filial piety (*hsiao*), so central for Confucian tradition, might appear unproblematic, but it raised any number of practical difficulties for the missionaries. Filial piety was used to justify polygamy. Though most Chinese men could afford only one wife, many wealthy Confucian scholars had several wives to ensure progeny to honor them and their ancestors. Here the Jesuits drew the line. If any Confucian scholar wished to convert to Christianity, he first had to promise to make do with one wife. Accommodation to Chinese culture and mores clearly had its limits. An even knottier question, however, was whether those limits excluded the practice of the "Chinese rites."

The observance of filial piety in China was not left to happenstance or sentiment. It was determined by detailed rituals and rules of propriety. An obedient son was duty-bound to care for his elderly parents during their lifetime and to render them a proper funeral and burial after their death. Even after burial, deceased parents and ancestors must be remembered in each home with memorial tablets inscribed with their names and set up on family altars or shrines. Mourners performed various gestures of respect before the tablets—kneeling, bowing, lighting candles, burning incense. On certain prescribed occasions, families gathered, set offerings of food and drink before the shrines, and later shared in a common meal. Similar rites were prescribed to honor Confucius at shrines set up to honor "Master K'ung the most holy teacher of antiquity."[19]

From their first entry into China and its Confucian circles, Ricci and the other Jesuits had to confront the question of these ancestral and Confucian rites. How should one interpret these symbolic gestures? Were they religious or merely civil and social? Was Confucius being honored as divine? Did the Chinese believe that the spirits of the dead were somehow present in the memorial tablets inscribed with their names? The difficulty in determining the meaning of the rites was that several of their components—candles, incense, profound bows, the offering of food and drink—could appear religious in a Western context. But this was China, where the profound kowtow was simply the appropriate gesture of respect to be shown high-ranking civil officials. Was such a gesture to be taken as worship when directed to a memorial tablet?

Ricci's opinions on the ancestral and Confucian rites were at once sympathetic and discriminating, obviously drawn from conversations with Confucian scholars and their answers to his pointed questions. Ricci relates in his journals that the whole idea of the rituals honoring one's ancestors was "to serve them in death as though they were alive." Food is set out for the deceased "because they know of no other way to show their love and grateful spirit toward them." Ricci relates being told that "this ceremony was begun more for the living than for the dead," to teach children how to respect living parents, seeing how they were honored in death. The Chinese did not regard their deceased ancestors as gods, nor did they ask them for favors. The same could be said of the rites honoring Confucius. Though candles are lighted and incense burned to express gratitude for Master K'ung's teachings, this was done without prayers or petitions to him. So the rites were free of idolatry and "perhaps" superstition.[20]

Ricci's qualifying "perhaps" derived from his awareness that superstition was rife among the poorer, uneducated Chinese, many of whom did worship Confucius as a god and did practice the ancestral rites as a form of magic. But Ricci believed that such misunderstanding did not vitiate the original and essential non-religious nature of the rites, which he saw as legitimate and good. Superstition was not inherent in the rites. They did not have to be abolished just because they could be abused. Ricci had only to remember how uneducated peasants back home in Europe could misuse relics, rosaries, and any number of other Catholic sacramental signs and symbols. Did Europeans place flowers on graves for the dead to smell them?

As superior of the Jesuit mission in China, Ricci issued an historic directive on the rites. Although the text of that directive no longer exists, we know its contents: that allowing Chinese Christians to observe the ancestral and Confucian rites is licit and even indispensable for Christian missionary work. There was no conclusive evidence that the rites were inherently superstitious and much evidence that excluded such a conception.[21] When they use the word "sacrifice" to describe the food brought to the Confucian ceremonies, it is "in a broad and indefinite sense." The ceremonies are not false worship because the Chinese honor Confucius as a great philosopher and teacher, not a god.[22]

Ricci's years in Beijing were the most productive yet for the missionary. Within the first five years there were over a hundred converts in Beijing, and by 1608 more than two thousand Christians in China altogether. [23] Most of the converts were from the ordinary ranks of Chinese society, merchants, craftsmen, and peasants, but they also included some of the intellectual elite and high-ranking officials.[24] The number of Christians was "not as great as might be wished," Ricci wrote, but he saw his task as one of preparing the way for others. Not harvesting nor even sowing the seed, but merely, as he put it, "clearing the forest."[25]

Given the intensity of his labors, Ricci did not expect to live a long life. Beijing in 1610 was filled with candidates for the triennial examinations, so the press of visitors eager to meet Ricci was even greater than usual. There were some days when he hardly had time to rest or eat until late in the evening. His labors took their toll. On May 3, he fell seriously ill and a week later, on May 11, he died. Among his last words he said, "I am leaving you before an open door which leads to great merits, but not without great effort and many dangers."[26] Ricci's words were uncannily prescient. Merit, effort, danger—his successors would encounter all three.

A Humanist Legacy

Ricci never met, let alone conversed with, the emperor. But among the Jesuits who took up his mantle, two of them— Adam Schall and Ferdinand Verbiest—did meet and converse with the Chinese emperors of their day. Similarly noteworthy is Roberto de Nobili, who explicitly appealed to

Ricci as a precedent when he sought to accommodate Christianity to Brahmin culture in India. And it appeared for a time that accommodation to culture, as envisioned by Valignano and practiced by Ricci, had won the day. As the Catholic Church had once wedded the Bible with late Hellenistic and Roman philosophy and letters to produce the Christian West, it would have to do the same in China and India to produce a Catholic East. That was what Ricci hoped and worked for, and there were Jesuits willing to follow his example so long as the door Ricci left behind remained open. Such, however, was not to be the case.

"The Chinese rites controversy," as it came to be called, erupted thirty-five years after Ricci's death, in 1645. Its tortured three-hundred year history would involve Jesuits, Dominicans, Franciscans, twenty-six popes, a host of Vatican cardinals, and a Chinese emperor. Even a summary narrative of the controversy would be too convoluted to rehearse here. Suffice it to say that Ricci's humanistic directive was overturned, when, in 1704, the Vatican forbade Chinese Catholics to have any part in the ritual practices honoring their ancestors or Confucius. The ruling meant in effect that, to become Christian, converts had to cease being Chinese, since it forbade them to do what, for Chinese culture, was simply requisite decency and good manners. That same year, 1704, the door began to close on accommodation in India as well. For the next two hundred years Catholic Christianity in China and India would remain alien western implants.

In 1939 the Vatican overturned the fateful decision regarding the Chinese ancestral and Confucian rites. Their reasons for doing so were essentially the same as those Ricci had offered three hundred years earlier. In 1965 the Second Vatican Council not only allowed but called for the adaptation of Christian life to indigenous cultures. It declared that "accommodated preaching" is the "law of all evangelization."[27] One can only conjecture how different China, India, and the Catholic Church might be today if those decisions had been made two hundred and fifty years earlier. Instead, all we can say is that the rites controversies in China and India are cautionary tales about the risks entailed in attributing too much omniscience to a remote centralized authority.

Four hundred years after Valignano and Ricci, their idea of accommodating Christianity to non-Western cultures enjoys a new beginning. The highest authorities in the Catholic Church have given official approval, at least in theory, to the concept of inculturation. In an era in which crosscultural studies and interreligious dialogue have become routine, it bears remembering that Matteo Ricci was the first Westerner to venture such undertakings. Granted, his motives were to convert the Chinese to Catholicism, and to that end he studied ancient Chinese texts and entered into conversation with Chinese scholars on matters of morality and religion. But the first practice was deeply rooted in his humanist training; the second in his Jesuit spirituality.

Going back to Ignatius, conversation is an integral part of the Spiritual Exercises and of the Jesuit "manner of proceeding." Today, at least as Ricci practiced it, we may prefer to call it dialogue. Considerable thought and literature has been devoted in recent years to the concept of dialogue—how it differs from debate; how it requires sympathetic listening and the willingness to learn, to be enriched, even to be changed.[28] Ricci's dialogues with Confucian scholars resulted in the conversion of any number of them to Christianity. But those dialogues and his study of Confucian texts converted Ricci as well. As he learned and as we now better appreciate, dialogue can have profound, unintended consequences. Thanks to dialogue, Ricci changed not only his dress and lifestyle, but his thinking and attitudes, as he acquired a profound admiration for a culture vastly different from his own. Ricci was not uncritical of China—its widespread superstition and social order, for example. But, notwithstanding its serious failings from a Western and Christian point of view, there was still much that was worthy of respect.

Along these lines, theologians today have gone far beyond Ricci.[29] He had a distinct bias against Buddhism. He did not study it deeply enough to realize Buddhist affinities with certain Christian mystic traditions, and contemporary theologians who have studied Buddhism and engaged in Buddhist-Christian dialogue have described the two traditions as complementary. Ricci's efforts at adaptation (or inculturation, as it is called today), while respected as pioneering, have been criticized for too neatly separating Asian culture from its religious roots and content. Not Ricci's blind spot toward Buddhism or his other shortcomings, however, but his sympathetic reading of Confucius is what deserves our respectful consideration. His humanity and warmth are what inspire us. His humanism is what allowed him to transcend cultures.

Ricci's Jesuit, humanist education encouraged him not only to read but to find value and beauty in the pre-Christian classics of Greek and Latin antiquity. Wisdom, for Renaissance humanists, was universal; truth was where you found it. Ricci was the first Westerner to find wisdom and truth expressed in Chinese ideographs. Nothing human was foreign to him because nothing human was merely human. As a Jesuit, Ricci was trained to see God in all things. That came to include the faces of the Chinese he called friends.

Notes

1. Matteo Ricci, *China in the Sixteenth Century: The Journals of Matthew Ricci: 1583-1610*, trans. Louis J. Gallagher (New York: Random House, 1953), 30.

2. Ricci, *Journals*, 93.

3. For a convenient history of Catholic thinking in this area, see Francis A. Sullivan, *Salvation Outside the Church? Tracing the History of the Catholic Response* (New York: Paulist, 1992), especially 52-60, 88-94.

4. *The Letters and Instructions of Francis Xavier*, trans. M. Joseph

Costelloe (St. Louis: Institute of Jesuit Sources, 1992), 15.

5. Andrew C. Ross, *A Vision Betrayed: The Jesuits in Japan and China, 1542-1742* (Maryknoll, NY: Orbis, 1994), 17.

6. Georg Schurhammer, *Francis Xavier, His Life and Times*, vol. 4, trans. M. Joseph Costelloe (Rome: Jesuit Historical Institute, 1982), 216-219.

7. The most thorough treatment on Valignano in English is Josef Franz Schütte, *Valignano's Mission Principles for Japan*, 2 vols., trans. John J. Coyne (St. Louis: Institute of Jesuit Sources, 1980). Another fine scholarly book-length study is J. F. Moran, *The Japanese and the Jesuits: Alessandro Valignano in Sixteenth Century Japan* (London: Routledge, 1993). Excellent shorter treatments are to be found in George H. Dunne, *Generation of Giants: The Story of the Jesuits in China in the Last Decades of the Ming Dynasty* (Notre Dame: University of Notre Dame Press, 1962) and Ross.

8. Moran, 54.

9. *Advertimentos e avisos acerca dos customes e catangues de Jappão.* For a detailed description of its contents in English see Schütte, vol. 2, 155-190.

10. Ibid., 163.

11. Amid his detailed instructions, time and again Ignatius would add the proviso that they should be followed unless circumstances indicate it would be better to do otherwise.

12. The most complete biography of Ricci is the two-volume work of Henri Bernard, *Le Père Matthieu Ricci et la Société Chinoise de son temps (1552-1610)* (Tientsin: Hautes Études, 1937). In English there is the scholarly biography of Jonathan D. Spence, *The Memory Palace of Matteo Ricci* (New York: Viking, 1984) and the more popular biography by Vincent Cronin, *The Wise Man from the West* (New York: E. P. Dutton, 1955). All of them draw on Ricci's *Journals*. Shorter treatments of Ricci's life and career are to be found in Dunne and Ross.

13. Ricci's prodigious memory and his *Treatise on Mnemonic Arts* are the principal focus of Spence's biography.

14. Ross, 123.

15. Ricci, *Journals*, 94.

16. See Julia Ching, *Confucianism and Christianity: A Comparative*

Study (Tokyo: Kodansha International, 1977), 97.

17. Ricci drew from a variety of sources, including an anthology contained in the mission library, *Sententiae et Exempla*, compiled by the Portuguese humanist Andreas de Resende (Eborensis). See Pasquale M. D'Elia, "Il Trattato sull'Amicizia," *Studia Missionalia* 7 (1952): 425-515, and "Further Notes on Matteo Ricci's *De Amicitia*," *Monumenta serica* 15 (1956): 356-377.

18. Ross, 148-149.

19. George Minamiki, *The Chinese Rites Controversy from Its Beginnings to Modern Times* (Chicago: Loyola University, 1985), 3-10.

20. Minamiki, 17-20. See also Ricci, *Journals*, 96-97.

21. Ray R. Noll, ed., *100 Roman Documents Concerning the Chinese Rites Controversy (1645-1941)* trans. Donald F. St. Sure (San Francisco: Ricci Institute, University of San Francisco, 1992), vii.

22. Rule, *K'ung-tzu or Confucius*, 47.

23. Dunne, 101, 104.

24. Ross, 166. Ross argues against the claim that Jesuits, unlike other religious orders, preferred a "top down" missionary strategy that favored the elite over the ordinary people of China. It was the Jesuits' acceptance by the scholars that made their outreach to the masses possible.

25. Cited in Tacchi Venturi, *Opere Storiche del P. Matteo Ricci*, vol. 2 (Macerata, Italy: Filippo Gioretti, 1913), 246-247.

26. Ricci, *Journals*, 563; Cronin, 272.

27. *Dogmatic Constitution on the Church in the Modern World*, 44; *Decree on Missions*, 22.

28. On the nature and potential impact of dialogue, see Leonard Swidler, "The Dialogue Decalogue: Ground Rules for Interreligious, Interideological Dialogue," *Journal of Ecumenical Studies* (Winter, 1983): 1-4.

29. The work of the Sri Lankan Jesuit Aloysius Pieris is especially notable in this respect. See his *Love Meets Wisdom: A Christian Experience of Buddhism* (Maryknoll, NY: Orbis, 1988); *An Asian Theology of Liberation* (Maryknoll, NY: Orbis, 1988); *Fire and Water: Basic Issues in Asian Buddhism and Christianity* (Maryknoll, NY: Orbis, 1996).

Alexandre de Rhodes' Mission in Vietnam: Evangelization and Inculturation

Peter C. Phan
Warren-Blanding Distinguished Professor of Religion and Culture
The Catholic University of America

Historical records suggest that Christianity made its first appearance in Vietnam in the sixteenth century.[1] However, it was only with the arrival of the Jesuits in Cochinchina that Christianity began to strike root. On January 6, 1615 Valentino de Carvalho, then the provincial of Japan, sent three Jesuits, Fathers Francesco Buzomi and Diego Carvalho, and Brother António Dias, to Cochinchina. Between 1616 and 1623, eleven other Jesuits joined the mission. In December 1624, another group of seven Jesuits, among whom was Alexandre de Rhodes, arrived in Cochinchina.[2]

Though not the first to arrive in Vietnam, de Rhodes is often proclaimed the founder of Vietnamese Christianity. No doubt he deserves this accolade. First, he carried out a highly successful mission in both parts of Vietnam, Tonkin and Cochinchina. Second, he wrote two priceless memoirs on Vietnamese society in the seventeenth century and on the beginnings of Vietnamese Christianity,[3] as well as a dictionary and a catechism in Vietnamese, in the Romanized script.[4] Third, he successfully lobbied for the establishment of a hierarchy in Vietnam. In this essay I will give a very brief account of de Rhodes' mission in Vietnam and then discuss his adaptations and innovations in the fields of culture and liturgy.

De Rhodes' First Mission in Cochinchina (1624-1626)

Born in Avignon on March 15, 1593, Alexandre de Rhodes joined the Jesuit novitiate in Rome to pursue his missionary vocation.[5] Shortly after his priestly ordination in 1618, de Rhodes was granted permission to go to the mission in Japan by Superior General Mutio Vitelleschi. On July 20, 1619, de Rhodes left Lisbon, and after six months and ten days arrived in Goa. After a lengthy delay in Goa, on April 22, 1622, de Rhodes resumed his journey to Macao where he arrived on May 29, 1623. De Rhodes stayed at the Jesuit college Madre de Deus, preparing himself for his work in Japan by learning the Japanese language.

De Rhodes' dream of being a missionary in Japan was not to be realized. Because of persecutions there, de Rhodes' superiors thought it wise to send him instead to Cochinchina. Although there was a king of the Le dynasty in seventeenth-century Vietnam, he was in fact nothing more than a puppet; real political power lay in the hands of two clans. The north, known to the West as Tonkin, was under the Trinh clan, and the center, known then as Cochinchina, was under the Nguyen clan. Continuous warfare was conducted between the two rival clans for total control of the country with no definitive results. De Rhodes' entire ministry in Vietnam was carried out during this struggle for power between Tonkin and Cochinchina.[6]

There were three Jesuit residences in Cochinchina when de Rhodes arrived in the country at the end of 1624. He was assigned to that of Thanh Chiem to study the language under the guidance of Francisco de Pina.[7] Meanwhile Andrea Palmiero, the Jesuit visitor, was planning to send missionaries to Tonkin. In July 1626, de Rhodes and Pêro Marques were recalled to Macao to prepare for their mission in Tonkin.

De Rhodes' Mission in Tonkin (1627-1630)

On March 1627, the two missionaries boarded a Portuguese merchant ship for Tonkin and arrived at Cua Bang (today Ba Lang) on March 19, 1627. Shortly afterwards, they met Lord Trinh Trang who was on his way to war against Cochinchina. When Lord Trinh Trang returned in defeat from his military expedition, the missionaries accompanied him to Thang Long, the capital, and there began their mission in earnest.

The great number of conversions aroused the opposition of eunuchs, Buddhist monks, and the concubines dismissed by their husbands who had decided to become Christian. One of the monks accused the missionaries of joining in a plot against Lord Trinh Trang. As a result, on May 28, 1628, Lord Trinh Trang issued a decree forbidding his subjects, under pain of death, to meet with the missionaries or to embrace the religion they preached.

However, the lord tolerated the presence of de Rhodes and Marques in the hope that they would attract Portuguese traders. When the Portuguese ships did not come during that sailing season, the lord expelled the missionaries. In March 1629, they left for the south with the plan to return to Macao. However, in November, when two Jesuits, Gaspar do Amaral and Paul Saito, arrived, de Rhodes and Marques returned to the capital in their company. At first, Lord Trinh Trang tolerated their presence, but after six months, when the Portuguese ship returned to Macao, he ordered them to board the ship and leave the country.

In May 1630, de Rhodes left Tonkin, never to return. He had worked there for more than three years. By numerical standards alone, his mission had been a huge success: when he departed, there were 5,602 Christians.[8]

Banished from Tonkin de Rhodes returned to Macao and stayed there for ten years during which he taught theology at the Madre de Deus College and took care of Chinese Christians. However, in 1639, events in Cochinchina once again made de Rhodes' missionary experience highly desir-

able. There were then some 15,000 Christians and 20 churches in central Vietnam.[9] In 1639, the lord of Cochinchina,
Nguyen Phuoc Lan, who suspected that the missionaries
had assisted his brother's rebellion against him, ordered the
seven Jesuits to leave the country.

De Rhodes' Second Mission to Cochinchina (1640-1645)

Eager to continue the mission in Cochinchina, the new visitor Antonio Rubino canvassed for someone to send there. De
Rhodes volunteered and was accepted. Thus began de
Rhodes' second mission to Cochinchina. It was divided into
four trips and lasted a total of fifty months, from 1640 to
1645. As a whole, it was far more difficult and eventful than
his mission in Tonkin. Four times he was exiled from the
country.

During the fifty months de Rhodes spent in Cochinchina
between 1640 and 1645, he baptized some 3,400 people, not
counting the baptisms administered by his catechists.
Compared with his mission in Tonkin, which produced 5,602
conversions, de Rhodes' second mission in Cochinchina produced significantly fewer conversions, though the mission
was much longer and much more strenuous (fifty versus
thirty-eight months). On July 3, 1645, sentenced to perpetual
exile from Cochinchina, de Rhodes left Vietnam for Macao.

Return to Rome and the Establishment of the Hierarchy in Vietnam

De Rhodes' superiors in Macao decided that a man of his
experience could render a vast service to the missions by
going back to Europe to fetch spiritual and temporal help. In
December 1645, de Rhodes began his return journey to Rome.
Immediately after his arrival on June 27, 1649, he set out to
realize his plan of having a hierarchy established in Vietnam.

On September 11, 1652, de Rhodes left for Paris where he
found three priests of the *Société des Bons Amis* who were
judged worthy candidates for the episcopacy, among whom

was François Pallu. On learning that Rome was about to send French bishops to Vietnam, Portugal voiced fierce opposition. Meanwhile the Jesuit General, believing that de Rhodes' presence in the project of establishing a hierarchy in Vietnam would prevent it from being realized, decided to make him superior of the Jesuit mission in Persia. On November 16, 1654, de Rhodes left Marseilles for his new mission where he died on November 5, 1660. But his dream of having a hierarchy for Vietnam was fulfilled shortly before his death when on September 9, 1659, Propaganda Fide published a decree, confirmed by Pope Alexander VII, establishing two apostolic vicariates with two bishops: François Pallu and Pierre Lambert de la Motte.[10]

De Rhodes and Cultural Practices

Like his fellow Jesuit missionaries Matteo Ricci in China and Roberto de Nobili in India, de Rhodes was profoundly sensitive to the cultural and religious traditions of the people he was evangelizing. He was convinced that successful missionary work required not only mastery of the native language but also familiarity with the people's customs and culture. That de Rhodes took enormous pains to learn about the countries and peoples he evangelized is testified by his many memoirs in which he provided us with a detailed and for the most part surprisingly accurate account of the socio-political histories, cultural practices, and religious traditions of both Tonkin and Cochinchina. In addition, he also described the ways in which he attempted to inculturate the Christian faith and practices into the local situation. In this section we will examine some of the ways in which de Rhodes attempted to meet these challenges in the areas of cultural practices and liturgical celebrations.

De Rhodes' profound knowledge of the Vietnamese language no doubt contributed to the astounding achievements of his mission. In Salsette near Goa he noticed how his countryman Etienne Crucius' perfect mastery of the local dialects

facilitated large-scale conversions. His own language studies
in Central Vietnam during the years 1624-1626, and his relative lack of success among the Chinese in Macao during the
decade 1630-1640 because of his inability to preach in their
tongue, convinced de Rhodes that mastery of the languages
of the peoples to be evangelized was the first and fundamental condition for the effective preaching of the gospel.[11]
It may be said that learning local languages well is the *sine
qua non* first stage of inculturation that missionaries must
undergo. This first stage is all the more urgent if language is
not merely a means of communication but a "house of
Being," a way of *experiencing* reality of which religion is an
expression. Language, in the words of Sri Lankan theologian
Aloysius Pieris, is indeed a *theologia inchoativa*.[12]

De Rhodes' belief that language is incipient theology is
implied in his view that the Hebrew language was the only
valid medium to transmit God's revealed teachings and that
nations that lost the Hebrew language after the confusion of
languages at Babel, e.g., China, fell into heresies such as
Confucianism, Taoism, and Buddhism.[13]

Besides knowledge of the language, de Rhodes also vehemently insisted on the need for missionaries to adapt to, and
for indigenous neophytes to preserve, local cultural practices
that were not contrary to Christian morality. He was scandalized by the fact that Indian Christians in Goa were
required to abandon their native costumes and to dress in
the Portuguese fashion. He also vigorously protested against
the obligation imposed upon Chinese male Christians to
wear their hair short.

De Rhodes' two criteria for judging the acceptability of a
particular cultural practice were whether it was required by
Jesus himself and whether it was opposed to the gospel.
These norms are implied both in his disagreement concerning the demands placed on the Indian Christians ("I don't
know why they are asked to do things that the Lord would
not have asked of them")[14] and his statement to Chinese

male Christians who were compelled to cut off their long hair ("I used to tell them that the gospel obliged them to lop off their spiritual errors but not their long hair").[15]

In his description of the "temporal state" of Tonkin de Rhodes recounted several cultural customs some of which he regarded religiously neutral, others morally objectionable.[16] Among the latter was polygamy. De Rhodes' opposition to this practice was one of the reasons for his expulsion from Tonkin. De Rhodes considered it immoral and made the dismissal of "concubines" a condition for the reception of baptism. No doubt, for him, polygamy was both contrary to the gospel and forbidden by Jesus, the two criteria he used to adjudicate the acceptability of a cultural practice.

On biblical grounds, he condemns polygamy by appealing to the Genesis account of the creation of one man and one woman.[17] In his exposition of the sixth commandment, he explicitly invokes both God's law and Christ's teaching against polygamy: "A legitimate marriage is one of one man and one woman so that as long as one partner is alive, no other partner may be taken. Consequently, polygamy as well as divorce is contrary to the divine law. Indeed, at the beginning, it was not so, as the Lord Jesus himself has taught with his own divine mouth. In fact, at the beginning, God gave Adam only one woman, Eve, and he remained with her until his death, for nine hundred thirty years."[18]

In addition to these Christian grounds, de Rhodes also sought to buttress his opposition to polygamy by appealing to a Vietnamese proverb: "*Hai vo chong gui xuong gui thit nhau,*" literally, the husband and the wife, give one another their bones and flesh. In itself the proverb is no argument against polygamy; it simply affirms the mutual commitment between the husband and the wife, and in principle can be applied to the husband and his "concubines" since the latter are truly and legally his wives. Nevertheless, it serves as an instructive example of how de Rhodes attempted to inculturate a Christian doctrine and practice, especially when it repudiates a local custom.

Besides outright rejection, de Rhodes also attempted either to impose a Christian meaning to theologically neutral cultural practices or to transform them in such a way that their potentially objectionable elements are purified. As an example of the first strategy, de Rhodes took advantage of a rather curious practice in Tonkin as an entry point for evangelization:

> I noted one custom among them that might suggest that our holy faith had been preached at one time in that kingdom, where nevertheless all memory of it has been obliterated by now. As soon as children were born, I often saw the parents put a crossmark on their foreheads with charcoal or ink. I asked them what good this would do to the child and why they daubed this mark on its forehead. "That," they used to tell me, "is to chase away the devil and keep him from harming the child." I immediately rejoined, "But how could that frighten devils, who are spirits?" They admitted to me they knew nothing more about it, but I did not neglect to disclose its secret to them by explaining the power of the holy cross. This often served me as a means of converting them.[19]

With regard to other cultural practices, de Rhodes neutralized their potentially superstitious elements by christianizing them. An example of this second strategy is the oath of allegiance that soldiers had to swear to the lord of Tonkin. Once a year, toward the end of the sixth month of the lunar calendar (roughly July), in the presence of a literary doctor representing the lord, every soldier had to pronounce aloud the oath of fidelity to the lord in front of a richly decorated altar "dedicated to the gods or rather to the devils."[20] After the swearing ceremony, each soldier received from the doctor a certificate marked with *minh* (clearly), or *bat minh* (not clearly), or *thuan* (average), indicating the degree of his loyalty to the lord. According to these grades, the soldier would be rewarded with a cloak of various length and quality.

The danger of swearing loyalty to the lord consisted for Christians in its association with gods and devils and its superstitious formula. A Christian soldier, with de Rhodes' approval, substituted the official formula with one inspired by the Christian faith: "I swear to the true God of heaven and earth, Father, Son, and Holy Spirit, the company of the blessed spirits, and the whole court of heaven that I shall render faithful service to my king (Trinh Trang) until death. If I lie, if I swear falsely, and against my conscience, I shall be glad to be killed at this moment by the true God, the Lord of heaven and earth, and be consumed by God's lightnings."[21]

Another example has to do with the celebration of Tet, the Vietnamese New Year, arguably the most solemn cultural feast in Vietnam. The Vietnamese had the custom of erecting, on the evening of the last day of the year, a bamboo pole (*cay neu*) in front of their house to invite their deceased parents (*ruoc ong ba*) to come and share in the family's celebration of the New Year. This pole is about 15 to 18 feet tall, higher than the roof of the house. Near the top of the pole is attached a small wicker basket or a bag containing a few mouthfuls of areca nut and betel (*mieng trau*) and several pieces of gilded paper money (*tien ma*).

The purpose of this custom is to welcome and assist the deceased parents. Areca and betel are the host's typical welcoming offerings to guests, and money is given to dead parents so that they may pay their debts before the beginning of the New Year. The Vietnamese believe that it is a bad omen not to pay before the New Year debts incurred during the previous year. Obviously, the dead ancestors are believed to have the same needs as the living, so that they are provided with the same things that the living require in their daily life. The bamboo pole serves as a sign to direct the ancestors to the houses of their descendants where they are invited.[22]

De Rhodes regarded the custom of erecting the bamboo pole, especially the offering of paper money to ancestors with which they may pay their debts, as nothing but "foolish imagination" and "superstition."[23] However, the New Year was such a culturally central celebration and afforded such a pastorally enriching opportunity that he was determined to keep the custom and at the same time transform the elements he deemed objectionable. He advised the Christians to attach to the *cay neu* a crucifix rather than the wicker basket or the bag with offerings: "One could see almost on all the streets of the city this venerable sign of our salvation raised above the housetops, causing terror to demons and joy to angels. The lord himself saw it as he was carried around the principal streets on New Year's Day.... Seeing these crosses raised high, he said: That is the sign of the Christians."[24]

De Rhodes also invested the New Year celebrations with Christian meanings. The Vietnamese celebrate the New Year in three days: the first day (*mong mot*) is reserved to the cult of ancestors; the second (*mong hai*) to near relatives; and the third (*mong ba*) to the dead. De Rhodes, on the other hand, asked the Christians to dedicate the three days to the Trinity: "The first day in memory of the benefits of creation and conservation, which is dedicated to God the Father; the second in thanksgiving for the inestimable benefit of redemption, which is dedicated to God the Son; and the third in humble gratitude to the Holy Spirit for the grace of being called to be a Christian."[25]

Finally, not only was de Rhodes interested in christianizing Vietnamese cultural customs but he was also careful not to introduce practices that would set Christians apart as a culturally separate group. During his first stay in Cochinchina, the Christian community ran into a potentially fatal difficulty. Lord Nguyen Phuoc Nguyen had issued an edict forbidding Christians to wear images, crosses, and rosaries around their necks. As de Rhodes noted, many Christians considered it cowardice unworthy of the

Christian name to conceal the insignia of their faith, and were ready to shed their blood in defiance of the lord's edict.

De Rhodes himself had nothing but the greatest reverence for religious objects and a profound admiration for those who wore them.[26] However, in this case, the outward display of religious objects, besides exposing the Christians to unnecessary death, would set them culturally apart from the other Vietnamese, just as Portuguese fashion set Indian Christians, and short hair set Chinese male Christians, apart from their compatriots. For all these reasons, de Rhodes and his fellow Jesuits persuaded, not without difficulty, the Christians to forgo wearing these sacred objects. In this way, the Vietnamese Christians "gave unbelievers no excuse for showing disrespect for the piety of our Christians."[27]

In sum, de Rhodes' attitude toward Vietnamese cultural practices was subtle and complex. (1) Generally, those practices he considered morally unacceptable, he would firmly reject, appealing to the law of the gospel and the teaching of Christ, his twin criteria for acceptability, and when possible, invoking Vietnamese wisdom embodied in proverbs and sayings to support his position. (2) Practices that were apparently good, he preserved and gave them a Christian meaning. (3) Practices that were in his judgment liable to superstition but possessed a strong potential for pastoral and spiritual enrichment, he purified by omitting their objectionable elements or by transforming them with a Christian interpretation. (4) Finally, he was in principle opposed to introducing into Vietnamese culture Christian practices that, though laudable in themselves, would set the Vietnamese Christians culturally apart from their compatriots.

Adaptations of Christian Liturgy

So far we have seen how de Rhodes modified or substituted certain Vietnamese cultural and religious usages. We will now investigate de Rhodes' reverse attempts to help the Vietnamese make sense of Christian liturgical celebrations.

De Rhodes reported that the Vietnamese Christians celebrated Christmas with great solemnity. Most interesting is
his practice of administering baptism *in public* and *during the
Mass* so that the connection between the physical birth of
Jesus and the spiritual birth of catechumens would be made
transparent. The congregation sang, besides religious songs,
Christmas carols, which means they had been translated into
Vietnamese. Furthermore, de Rhodes respected the cultural
custom of not allowing women to go out at night, so that he
told them to come to the Christmas Day Mass only. After the
Mass, he exposed the statue of the Infant Jesus for the faith-
ful's adoration.[28]

On the feast of the Purification of the Virgin, de Rhodes
organized the solemn blessing of the candles. The catechumens carried them during the procession into the church and
afterward were allowed to take them home. De Rhodes
noted that they had these candles lighted when they were on
their deathbed to prepare for a holy death. Moreover, these
candles also helped Christians break the taboo common
among the Vietnamese of not using the word "death" but
rather a circumlocution, especially in front of a person of
rank.[29]

With regard to fasting, de Rhodes noted that Vietnamese
non-Christians observed an extremely rigorous fast in honor
of their "idols." They abstained not only from meat and eggs
but also from milk products and fish of all kinds, not merely
for a few months but for their whole lives. Given this custom, de Rhodes encouraged Christians to practice fasting
beyond the minimum church requirements, not only during
Lent but also during Advent.[30]

On Palm Sunday, there was the blessing of the palms in
which not only Christians but also pagans participated.
Since there were no olive trees in Vietnam, de Rhodes substituted olive branches with those of local coconut trees.
Christians kept these blessed branches at home to chase
away demons and evil spirits. On Holy Friday the cross was

exposed for veneration by the faithful.[31]

One of de Rhodes' most interesting paraliturgical innovations (and still in use) is what is known as *ngam dung*, that is, standing meditation. To enable the Christians to participate in the liturgy of Holy Week, in particular the Tenebrae, and to obviate problems caused by their ignorance of Latin, de Rhodes composed in Vietnamese the mysteries of the Passion in 15 *ngam* (meditations). Each of the meditations is declaimed, with the accompaniment of drum and gong, by a member of the faithful who stands (*dung*) on a platform in the middle of the church. Behind the platform there is a crucifix and a 15-branch candelabrum. At the end of each meditation, a candle is extinguished, followed by the common recital of one Our Father, seven Hail Marys, and one Glory Be. This well-attended liturgy, which resembles the classical Vietnamese theater (*cheo, tuong*), with its dialogues between the assembly and the declaimer, and the use of drum and gong, is still celebrated in many parts of Vietnam on every Friday of Lent and each evening of the Holy Week.[32]

De Rhodes has not provided us with detailed information on how he celebrated the sacraments and how he adapted them to the needs of the Vietnamese. Concerning the celebration of the Eucharist, given the fact the mission in China had failed to make use of Pope Paul V's authorization to celebrate the Mass, recite the breviary, and administer the sacraments in Chinese, it is highly likely that de Rhodes celebrated the Mass in Latin rather than in Vietnamese.[33] Furthermore, we learn that de Rhodes celebrated the Mass with his head uncovered. In China as well as in Vietnam, no one was permitted to appear before the king with the head uncovered, except criminals as a sign of shame. De Rhodes justified his practice of celebrating the Mass with the head uncovered with the argument that while the priest appears before God as the representative of Christ, he is also the representative of sinners imploring God for the remission of their sins. Hence, he can appear before God with the head uncovered.[34]

For those who could not attend Sunday Mass because of distance or because of the absence of the priest, de Rhodes encouraged them to meet together for prayer and devotions.[35] Moreover, a calendar was composed and distributed to Christians to facilitate remembrance of Sundays, holidays of obligation, and fast days.[36]

It is known that in his administration of baptism de Rhodes used the baptismal formula in Vietnamese. His Vietnamese baptismal formula is: *"Tao rua may, nhan nhat danh Cha, va Con, va Spirito Santo. Amen."*[37] For reasons unexplained, de Rhodes left the words *"Spirito Santo"* untranslated, even though he could easily have found the Vietnamese equivalents for them.[38] The reason de Rhodes used the Vietnamese formula for baptism is probably so that it could be used in the administration of the sacrament by catechists and other lay Vietnamese Christians who did not know Latin.

With regard to the baptismal rites themselves, de Rhodes took pains to explain gestures and things that may suggest magic. He reported that once as he was about to baptize 80 catechumens and was using the blessed salt in a plate as part of the ceremony, a man rushed into the church and shouted to the catechumens: "Wretched people! Be careful! He is performing sorcery with the thing in the plate!" De Rhodes had to explain to the people that the plate contained nothing but ordinary salt that had been blessed.[39]

In the administration of the sacrament of penance, de Rhodes found that the practice of auricular confession for women, even in public, with a board separating the confessor from the penitent, was offensive to the Vietnamese, especially to pagans. Once, de Rhodes relates, soldiers came into the church to listen to what the women were telling him. He resolved the problem by using two adjoining houses, the women staying in the one house and making their confessions through the wall to the priest who stayed in the other.[40]

De Rhodes repeatedly referred to books of prayers that he dictated to those who were leaders of the community so they could teach them to others.[41] Unfortunately, no such books survived to help us form an idea of how de Rhodes translated what he calls "Catholic prayers." Of course, these were not liturgical texts, as de Rhodes still used Latin for sacramental celebrations. There is no doubt that such prayers include the Our Father, the Hail Mary, the Glory Be, the acts of faith, hope, and charity, the act of contrition, the Apostles' Creed, morning and evening prayers, and various litanies.[42]

Conclusion

The challenges to de Rhodes' mission to Vietnam were multiple and diverse. They came from the Vietnamese cultural practices and religious traditions, from Christian liturgical celebrations, and from the very tasks of evangelization and catechesis. To meet all these challenges de Rhodes availed himself of all the means at his disposal: polemics against errors, adaptation of cultural customs, translation of Christian texts, and inculturation of Christian practices.

Notes

1. This essay is part of my work entitled *Mission and Catechesis: Alexandre de Rhodes and Inculturation in Seventeenth-Century Vietnam* (Maryknoll, NY: Orbis Books, 1998). All translations of de Rhodes' writings are mine. For earlier studies on de Rhodes, see the unpublished doctoral dissertations of Nguyen Khac Xuyen, "Le Catéchisme en langue vietnamienne romanisée du P. Alexandre de Rhodes" (Pontificia Universitas Gregoriana, 1956); Placide Tan Phat, "Méthodes de catéchèse et de conversion du Père Alexandre de Rhodes" (Institut Catholique de Paris, 1963); Do Quang Chinh, "La Mission au Viet-Nam 1624-1630 et 1640-1645 d'Alexandre de Rhodes" (Sorbonne, 1969); and Nguyen Chi Thiet, "Le Catéchisme du Père Alexandre de Rhodes et l'âme vietnamienne" (Pontificia Universitas Urbaniana, 1970). I am deeply grateful to Dr. Do Quang Chinh for his generous assistance in providing me with archival

materials on de Rhodes.

2. Besides de Rhodes, there were four Portuguese priests (Gabriel de Martos, Gaspar Luís, António de Fontes, and Manoel Gonzales), one Italian priest (Gerolamo Maiorica), and one Japanese priest (Michael Maki). See de Rhodes' letter written from Cochinchina on June 16, 1625 to Father Nuno Mascarenhas, Assistant for Portugal, in *Archivum Romanum Societatis Iesu, Jap.-Sin.* 68, f. 13 rv (henceforth: *ARSI, JS*).

3. The first work is entitled *Histoire du Royaume de Tunquin, et des grands progrez que la predication de l'Evangile y a faits en la conversion des infideles. Depuis l'année 1627 jusques à l'Année 1646. Composée en latin par le R. P. Alexandre de Rhodes, de la Compagnie de Jesus. Et traduite en françois par le R. P. Henry Albi, de la mesme Compagnie* (Lyon, 1651). (henceforth: *Histoire du Royaume.*) The second work is entitled *Divers voyages et missions du P. Alexandre de Rhodes en la Chine, & autres Royaumes de l'Orient. Avec son retour en Europe par la Perse & l'Arménie. Le tout divisé en trois parties.* (henceforth: *Divers voyages*).

4. The dictionary is entitled *Dictionarium annamiticum, lusitanum, et latinum ope Sacrae Congregationis de Propaganda Fide in lucem editum ab Alexandro de Rhodes è Societate Jesu, ejusdemque Sacrae Congregationis Missionario Apostolico* (Rome, 1651) and is composed of three parts: the first part, with a separate pagination (31 pages) is an essay on Vietnamese grammar, entitled *Linguae Annamiticae seu Tunchinensis brevis declaratio*; the second part is the dictionary proper, entitled *Dictionarium Annamiticum seu Tunchinense cum Lusitana, et Latina declaratione*; and the last part, unpaginated, entitled *Index Latini sermonis*, is an index of Latin words followed by the numbers of the pages in which they occur in the second part. The catechism is entitled *Cathechismus pro iis, qui volunt suscipere Baptismum, in Octo dies divisus. Phep giang tam ngay cho ke muan chiu phep rua toi, ma beao dao thanh duc Chua Bloi. Ope sacrae Congregationis de Propaganda Fide in lucem editus. Ab Alexandro de Rhodes è Societate Jesu, ejusdemque Sacrae Congregationsi Missionario Apostolico* (Rome, 1651) (henceforth: *Cathechismus*). For a discussion of the history, structure, method and theological message of the *Catechismus* see my *Mission and Catechesis*, 107-202. With regard to the alphabetization of the Vietnamese language, de Rhodes was not its inventor but perfecter and popularizer. In this work he derived

much help from the unpublished dictionaries of Gaspar do Amaral and António Barbosa, both now lost. After being confined to Roman Catholics for two centuries, the Romanized script became the national script (*quoc ngu*) at the beginning of this century, replacing both Chinese and *chu nom* (the demotic script).

5. For a detailed biography of de Rhodes, see the excellent dissertation of Do Quang Chinh.

6. For a full description of de Rhodes' mission in Vietnam, see ibid. For more detail on seventeenth-century Vietnam see my *Mission and Catechesis*, ch. 1.

7. The other two residences were located at Hoi An and Nuoc Man (Qui Nhon).

8. António Francisco Cardim, *Relation de ce qui s'est passé depuis quelque années, jusques à l'An 1644 au Japon, à la Cochinchine, au Malabar, en l'Isle de Ceilan, & en plusieurs autres Isles & Royaumes de l'Orient compris le nom des Provinces du Japon & du Malabar, de la Compagnie de Jésus. Divisée en deux Parties selon ces deux Provinces* (Paris, 1646), 85.

9. This number is given by B. Roboredo in his report "Relaçao das perseguiçoes da Missam de Cochinchina desde Dezembro de 1640 ate Abril de 1641," *ARSI JS* 70, f. 1r. According to de Rhodes, the number is 12,000 (*Divers voyages*, 117).

10. For a history of Vietnamese Christianity in the seventeenth century, see Henri Chappoulie, *Aux origines d'une Eglise. Rome et les Missions d'Indochine au XVIIe siècle* (Paris: Blou et Gay, 1943), 2 vols. and Nguyen Huu Trong, *Les origines du clergé vietnamien* (Saigon: Tinh Viet, 1959).

11. See *Divers voyages*, 72-73.

12. *An Asian Theology of Liberation* (Maryknoll: Orbis Books, 1988), 70-71.

13. See *Cathechismus*, 103-104. De Rhodes seems to have derived this understanding of the Hebrew language from Augustine. See *City of God*, bk XVI, c 11. For de Rhodes' view of Confucianism, Taoism, and Buddhism see my *Mission and Catechesis*, 82-92.

14. *Divers voyages*, 21.

15 *Divers voyages*, 21.

16. See *Histoire du Royaume*, 93-109; 112-16. I leave aside the *religious*

practices which de Rhodes described under the heading of the three "superstitious sects" and the cult of ancestors. I will discuss them in the next section.

17. See *Cathechismus*, 77-78.

18. *Cathechismus*, 299-300.

19. *Divers voyages*, 86-87. See also *Histoire du Royaume*, 103-104. This custom, not reported by any other missionary, is probably part of the practices to protect the child from the harms of the evil spirits. Other practices include not naming the child with the name of an older child who has died, that is, taken away by the evil spirits, and naming the child with obscene names. In both cases, the intent is to deceive the evil spirits into thinking that the child is so ugly that it is not worth taking him or her away. See *Histoire du Royaume*, 112-13.

20. *Histoire du Royaume*, 35.

21. Ibid., 37.

22. See ibid., 105. In certain parts of Vietnam, people paint the alleys leading to the house with white chalk with the same intention.

23. Ibid., 105. As to the practice of paying all one's debts before the New Year, de Rhodes found it quite laudable. But he considered it vitiated by the superstitious motives which inspired it, namely, to avoid bad luck in the coming year or to avoid bringing shame to one's ancestors.

24. Ibid., 201.

25. Ibid.

26. See his admiration for the piety of Tonkinese Christians: "They each wear two crosses, one on the breast and the other up their sleeve; and they say the former serve as their shield, the latter as their sword. They never travel abroad without taking with them their little oratories, which they open up as soon as their reach their lodgings" (*Divers voyages*, 101-102).

27. Ibid., 78.

28 See *Histoire du Royaume*, 200.

29. Ibid., 201-02.

30. Ibid., 202-03.

31. Ibid., 203.

32. Ibid., 203-04.

33. On June 27, 1615 the Holy Office issued the instruction *Romanae Sedis Antistes* allowing the Chinese mission three things: to wear a head cover during the divine offices; to translate the Bible into literary Chinese; and for future Chinese priests to celebrate the Mass, recite the breviary, and administer the sacraments in literary Chinese. Whereas the first authorization was immediately enacted, the last two were postponed *sine die*. In September 9, 1659 Pope Alexander VII issued the bull *Super Cathedram* permitting the ordination to the priesthood of Chinese men who could read Latin, even though they could not understand it. For the question of Chinese liturgies, see François Bontinck, *La Lutte autour de la liturgie chinoise aux XVIIe et XVIIIe siècles* (Louvain: Éditions Nauwelaerts, 1962).

34. See Tissanier, 270.

35. This practice was extremely important for the faith life of the Christian community, especially because most of the time during 1640-1645 de Rhodes was practically the only priest for the entire Vietnam. We are told that near the border between Tonkin and Cochinchina, "there were at least a thousand Christians who were living very holy lives although they had never seen a priest" (*Divers voyages*, 181).

36. See *Histoire du Royaume*, 249.

37. Literally, the formula means: "I wash you, in the one name of the Father, the Son, and the Holy Spirit." De Rhodes' translation of the baptismal formula was subjected to discussion by the Jesuits both in Macao and Vietnam between 1640 and 1645. In 1645, a meeting was held in Macao to discuss it, presided over by João Cabral and Alvare de Semedo, vice-provincials of Japan and China respectively. At the meeting, the baptismal formula in Vietnamese proposed for approval reads: *Tao rua may nhan danh Cha, va Con, va Spirito santo*, literally, "I wash you in the name of the Father, and the Son, and the Holy Spirit." Note the absence of the word *"nhat,"* i.e., "one" after the word *"nhan."* At the end of the meeting, 31 of 35 fathers, half of whom were professors of theology and several of whom knew Vietnamese, approved this formula and rejected the formula proposed by de Rhodes.

38. The Vietnamese words for Holy Spirit is *Thanh Than*. The current baptismal formula is: *"Cha rua con, nhan danh Cha va Con va Thanh Than."*

39. See *Histoire du Royaume*, 194-95.

40. Ibid., 247. Of course, auricular confession, possibly in a confessional box, was the only form of celebrating the sacrament of penance available in the seventeenth century. It is the close proximity between the foreign priest and the female penitent and the *sotto voce* confession that caused the scandal.

41. See, for example, *Histoire du Royaume*, 139, 145-46, 236. On Day Four of *Cathechismus*, de Rhodes says that at this stage catechumens should be given the Our Father, the Hail Mary, and the Apostles' Creed to learn by heart (133).

42. Of course, de Rhodes may not have been the first to translate these prayers into Vietnamese. It is likely that other Jesuits, in particular Francisco de Pina, might have already translated them.

Practicing the Freedom of God: Formation in Early Baptist Life

Philip E. Thompson
Adjunct Professor of Religion and Philosophy
Chowan College

Introduction

Recent years have witnessed the awakening of some Baptists to issues concerning spiritual formation.[1] This is a laudable development in Baptist life; yet I hope that I might be excused for finding in it reason to lament. Students of liturgy tell us that prayer and worship without lament are deficient.[2] This essay is born of my prayer for my tradition.

My chief lament is that this development is not leading Baptists to seek guidance in their newfound path within their own tradition. Indeed, the path seems at present to be carrying them still further away from their heritage. Two related concerns stand out. First, there has long been an (erroneous) assumption that Baptist theology has remained fairly constant throughout the four centuries of Baptist existence. A punctiliar, voluntarist, individualist, conversionist soteriology bequeathed to Baptists by revivalism in the late eighteenth and nineteenth centuries has been retrojected onto the earliest Baptists. Thus, Baptist heritage may be perceived as deficient in resources for thinking about spiritual formation.[3] Second, by reason of the regnant soteriology, Baptists have perhaps been rendered vulnerable to one-sidedness in matters of spirituality, focusing too exclusively on the individual.[4] Even when Baptist heritage is studied, then, the conventional (i.e., individualist) parameters seem to prevent discovery of some of our more valuable heirlooms.[5] I will examine the nexus of Christian formation in early Baptist life and thought in order to recover some of these heirlooms.

Gordon W. Lathrop describes the process of formation as taking place within a juxtaposition of the name of Jesus to a complex of ritual acts; setting remembrance of Jesus alongside human acts, that a word of transforming grace may be heard.[6] The occasion for this is given in the more obvious juxtapositions within the actual ordo of worship, its structure of gathering, reading and hearing, instructing, washing and eating, and departing.[7] Yet the ordo is not merely a reenactment of the story of Jesus, allowing the contemporary to disappear behind or into the past. In faith, the ordo of worship brings the particular life of local worshiping communities into God's work, opening both to mutual interpretation.[8] To "follow Jesus" is to live life in community and in the world in accordance with such interpretation.

My purpose is to inquire into the dynamics of juxtaposition, the interpretation, the way of following Jesus, that was characteristic of early Baptists. I contend that the spiritual history of Baptists began with a juxtaposition of a certain theological conviction to the ordo of worship, and indeed to the whole of ecclesial life. The conviction was that God must be free. This juxtaposition produced a tension that informed the Baptists' understanding of the process of Christian formation. I will examine chiefly British Baptists during the first two centuries of their existence, though with occasional glances across the Atlantic to America.

The God Who Forms Persons in Freedom

Lathrop notes that truthful speech about God requires always at least two words.[9] Baptists spoke two words concerning God's freedom. First, God is free *from* any sort of control by creation in God's work of redemption. Second, God also is free *for* using creation in the same work of redemption. The younger Robert Hall signaled both of these in a treatise on the Holy Spirit.

> We are most ready to acknowledge that the assistance you need is free and gratuitous, neither given to our deservings, nor flowing from any connection subsisting betwixt our endeavors and the exertion of divine agency. The Spirit of God is a free Spirit, and it is impossible to conceive how either faith or prayer should have an intrinsic efficacy in drawing down influence from heaven. There is, however, a connection established by divine vouchsafement, which entitles believers to expect, in the use of means, such measures of gracious assistance as are requisite to sustain and support them in their religious course.[10]

We may now turn to specific aspects of God's twofold freedom.

Part of the early Baptists' inheritance from the Reformed tradition was their insistence upon the absolute difference between the Creator and creation. Corresponding to this ontological gap was an "epistemological gap." Created beings cannot on their own know God. Presumption otherwise was fraught with the danger of idolatry. This conviction found ample witness in the first articles of a number of confessions and catechisms:

> That God as he is in himselfe, cannot be comprehended of any but himselfe, dwelling in that inaccessible light, that no eye can attaine unto, whom never man saw nor can see... ("First London Confession," 1644, Particular Baptist)[11]

> We believe and profess, that there is only one true God, who is our God; who is eternal,

> almighty, unchangeable, infinite, and incomprehensible;... ("Midlands Confession," 1655, Particular Baptist)[12]

> We believe and are verily confident, that there is but one God the Father, of whom are all things, from everlasting to everlasting, glorious, and unwordable in all his attributes. ("Standard Confession," 1660, General Baptist)[13]

> We verily believe, that there is but one, only living and true God; whose subsistence is in and of himself, whose essence cannot be comprehended by any but himself... ("Orthodox Creed," 1678, General Baptist)[14]

Reflecting this conviction, the preeminent Baptist theologian of the seventeenth century, General Baptist bishop Thomas Grantham, began his discussion on the knowledge of God by asking "in what respect we ought to be ignorant of him." This was because God has "reserved the discovery of himself in great measure."[15] If there is knowledge of God, it is given to us by God accommodating to our need and capacity.[16] In this accommodation God holds forth grace to humankind.

Knowledge of God comes only from the one Word of God, Jesus Christ. A hymn by Benjamin Keach put the matter succinctly:

> Thou dost, Lord, represent to us
> God, whom we cannot see;
> He dwells in light inaccessible,
> Which can't approachéd be.[17]

Even this knowledge is not simply ours for the taking. To worship Christ is not to exercise control. The early Baptists were too zealous to guard God's freedom to allow such impudence. They discussed, and hymned, this imparting of knowledge and grace in terms of a theology of Word and Spirit.

> The efficacy of thy Word

Does in the Spirit lye,
It an impression ne'er will make,
If he don't it apply.[18]

Yet the early Baptists added another consideration, one quite out of keeping with the sensitivities and sensibilities of many contemporary Baptists. The Word and Spirit were not together released for private consumption. Our Baptists did not speak of the Spirit residing in the individual heart, making the Word comprehensible for the individual. The ontological gap rendered this impossible.[19] There had to be mediation. After speaking of saving knowledge coming only from the Lamb slain from the foundation of the world, Grantham's "St. Paul's Catechism" asked, concerning the proper "guide in these soul-concernments," Would it be the testimony of Scripture, the action of the Holy Spirit, or the Holy Church? Grantham's surprising answer was, "There is no doubt that these three agree in one testimony."[20] Christ indwells the Church by the Holy Spirit, Grantham noted, and through the Spirit the Church is the habitation of God.[21]

This understanding was not peculiar to Grantham, but found wider attestation among Baptists. Of the Third Person and the Church, John Bunyan wrote, "He will in this House our helper be."[22] The "Somerset Confession" declared that God in Christ works:

> ...teaching and revealing the mysteries of the kingdom, and will of God to us..., giving gifts in his church for the work of the ministry, and edifying the body of Christ ... that through the powerful teachings of the Lord, by his Spirit in his church, they might grow up into him (Eph. 4:15), be conformed to his will (Ezek. 36:27; I Pet. 1:2), and sing praises to his name (Heb. 2:12; I Cor. 14:15).[23]

Themes sounded in this confessional statement indicate what at heart early Baptists meant by religion. After noting that religion is often defined either etymologically, as that which binds (*religare*) human beings to God, or functionally, as worship such as God's majesty requires, Grantham opted for a definition based upon Titus 2:11–14.[24]

> For the grace of God has appeared, bringing sal-
> vation to all, training us to renounce impiety and
> worldly passions, and in the present age to live
> lives that are self-controlled, upright, and godly,
> while we wait for the blessed hope and the mani-
> festation of the glory of our great God and Savior,
> Jesus Christ. He it is who gave himself for us that
> he might redeem us from all iniquity and purify
> for himself a people of his own who are zealous
> for good deeds. (NRSV)

This work was God's alone. Grantham noted with approval Tertullian's dictum that "We are not born, but made, Christians," adding himself, "...nor are we made such by man, but by God."[25] Yet this religion must itself be spoken of within the juxtaposition of both aspects of God's freedom. The formation for which religion aimed meant regularly "for Men to be imbodied as his Church and Family, by the just observation of His ordinances."[26]

The Church's Relation to God's Work of Formation

The Church was thus the principal locus of God's freedom for using the things of creation as means of grace. We need to be aware that the tension created by the Baptists' juxtaposition of the two words of God's freedom was a lively one. Each always remained close by the other. While the Church was indeed the place in which God was held to be present and active for redemption by the Holy Spirit, human beings explicitly could not presume to possess salvation simply by possessing the means. God remained free from the Church in matters of salvation, and so stood over against the Church when the aforesaid presumption manifested itself. John

Smyth noted that the danger lay not only with Popes and prelates, but with presbyteries and even local congregations to claim that the power of Christ was in and with them. But this was to rob Christ, and to "make themselves even Christ himself..."[27]

It was not the Church, according to the early Baptists, or even the gospel and book by which the gospel is given witness, that gave salvation; but the One worshiped in the Church and testified to in the gospel. In a remarkable passage from "St. Paul's Catechism," the question of persons who do not have access to the means of Church, Scripture, and Christian rites was posed. "Many who never had the means to know the Mediator particularly and distinctly, must yet have salvation by Him," began the answer. "All that know the Lord to be such a God as do's exercise loving Kindness, Judgment, and Righteousness on Earth do know this Mediator virtually and believing on the Lord as such, do know him savingly." "I see," came the response, "that it is not good for us to pride up ourselves against the Nations, which have not the gospel as we have."[28]

The Church could not be so foolish as to presuppose the presence of the Spirit in it as a possession. Nor could it be so foolish as to think that God was confined to it in the work of redemption. Yet neither could those to whom the means had been given pride up themselves and presume to be free from them. Indeed, Baptist catechesis urged "diligent use of all outward and ordinary means whereby Christ communicates to us the benefits of redemption."[29]

While early Baptists believed God to be free from the Church, human beings were not seen as likewise free, precisely because of God's freedom *for* the Church in the work of redemption. So they could say in the "Orthodox Creed" that it is to the Church "and not elsewhere, all persons that seek for eternal life, should *gladly* join themselves."[30] In the Church were to be found the "few solemn Rites by command from Heaven, to commemorate the Love of God in the Gift of his Son; and for Christians to express their Unity and Communion in the Mystery of the gospel."[31]

The Means of Formation

We turn now to discuss the ways in which the early Baptists believed God, particularly the Second and Third Persons of the Holy Trinity, works in and through the life of the Church. We must keep in mind at every turn that while we make assertions concerning God's freedom for all these good things of the Church's life together, the first word of God's freedom from all of them stands nearby in judgment of human pride. Early Baptists called these means of God's grace "ordinances" in a sense larger than that usually intended by contemporary Baptists. We will return to this shortly. These ordinances were likened to spectacles that enabled persons to see divine things from which they otherwise were hindered.[32]

The context in which these ordinances were found was the Church's corporate worship. While not discouraging private or family worship, indeed even while encouraging both, primacy was placed upon the worship that took place in the gathered community. Employing the words of Psalm 87, Benjamin Keach declared, "...God loves the gates of Sion more than all the dwelling places of Jacob; Therefore the Publick worship of God is to be preferred before private." He continued soon thereafter, "O pray to be fitted for publick worship!"[33] It was in the worship of the gathered community that God was most glorified, that God's grace was preeminently available by the power of the Holy Spirit, and that spiritual advantage for the upbuilding of the Church was most to be got.[34]

This grace was made available by the Word by the Holy Spirit in the media of worship. Among these media was the ordinance of preaching. In like fashion to worship, private devotional reading of Scripture was not discouraged. Indeed, Benjamin Keach called it a pasture in which God's people are fed.[35] Yet Keach also declared that "[t]he gospel is the instrumental means, through the Spirits Operations of the Sinner's Reconciliation to God... an Instrument of his Power, or a powerful means ordained of God to this purpose... *where it is proclaimed and received.*"[36] "How is the Word made effectual to salvation?" queried the "Baptist Catechism." "The Spirit of God makes the reading, *but especially the preaching of the Word* an effectual means of convincing and converting sinners, and *of building them up in holiness and comfort*, through faith unto salvation."[37]

Closely related to proclamation, the pastoral office itself was an ordinance of God, a means of God's free work for salvation through things of creation. Our Baptists warned against pastoral autocracy, and indeed left no place for it, calling the Church the next "lord" under Christ.[38] Still, there was a particular role for Christ's ministers, one described largely in terms of guidance. This was given striking expression in Bunyan's *The Pilgrim's Progress*. There we find the odd, even disconcerting, portrait of the man who could beget children, travail in birth, "and nurse them himself once they are born." He is the one "whom the Lord of the place whither thou art going hath authorized to be thy guide...."[39]

Another ordinance was prayer. "You may as well live without eating," Keach admonished, "as spiritually live without praying.... He that casts off prayer casts off God."[40] As with worship and the Word, private exercise of this ordinance was not denied. Perhaps in this instance, the private was given more place than the public.[41] Still, public prayer was in no wise relegated to unimportance. Bunyan described prayer as "an Ordinance of God, and that to be used both in Publick and Private... through Christ, in the strength and assistance of the Holy Spirit, for such things as God hath promised... for the good of the Church, with submission, in Faith, to the will of God."[42] John Smyth held prayer to be an "action of Communion" with Christ and "in a true visible communion of Saints as the Lord hath appointed..."[43] In prayer, the Spirit came close to the Church to bring to remembrance the things of Christ.[44]

The sacraments of baptism and the Lord's Supper were also among God's ordinances. A word of clarification is in order here. Given the (presumed to be historical) non- or anti-sacramentalist view of many contemporary Baptists in America, the early Baptists' use of the word "sacrament" may cause some consternation. It may be tempting to argue that they called baptism and the Supper "sacraments" because that was the linguistic convention of their day. Early Baptists meant by "sacrament," however, what contemporary Baptists mean by "ordinance."

This argument, as tempting as it may be, would simply be wrong. The early Baptists were careful in their terminology. As we noted above, they numbered several ordinances of ecclesial life by which God works for salvation. Two of these were sacraments. In Keach's catechism, *The Child's Delight*, the question was asked, "What are those gospel Ordinances called Sacraments, which do confirm us in this Faith?"[45] This shows a precision not commonly acknowledged. Not only did they employ carefully a sacramental terminology, early Baptists held a sacramental understanding of the two rites. "And as [Israel] had the manna to nourish them in the wilderness to Canaan," Baptists confessed in the "Orthodox Creed," "so have we the sacraments to nourish us in the church, and in our wilderness-condition, till we come to heaven."[46] Of the water and table Bunyan exclaimed, "Here's such as helpeth Man's Salvation."[47] William Kiffin, in his debate with Bunyan, stated the matter plainly. The one who does not care for "Christ sacramental" does not care for "Christ God." Kiffin explained that the latter draws near to us in the former.[48]

While I must be altogether too brief in my examination of the sacraments themselves, letting summary suffice where deeper discussion is required, I will be a bit more detailed in discussing baptism. That sacrament was given fuller treatment by the early Baptist writers themselves. Most basically, our Baptists believed that God the Spirit acts redemptively in the rite of baptism. This stands in marked contrast to the dominant contemporary understandings that baptism is either an obligation placed upon the regenerate in order to formalize membership in a local congregation, or a ritual depiction of the conversion experience. A hymn penned by Benjamin Beddome petitioned:

> Eternal Spirit, heavenly Dove,
> On these baptismal waters move;
> That we thro' energy divine,
> May have the substance with the sign.[49]

What was this substance? Grantham noted that "it is Christ who is held forth in Baptism, which saveth."[50] While baptism was for the early Baptists the "sacrament of initiation," it was foremost the "sacrament of regeneration." They interpreted regeneration in light of the process of formation, and spoke of two aspects. First there was mortification, putting to death the old nature. Baptists in America sang:

> O may they find beneath the wave,
> That Christ is in the liquid grave;
> May they sink deep in love divine,
> And feel the death of self and sin.[51]

The second aspect of regeneration was vivification; rising to new life in Christ and also in Christ's Body, the Church. "[T]hat first is called burial with Christ, the second a rising with Christ, the sacrament of both of these is Baptism..."[52] Morgan Edwards recorded a baptismal prayer from colonial America that bears quoting at length:

> Is baptism a symbol of the death, burial and resurrection of Christ; of the resurrection of the body; and of death to sin, and rising in the newness of life?... Let us pray, Hear, O Lord Jesus! for

he that is risen to be baptized calleth upon thy
name! Thou that didst come from Galilee to
Jordan come now also from heaven to _ and meet
us on the banks of this river; for we repair hither
for the sake of fulfilling all righteousness! Lamb
of God, which taketh away the sin of the world
meet thy disciples! We know that thou art present
every where, but ah! let it not be here as at first on
the banks of the Jordan when thou didst stand
among the croud, and they knew it not! O let us
find the messiah here! *Thou that comest by water,
and art witnessed to of the water come by this water.*
Let this laver of regeneration bear testimony to
thee. *And afford us communion with thee in thy baptism; for in the water and in the floods thy presence is
promised!...* Behold the suppliant of pardon, sanctification, and salvation on coming to that which
encourages his expectation of the necessary blessings! Accept his person... Henceforth be thou his,
and he thine; for it is his will to put on Christ by
baptism; to become a christian openly; to take thy
yoke and burden on his shoulder; and to learn
obedience of the meek and lowly Jesus! *Let his life
be alike figure to his baptism ...*[53]

For this to be so, the new life needed to be nourished.

Nourishment came through the Lord's Supper, which
Grantham likened to a family feast with Christ at the head.
"Yea, here Christ gathers his People together at his own
Table, as one Family. And it is that Table, to which all Saints
are to approach with such preparation as may render them
fit for communion in the Mystical Body, the Church, which
is also called Christ, because of that unity they have with
him, and one another in him."[54] The spiritual presence of
Christ in the Supper was affirmed with wide consent.[55]
Because of the special presence of Christ in the sacrament,
Grantham gave the Supper priority over even proclamation
of the Word in establishing persons in God's grace.[56] Since

the nourishment was through communion with Christ by the Spirit, our Baptists believed that the Supper formed persons in the image of Christ. This made it necessary for formation.

> It teacheth Humility because it setteth forth Christ in the greatest of his self-abasement, yea the depth of his Humility shewed forth in his bearing the revilings, contradictions, and murther of his enemies... Let no man strive therefore against this gospel precept, because (as they are pleased to speak) it is a low ministration, sith what may rightly be said of its small beauty in the Judgment of men, doth argue the necessity of the true usefulness of it, being therein made fit to set forth Christ in his humiliation, and consequently the conformity of the Church to Christ in his abasement which she must learn during the time her Lord exercises her under the word of his patience.[57]

The question arises: how did the early Baptists conceive of this conformity, both its content and scope?

The Goal of Formation

The Baptists envisioned the end of God's free work in the Church to be sanctification; of individuals certainly, but also of the Church. Where contemporary Baptists in America generally fail to hold together the individual and community, the early Baptists did so quite carefully. We may see this in their hymns. They sang:

> O draw *me* my dear Saviour then
> With thy strong cord of Love,
> And *we* will all run after thee
> as fast as we can move.[58]

and

> O Blessed Day when *we* can say,
> Lord Jesus, thou art *mine!*
> O Blessed Day when *we* can say,
> Lord Jesus, *I* am thine!

and perhaps most poetically in the eucharistic hymn:

> O Let but me and this Church be
> a garden of delight...[59]

They could speak of the Church as a collective singular, even as having one heart.[60] As we noted above, Grantham's definition of religion focused upon the formation of a people.[61]

Our Baptists described sanctification as the formation of believers and the Church in a certain habit (*habitus*) of virtue. "In a word," noted Keach, "All Grace is from the Spirit; and it is by the Aid and Assistance of the Spirit, that we are enabled to exercise that Grace: for as he first formed the Habit in our Souls, so it is he helps us to do the Act also, or that [he] doth influence us in the Exercise thereof."[62] Our Baptists also hymned this belief:

> Father of mercies, send thy grace,
> All powerful from above,
> To form in our obedient souls,
> The image of thy love.[63]

The virtues that comprised this image in God's People included love, burden-bearing, forgiveness, goodwill toward enemies, sincerity, meekness, temperance, patience, hospitality, humility, and compassionate service to the poor.[64] As these virtues were formed in individuals and the Church, they were, by the free work of God, taken into the ongoing story of God's redemptive work in the world through Christ.

As the Church and its members were formed in the image of God's love, Christ, God's redemptive work in and toward the Church became of one piece with God's work beyond the

Church. The "Orthodox Creed," for instance, spoke of the obligation of Christians to relieve the poor within the community of faith. Yet it was not to be confined there, but was to extend "to all as we have opportunity and ability to be doing good."[65] This good work would be that ". . . it sympathize with the Afflicted, Succour the Tempted, and Reliev the Poor and Distressed; Rejoicing with them that Rejoice, and Mourning with them that Mourn." Such, Keach noted, is the beauty and glory of the Church.[66]

Conclusion

Baptists are coming to give long overdue attention to matters of spiritual formation. This brief survey indicates that many resources for formation lie untapped in Baptist heritage itself. Thus the present-day concern holds the possibility of being, and I hope that it indeed may be, an entry point into something else long overdue in Baptist life: sustained dialogue with our own tradition. Such dialogue holds the promise of steering Baptists from a one-sided spirituality through its emphasis upon formation that may properly be called both ecclesial and liturgical.

Notes

1. For instance, the 1998 Cooperative Baptist Fellowship General Assembly devoted much attention to spirituality.

2. Don E. Saliers, *Worship Come to Its Senses* (Nashville: Abingdon Press, 1996), 56-64.

3. Cf. E. Glenn Hinson, "The Future of the Baptist Tradition," in *Are Southern Baptists "Evangelicals"?* ed. James Leo Garrett, Jr., E. Glenn Hinson, and James E. Tull (Macon, GA: Mercer University Press, 1983), 190, who argues that early Baptists "could not grasp the communal nuances of faith which Roman Catholics, Anglicans, and other Protestants" discerned. He includes a number of practices associated with spiritual formation in these communal nuances.

4. Cf. Sarah Zimmerman, "Call to Spiritual Formation Challenges Baptist Lifestyles," *Fellowship!* 8 (December, 1998): 1-3. James Wm. McClendon, Jr., gives needed words of caution to those who would too quickly discard this sort of spiritual life, however. "Toward a Conversionist Spirituality," in *Ties That Bind: Life Together in the Baptist Vision*, ed. Gary A. Furr and Curtis W. Freeman (Macon, GA: Smyth & Helwys Publishing, Inc., 1994), 23-32.

5. This is seen in William Lloyd Allen, "Mining Baptist History and Traditions for Spirituality: Paradigm Sifting for Ores of a Different Color," *Perspectives in Religious Studies* 25 (Spring 1998): 43-61. He notes, p. 47, "Few would disagree that the heart of the Baptist tradition is more closely related to personal and experiential religious expressions than propositional or institutional ones," and so contrasts individual affective versus individual rational approaches to spiritual life. He is not wrong to do this, but seems unaware that there are other, more differently colored still, approaches that are not so individualistic.

6. Gordon W. Lathrop, *Holy Things: A Liturgical Theology* (Minneapolis, MN: Fortress Press, 1993), 22-23.

7. Ibid., 33. By this, he means not simply the rubrics of a "worship service," but also the larger daily, weekly, and yearly rhythms of the liturgy. He also is not referring simply to what is popularly called "high" liturgy. The juxtaposition of silence and speech in a Quaker meeting would equally be an example.

8. Ibid., 65-79.

9. Ibid., 121, n.9.

10. Robert Hall, the younger, *The Work of the Holy Spirit or, The Means for Enjoying His Blessed Influences*, in *The Works of the Rev. Robert Hall, A.M.* ed. Olinthus Gregory and Joseph Belcher (New York: Harper & Brothers, Publishers, 1854), 240. This treatise was originally written in 1809.

11. William L. Lumpkin, *Baptist Confessions of Faith* (Valley Forge, PA: The Judson Press, 1959), 156. In all quotations I shall retain the original spelling.

12. Ibid., 198.

13. Ibid., 225.

14. Ibid., 298.

15. Thomas Grantham, *Christianismus Primitivus: or The Ancient Christian Religion* (London: np, 1678), Book Two, Part One, Chapter Two, Section One. (Due to irregularities in pagination, references from this work will be hereafter designated by CP book/part, chapter, and section. For instance, this citation would be CP, II/1.ii.1.)

16. Ibid. "[We must be] humbly content with that measure of the Knowledge of God, which his Word accommodates us with."

17. Benjamin Keach, *Spiritual Melody* (London: np, 1691), 49.

18. Ibid., 206.

19. Cf. Benjamin Keach, *Instructions for Children* (London: np, nd), 19, who noted that while God is "increated Spirit," we are finite, created spirits, and so have no more ontological connection to God spiritually than physically; and Thomas Grantham, *A Sigh for Peace* (London: np, 1671), 4-5, "[W]hen we speak of mens receiving this Holy Spirit, we do not mean that he dwells in them essentially *and personally*... But he dwells in them by manifestation and operation." Emphasis in the original.

20. Thomas Grantham, "St. Paul's Catechism" (London: np, 1687), 11-12.

21. Grantham, CP, II/1.iii.11.

22. John Bunyan, "A Discourse on the Building, Nature, Excellency and Government of the House of God," in *The Miscellaneous Works of John Bunyan*, vol. VI, *The Poems*, ed. Graham Midgley (Oxford: The Clarendon Press, 1980), 284.

23. Lumpkin, 207. Note the way in which the Second and Third Persons are held together in the context of the Church.

24. Grantham, CP, II/1.i.1.

25. Ibid., II/1.i.3.

26. Ibid., II/1.i.2.

27. John Smyth, "Parallels: Censures: Observations," in *The Works of John Smyth Fellow of Christ's College 1594-8*, vol. II (Cambridge: Cambridge University Press, 1915), 395.

28. Grantham, "St. Paul's Catechism," 11-12.

29. "The Baptist Catechism" (Grand Rapids, MI: Baker Book House, 1952), 38-39. The catechism was composed in either 1683 or

1684, and is attributed by some to Benjamin Keach, and by others to William Collins.

30. Lumpkin, 319. Emphasis mine.

31. Grantham, CP, I.13.

32. John Bunyan, "A Book for Boys and Girls," in *The Miscellaneous Works of John Bunyan*, vol. VI, *The Poems*, ed. Graham Midgley (Oxford: The Clarendon Press, 1980), 263.

33. Benjamin Keach, *The Glory of a True Church and its Discipline Display'd* (London: np, 1697), 63,67.

34. Ibid., 65-66.

35. Benjamin Keach, *A Golden Mine Opened* (London: Benjamin Keach, 1694), 130.

36. Benjamin Keach, *The Display of Glorious Grace or the Covenant of Peace Opened in Several Sermons* (London: S. Bridge, 1698), 121. Emphasis mine.

37. "Baptist Catechism," 39. Emphasis mine.

38. Smyth, 410, 523. Cf. Thomas Grantham, *The Paedo-Baptists Apology for the Baptized Churches* (London: np, 1671), 88-89; and idem "St. Paul's Catechism," 55-56.

39. John Bunyan, *The Pilgrim's Progress* in *The Works of John Bunyan*, vol. III, ed. George Offor (Glasgow: Blackie and Son, 1853), 98. Some Baptists interpret the one depicted as the local congregation. Cf. E. Glenn Hinson, "Baptists and Spirituality: A Community at Worship," *Review and Expositor* XXXIV (Fall 1987): 657. I followed Hinson's interpretation in my dissertation, reacting against abuses of the pastoral office by one faction in the Southern Baptist Convention. I had misgivings even then, however. The portrait would certainly have been of a woman had it been the Church.

40. Keach, *A Golden Mine Opened*, 134.

41. This was perhaps due to the violations of God's "freedom from" the early Baptists detected in public prayer. The traditional forms, bereft of the Spirit, were impotent to lead persons to right prayer. "Without which Spirit," Bunyan wrote, "though we had a thousand *Common Prayer Books*, yet we know not what we should pray for as we ought, being accompanied with those infirmities that make us absolutely uncapable [sic] of such as work." "I Will Pray With the Spirit and I will pray with the understanding also" in *The*

Miscellaneous Works of John Bunyan, vol. II, ed. Richard L. Greaves (Oxford: The Clarendon Press, 1976), 268.

42. Ibid., 235.

43. Smyth, 457-58.

44. Grantham, *A Sigh for Peace*, 3.

45. Benjamin Keach, *The Child's Delight: Or Instructions for Children and Youth* (London: William and Joseph Marshall, 1702), 38.

46. Lumpkin, 311-12.

47. John Bunyan, "A Discourse on the Building, Nature, Excellency and Government of the House of God," 276.

48. William Kiffin, *A Sober Discourse on the Right to Church Communion* (London: George Larkin, 1681), 42-43.

49. John Rippon, comp., *A Selection of Hymns From the Best Authors Intended to be an Appendix to Doctor Watts' Psalms and Hymns* (Philadelphia: Peter Stewart, 1803, originally printed in 1797), 460. Cf. 443, 449, 450, 453, and 468.

50. Grantham, "St. Paul's Catechism," 35-36.

51. Andrew Broaddus, *The Dover Selection of Spiritual Songs* (Richmond: R.I. Smith, 1829), 50.

52. Grantham, CP II/2.ii.4.

53. Morgan Edwards, *The Customs of Primitive Churches—or—A Set of propositions, relative to the name, materials [sic], constitution, power, officers, ordinances, rites, business, worship, discipline, government, & c. of a church; to which are added proofs from Scripture; and historical narratives of the manner in which most have been reduced to practice* (Philadelphia: np, 1774), 81-82. Emphasis mine.

54. Grantham, CP, II/2.vii.5.

55. Cf. Grantham, CP II/2.vii.4; Lumpkin, 293; and Rippon, 483, a hymn by Samuel Stennett in which the real presence of Christ is carefully, though unambiguously, defined:

> Here at thy table, Lord, we meet,
> To feed on food divine:
> Thy body is the bread we eat,
> Thy precious blood the wine.
> He that prepares this rich repast,

Himself comes down and dies;
And then invites us, thus to feast
Upon the sacrifice.

56. Grantham, CP II/2.vii.4,6, and 7.

57. Ibid., II/2.vii.6.

58. Keach, *Spiritual Melody*, 315. Emphasis mine.

59. Benjamin Keach, *A Feast of Fat Things Full of Marrow* (London: B.H. 1696), 88. Emphasis mine.

60. Ibid., 87. I believe it possible to argue that the early Baptists, far from being the radical individualists they are portrayed to be by some of their latter day namesakes, actually gave some degree of precedence to the community. While displaying generally a verbatim adherence to the "Westminster Shorter Catechism," the "Baptist Catechism" made some striking departures. In one case, to the question, "Did God leave all mankind to perish in the estate of sin and misery?" the Baptist piece did not answer as did its Presbyterian model, "God having out of his mere good pleasure, from all eternity, elected some to everlasting life ..." Rather, Baptists echoed the conviction, "God having out of his mere good pleasure, from all eternity, elected a people to everlasting life..." "Baptist Catechism," 20. Cf. "The Westminster Shorter Catechism" in *The Book of Confessions* (Louisville: The Office of the General Assembly, 1994), 182.

61. See above, 5-6.

62. Keach, *A Golden Mine Opened*, 260.

63. Rippon, 257.

64. Cf. Bunyan, "A Discourse of the Building, Nature, Excellency and Government of the House of God," 295-303.

65. Lumpkin, 323-24.

66. Keach, *The Glory of a True Church and Its Discipline Display'd*, 58.

Claude Heithaus and the Integration of St. Louis University: The Mystical Body of Christ and Jesuit Politics

Daniel Van Slyke
Doctoral Student in Historical Theology
Saint Louis University

Putting Heithaus in His Place:
The Historical Background

St. Louis was a completely segregated city in 1943. In the neighborhood of Grand and Lindell surrounding Saint Louis University (henceforth SLU), blacks were not allowed in hotels, barber shops, restaurants or theaters serving whites.[1] The city's citizens had proven themselves avid supporters of segregation. In 1916 a grassroots initiative driven by numerous "neighborhood improvement groups" mustered 52,220 votes in favor of legislation enforcing mandatory segregation.[2] The Supreme Court decided in 1917 that such segregation laws were unconstitutional, but the victory was hollow for black city residents. "Restrictive covenants" or "block agreements" among property owners forbidding them to sell their property to blacks were widespread. Since these agreements were enforceable in the courts, black residents were restricted by law to a limited number of squalid blocks in the downtown area until the Supreme Court declared such agreements unconstitutional in 1948.[3]

For the previous several decades the United States Catholic hierarchy had been vigorously expounding the importance of Catholic education for Catholic students.[4] While integration had been proceeding more or less haltingly in Catholic colleges and universities of the north, black Catholics were still unable to obtain a college or university education under Catholic auspices in Missouri in the 1940s.[5] All schools in the diocese of St. Louis remained segregated, and Archbishop Glennon of St. Louis firmly opposed integration.[6] Thus SLU did not seem a likely candidate to become the first university in a former slave state to admit blacks. Yet that is what it became when five black students enrolled in the summer programs of 1944.[7] In 1945 there were seventy-six black students at SLU, and Jesuit observers noted no friction between them and white students.[8] The following school year the University counted 150 blacks among its students.[9] How did such an abrupt change come about?

This paper examines the surprising but pivotal role Claude Herman Heithaus, S.J., played in bringing about the academic and social integration of SLU. His role centered on two deliberate public actions: a sermon delivered during a student Mass on Friday, February 11, 1944, and an article entitled "Why Not Christian Cannibalism?" published in the SLU student newspaper on March 16, 1945.

These works and his subsequent activism are surprising because before 1944 Heithaus exhibited no concern for the question of race relations, and his background suggests different interests. Claude Herman Heithaus was born in St. Louis on May 28, 1898. Although slender he attained a height of six-foot-two, and he carried himself with an "intensely serious" demeanor.[10] He was educated primarily in the St. Louis area, at St. Francis de Sales Parochial School,

St. Louis University High School, St. Stanislaus Seminary in Florissant, Missouri, and SLU.[11] His studies were interrupted for a time when he served in the armed forces during World War I. Second lieutenant Heithaus returned to SLU for his junior year in 1919, and his activities included founding *The University News*, the student paper which he would employ years later as an organ for social change.[12] Heithaus studied for his Ph.D. in archaeology at the University of London from October 1933 to September 1939.[13] During that period he traveled extensively taking photographs he would later utilize in his archaeology classes.[14]

By contrast, Heithaus' fellow Jesuits John and William Markoe lived faithful to a pledge they solemnly signed before the Blessed Sacrament when they were still seminarians in 1917: "to give and dedicate our whole lives and all our energies... for the work of the salvation of the Negroes in the United States."[15] The Jesuits of St. Louis and nearby Florissant, Missouri, had been engaged in small-scale missionary activities among black communities for over fifty years.[16] Segregation, however, remained the generally accepted norm within which the Church of St. Louis conducted its works among blacks. All the city's Catholic institutions were segregated, including St. Mary's Infirmary, which was in 1940 the largest Catholic hospital unit for blacks in the United States, and two black senior high schools—St. Joseph and St. Rita.[17]

On the national level, William challenged segregation and encouraged discussions on race questions with a series of articles in the Jesuit magazine *America* beginning in 1919.[18] He boldly attacked various forms of racism within the Catholic Church. On the local level, while still seminarians, the Markoe brothers organized extensive missionary activities among the blacks of downtown St. Louis in which Jesuit scholastics, nuns, and lay catechists both black and white played a role. When William first arrived he found that blacks did not even know they could be Catholics. By the time nine months had passed, over two hundred converts had been baptized. William opened a grade school for black children in the abandoned buildings of St. Nicholas' parish downtown.[19] In 1926 he became pastor of the all-black St. Elizabeth's parish, which also had a small grade school, and his brother joined him later as the co-pastor.[20] They turned the Church into "a hub of social activity," a center for efforts to improve interracial cooperation.[21]

The network of missionary activity which the Markoes and their companions set up in St. Louis greatly increased the number of black Catholics in the city and hence also the demand on their part for Catholic educational opportunities. This demand was evident in the overwhelming response from black parents who wanted their children enrolled at St. Nicholas grade school, as well as in the fact that many black youths on their own initiative were approaching SLU to be registered as students *before* the school was integrated. William's "policy to dissuade any of our fine Catholic Negro young people from going anywhere near the un-Catholic [because racist] school to apply for admission as students" seems to have been ignored by his parishioners.[22]

William became a persistent critic of the segregationist policy of the Archbishop, which is probably why he was removed from St. Louis in 1941.[23] In 1940 Heithaus arrived at SLU to teach archaeology; he had enough time to become acquainted with William before the latter's departure.[24] John, having overcome a serious drinking problem, returned to St. Louis and became pastor of the black parish of St. Malachy.[25] He and Heithaus worked together surreptitiously yet nonetheless effectively during the struggle over integrating SLU.[26] For example, once SLU was integrated they consulted with local black Catholic educational leaders Clarence Hunter and Creamus Evans and went out together to find and recruit black youths who had sufficient academic preparation for studies at the university.[27]

One more important Jesuit should be introduced here.

John LaFarge, S.J., "widely recognized as the most influential Catholic spokesman on black-white relations in the United States," was also a lifelong activist.[28] Through his position on the staff of *America* from 1926 until 1963 he engaged in "continual, almost day-by-day picking away at racism." In addition to publishing important books on the topic of race relations [29] he was active in promoting Catholic Interracial Councils and other groups seeking to improve race relations within the Church.[30] His approach stands in contrast with that of Heithaus and Markoe. LaFarge "never openly agitated or sullied his record for obedience," and he "never rushed history." "He instead tactfully cultivated open-minded bishops."[31] Rushing history is exactly what Heithaus sought to do when he dramatically entered the discussions on race relations.

President Holloran's Letter

It is clear that "Claude Heithaus did not begin the discussion of integration."[32] Already on February 2, 1943, a special committee met to consider "the Admission of Negroes to the University." Although the committee determined that the policy of segregation should not be changed immediately, a final motion was carried unanimously "that steps be taken to ascertain objectively the attitude of the students, the friends of the University and the graduates of the last twenty years with regard to the admission of negro students."[33] The Assistant-General for America and the Provincial of the Missouri Jesuits, Zacheus Maher and Peter Brooks, urged the trustees of the Missouri Province to discuss integration again in September of 1943. In turn the trustees urged the president of SLU, Patrick Holloran, S.J., to consider the admission of Negro students. Joseph Zuercher, who allowed the directive to stand, succeeded Brooks in December.[34]

Meanwhile Ms. Ethel Williams, a young black woman who graduated from a Catholic high school in Virginia, returned home to St. Louis hoping to continue her education in a Catholic college. Late in the fall of 1943 she and her mother, Mrs. Mattie Williams, consulted John Markoe regarding how to pursue this goal.[35] In turn Markoe consulted "with the President of St. Louis University and various members of the faculty to get their views on the possibility of integration." Holloran agreed to call a formal meeting of the deans and regents to discuss the matter with the priests of St. Malachy's. Before doing so, however, Holloran sought the opinion of the local supporters and alumni of the University.[36] For this purpose, he sent the following letter, dated January 26, 1944, to a select group of friends of SLU:

> I hope you will do this slight favor for the benefit of St. Louis University. Of late not a few individuals have been representing to me in various ways the advisability and necessity of our accepting Negro students at the University. This much should be said: there will never be any lowering of academic standards in the admission of colored students—they will satisfy all requirements or will not be considered; secondly, the number will never be great, simply because they have not—save in a few isolated cases—either the educational background requisite for admission to college, or the financial means. I do not think the number will reach twenty in the next twenty years.
>
> Before even contemplating such a step, I feel it my duty to learn the opinion of representative Catholic groups in the city and to be guided by that opinion. This school exists primarily for them and in many respects owes its existence to their parents and grandparents....Will you please answer the two questions on the enclosed card candidly? Do not sign it, but return it to me with just "Yes" or "No" written at the end of each question.

The enclosed card read: "Would you look favorably on St. Louis University accepting negro students? Would you be less inclined to send a son or daughter to St. Louis University if negro students were admitted?"[37]

The responses of the influential Catholics who received Holloran's letter do not seem to have survived, and different accounts of them are given. A recent article in the *St. Louis Post-Dispatch* claims that "Answers were mixed."[38] Faherty claims that Holloran received only one letter which opposed integration.[39] If indeed the majority of responses were positive, that might indicate the effect of Holloran's assurance that the Negro presence at SLU will be minimal, rather than a generally positive attitude towards integration.[40]

Nevertheless the responses were less momentous than the publicity which the letter received. The next day it was described and quoted at length in the *St. Louis Post-Dispatch*.[41] Shortly thereafter the letter became the object of a feature article in the *Pittsburgh Courier*.[42] C. Denny Holland's discussion of how the press received the letter is based on the testimony of John Markoe. He conspired with Raymond Crowley, the City Editor of the *Post-Dispatch*:

> ...the priest unexpectedly ran across the form letter sent out to the Alumni by the President of the University. He immediately took it to the City Editor of the *Post-Dispatch* with the suggestion that the support of his powerful paper would be most welcome and more effective before the scheduled meeting of the Regents and Deans at the St. Louis University than after it. The City Editor agreed and secured the approval of Mr. Pulitzer to launch a campaign against segregation at St. Louis University along with the paper's campaign against the University of Missouri. This public campaign started with the publication, over the violent protests of the President of St. Louis University, of his letter to the Alumni in an evening edition of the *St. Louis Post-Dispatch*. The next

morning the *St. Louis Globe Democrat* and *St. Louis Star* carried the story and the hue and cry was on.[43]

One of the people who heard this cry was Fr. Claude Heithaus.

By no means was integration a major concern of Holloran. His more prominent ambitions were to improve the financial situation of the university and to build new edifices for accommodating the influx of veterans anticipated after the War. To this purpose, he initiated a major fund drive.[44] His targeted donors were wealthy white Catholics. In his annual report on the university given in May 1945 at the first spring commencement after black students were admitted, he stated:

> Easily the most significant endeavor of the scholastic year at present drawing to a close was what was styled the St. Louis University Expansion Program. A goal of two million dollars was set, which, with funds already on hand, would make possible the erection of seven vitally needed new buildings.[45]

Holloran did not want to rush into something like integration, which could have offended potential donors. This consideration may explain his letter and the general caution (if not opposition) which he displayed towards integration.

Father Heithaus's Sermon

Let us return to February, 1944, when Heithaus was faculty moderator of the *University News* and Jack Maguire was its student editor. In a recent interview, Monsignor Jack Maguire recalled hearing of friction between Holloran and Heithaus during the two weeks between the public exposition of the former's letter and the delivery of the latter's sermon on February 11. Hence the sermon "was a very reasoned, deliberate thing... he had thought about his position very, very deeply."[46] According to George Dunne, a fellow Jesuit working to integrate the university, Heithaus "put the sermon through twenty drafts and submitted it to the judgment of three of the most highly respected Jesuits on the Faculty."[47]

Maguire related that the students "certainly understood the position of Father Heithaus and the logic behind it… but we understood the financial pressure behind Father Holloran too." He adds, "we were not at all attuned to the whole idea of integration"; the rhetoric of the time stressed equal opportunity, but not integration.[48] Maguire, however, represents the retrospective male point of view. Because of the War, however, few young men were then at the university:

> the overwhelming majority of students attending Mass that Friday morning were women. The enthusiasm and support of these and other women for the call for integration was instrumental in bringing about this change. These women identified with the struggle African Americans were undertaking to receive an education, having begun their own struggle not so many years before.[49]

The sermon intentionally appealed to a wider audience than the female students who were present for its delivery. This is evident in its content and in the fact that Heithaus planned not only to publish it (before it was delivered) in the *University News*, but he also was sure to send copies to the St. Louis daily newspapers.[50] Substantial segments of the sermon were printed in the *St. Louis Post-Dispatch* on the day it was delivered.[51] The next day the newspaper dragged Holloran into the spotlight: "I'm surprised that Father Heithaus spoke publicly on his personal opinion in the matter at this time. I told Father Heithaus so." The article went on to report that the "council of regents and deans of the university is still discussing the question as to whether the university should admit Negro students, Father Halloran

[sic] said, and has rarived [sic] at no conclusion."⁵² There is little doubt that such public attention forced University officials to look into the matter more urgently than they would have otherwise; and that was Heithaus's goal. He achieved it by basing his appeal on grounds of Catholic religion and ethics. He argued from Scripture, the teachings of the Popes, and the sacraments.

Heithaus begins in a striking manner by asserting that Muslims and atheists "are more Christ-like than many Christians" in "what concerns justice for the negro." He goes on to build up an unassailable theological argument, deeply rooted in the Catholic tradition, against discrimination and segregation:

> Our Lord and model, Jesus Christ, commanded His followers to teach all nations. He founded one church through which all were to be saved. He prayed that all might become one in Him. He incorporated all races and colors into His Mystical Body. He died that all might be united in the happiness of the Beatific Vision.⁵³

The argument proceeds with a series of juxtapositions between the teachings of Scripture and the Church and what "some people say," including the following:

> St. Paul says very explicitly... that in the Mystical Body of Christ, to which all Christians belong, there is absolutely no difference between one race and another. But some people say that if negroes are members of the Mystical Body, they are only nominal members.⁵⁴

This concern represents a major focus not only of the sermon, but also of the wider discussions about integrating SLU. "The Negro" *as such* is not the concern so much as the Negro *as Catholic*.

Thus in the postscript of Holloran's aforementioned letter

he explained:

> The weight of the appeal which has come to us
> has stressed the position of the Negro in the
> Catholic Church and the serious challenge of dis-
> crimination by a Catholic University against col-
> ored Catholics who find it impossible to obtain a
> Catholic education.[55]

Heithaus points out the irony of Catholic universities which admit "Protestants and Jews, Mormons and Mohammedeans, Buddhists and Brahmins, pagans and atheists," and yet slam their doors "in the face of Catholics, because their complexion happens to be brown or black."[56]

Yet Heithaus's most powerful and constant appeal is to the Mystical Body of Christ, as seen in the quotations above.[57] It is no coincidence that the previous year Pope Pius XII had issued *Mystici Corporis Christi*. This encyclical had been received by many as a call to various forms of action for social justice.[58] It also followed a period in which theologians—the French Jesuits Emile Mersch and Henri de Lubac being prominent—had been exploring the concept.[59] Among other things, the encyclical stressed the God-given unity of the Church, "by which all men of every race are united to Christ in the bond of brotherhood." [60] Certainly a Church segregated cannot be perceived as an unbroken unity. The Pope went on to explain that since Christians are baptized into Christ's Body, it is impossible to love Christ without loving them: "How can we claim to love the Divine Redeemer, if we hate those whom He has redeemed with His precious blood, so that He might make them members of His Mystical Body?"[61]

Heithaus was not the first to apply this doctrine to the question of race relations.[62] In *The Race Question and the Negro* LaFarge cited several Scripture passages under the heading of "The Mystical Body": 1 Corinthians 12:12–14, 20, 24–27; Colossians 1:12–22; Ephesians 4:5–15. The first of these contains the phrase: "For in one spirit were we all baptized into one body."[63] With such passages LaFarge gently nudged Catholics in the direction of improving race relations.

Heithaus was not so gentle. At a particularly poignant moment in the sermon, he asked his student audience to look at the Blessed Sacrament and ponder that black Christians are, like Christ, "hated and feared. Like Him, they are humiliated and despised. Like Him, they endure injustice and persecution. Like Him, they suffer meekly and in silence." These similes Heithaus followed with a call for all those present to make an act of reparation "[f]or the wrongs that have been done to the Mystical Body of Christ through the wronging of its colored members." Heithaus then asked the five hundred students present at Mass to repeat the following prayer:

> Lord Jesus, we are sorry and ashamed for all the wrongs that white men have done to Your Colored children. We are firmly resolved never again to have any part in them, and to do everything in our power to prevent them. Amen.[64]

This prayer was aimed at mobilizing the students to take an active part in integrating SLU. It also was calculated to allay the fears being expressed regarding integration: "Now some people say that if the Society of Jesus gives Catholic Negroes the Catholic education which the Church wishes them to have, our White students will walk out on us." He went on, "[l]et them ask our students first before they tell us what is in their minds.... For our students not only will not desert us... they will fight tooth and nail for the only University in this state that teaches and practices the religion of Christ." With this act of reparation Heithaus effectively both proved the falsity of such fears and convinced the students that this was a matter of *faith*. He then commissioned them to fight racism "even among your own parents."[65]

The *St. Louis Argus* editorialized the following week:

> Sermons of the kind which Father Heithaus
> preached to his students, we believe does [sic]
> more toward hastening the coming of the king-
> dom of God on earth than ten thousand sermons
> patterned after the empty conventionalities
> which we hear from many pulpits every
> Sunday.[66]

The *St. Louis American*, another local black paper, published the entire text of the sermon along with an interview of Heithaus. There he insisted that every Jesuit on the faculty of SLU "admits that the teachings of Christ, of St. Paul and of the Popes, with regard to race and race problems is binding in conscience on all Catholics." The black *American* reporter added his own opinion of Heithaus: "here is a real Christian, a man who is no hypocrite, hiding behind the cloak of pro-fessed love for all mankind." In the interview Heithaus clearly articulated the motivation behind the sermon: "The purpose of my sermon was to educate the students of the University and through them, their parents, which is more important, to their duties as true Catholics."[67]

How did the students respond? Maguire's testimony that they were not concerned with the question of integration was supported by the lack of articles on the topic in the *University News* preceding the sermon. In the first issue after it, an editorial written by two female students compared racism in America to "the Nazi arrogance" which was being fought in Europe. This was a significant accusation; articles reporting that alumni and students of SLU had been killed in the war hung like dark clouds over these issues of the *University News*. The editorial concluded with an assertion of the students' willingness to work for integration:

> The Catholic students of St. Louis University are
> ready and eager to do their part in breaking down
> all forms of racial intolerance. They literally
> believe: "What you do to these the least of my
> brethern [sic], you do also to Me." They have

enough faith to see Christ in the Negro.[68]

Not only the timing, but also the application of Christian morality to integration in the above statement demonstrate the influence of Heithaus's sermon. Some students were still thinking about integration in the February 25 issue.[69] But any manifest student interest in the topic faded thereafter; integration was not mentioned again in the school paper that school year.

Nevertheless, the career of this powerful sermon on integration extended far beyond St. Louis and its Jesuit university. A scrapbook in the Midwest Jesuit Archives, most likely compiled by Heithaus himself, contains clippings of articles covering the sermon from the *Pittsburgh Courier*, the *Chicago Defender*, the *Denver Star*, the *Catholic Worker*, and the *Catholic Herald Citizen* of Milwaukee. *Midwest Labor World* and LaFarge's *Interracial Review*, like the *St. Louis American*, quoted the text in its entirety.[70] Heithaus purposely provoked this media frenzy, and there is little doubt that it pressured Holloran and the University administration into taking swift and decisive action. But pressure also came from the Jesuit hierarchy. Maher wrote a letter to the Missouri Provincial stating, "Catholic U. is open to all. So should we be."[71]

Academic Integration and Social Segregation

The result was heralded in the local papers at the end of April: "St. Louis University Accepts Five Negroes As Students."[72] Holloran made the announcement public on April 25, 1944, just two months after Heithaus's sermon. The *St. Louis Post-Dispatch* quoted the president's explanation:

> in taking this action, the aim of the university is to make possible for those colored Catholics desirous of, and qualified for, college and university studies, the opportunity to obtain such an education in the environment which the Catholic Church wisely judges to be imperative for the

preservation of moral standards and the strength-
ening of their faith.[73]

This insistence upon the Catholicity of accepted blacks certainly represented a double standard, since members of
other faiths were admitted to SLU but blacks of other faiths
were still to be excluded. Holloran was also sure to emphasize "that the university's academic standards would not be
lowered." [74] He assured the public, and in particular the
Catholic community of potential donors, that the reasoning
behind the decision of the Board of Trustees and the Council
of Regents and Deans was deeply Catholic. Through the
lenses of prejudice concerning the intellectual capabilities of
blacks and in the presence of so few black Catholics, the decision of the SLU administration seemed principled but not at
all threatening.

This development did not occur without tension and conflict within the Jesuit community of St. Louis. Maguire's testimony that disagreement erupted between Heithaus and
Holloran before the sermon was delivered has already been
noted. The most detailed available first-hand account of the
events following the sermon is given by Dunne. "Father
Holloran," he writes, "was not pleased by Heithaus's sermon and wrote him a note the same day to tell him so." On
February 15, Holloran took Heithaus with him to consult the
Archbishop. In a letter from Heithaus to Zuercher dated
December 18, 1944, the former described the meeting
between himself, Holloran, and Glennon in great detail. The
Archbishop had vilified Heithaus, but "Heithaus, no wimp,
refused to be browbeaten and responded without equivoca-
tion to the articles of indictment."[75]

Speculating about the motivations of Holloran, which mirror those of Glennon, Reinert and Shore write:

> It is not clear whether Fr. Holloran was motivated
> chiefly by fears of how parents and alumni would
> react to the prospect of an integrated University,

or whether he actually believed that African
Americans did not belong at St. Louis University
because of their alleged intellectual or moral infe-
riority. What is evident is that concern over
parental reactions was made the principal argument against the integration of the University.[76]

Heithaus was also concerned with parental opinions,
although by contrast with Holloran he directed a Christian
moral appeal to parents through their children. Faherty
gives a more sympathetic presentation of Holloran's concerns:

He was trying to move the University back into
the mainstream of a city that rigidly followed the
Southern racial pattern. At the same time, he was
being challenged to lead that city in a most dramatic and tense social step, namely, to inaugurate
integration in education. One can readily understand his dilemma.[77]

The major part of Holloran's effort to "move the University"
was massive fundraising. He likely viewed Heithaus's agitation as a threat that could dissuade potential donors.

Returning from their meeting with the Archbishop,
Holloran informed Heithaus that Glennon had given him
approval for integration, but the charges against Heithaus
still stood. In his capacity as Rector of the Jesuit community,
he forbade Heithaus to speak in public on the racial issue.[78]
Heithaus was not removed from his position as assistant
professor of archaeology or as moderator of the *University
News*.[79]

Heithaus obeyed the injunction to public silence, although
he vehemently defended himself and attacked Holloran and
Glennon in "interminable and highly emotional letters to the
Provincial." Faherty writes, "The very length of these letters
in the late fall of 1944 suggest that Heithaus presumed that
the Provincial had nothing to do but read his letters." He

also may have worked behind the scenes to encourage further discussion on the issue of race relations. On November 15, 1944, LaFarge, who had privately lauded Heithaus's sermon,[80] delivered a lecture in St. Louis "On Interracial Topic," which was advertised in the *University News*.[81]

Heithaus gave a talk entitled "An Appeal to American Conscience" at the invitation of the League of Women Voters of St. Louis on October 3, 1944. From Friday morning Mass to the voting booths, women were a driving force behind integration. Heithaus began the talk by noting, "During the past six months I have received hundreds of letters about my attitude toward the Negro...over ninety percent...were unequivocal endorsements of the admission of Negroes to St. Louis University." He pointed out that those who opposed integration inevitably raised the specter of miscegenation: "'Do you expect my daughter to marry a Negro?' This is the great fear that paralyzes so many keen minds and freezes so many kindly hearts."[82] Faherty confirms that Holloran received letters from many white parents who "presumed that their sons and daughters would find members of the other race overwhelmingly charming and numerous intermarriages would follow."[83]

To allay such fears, Holloran made a fascinating compromise; he "decided to restrict integrated activities to the classroom."[84] In the commencement address of 1945 he articulated a twofold policy for the University based on the principle that "Freedom and justice do not require the complete identification of all men, nor do distinctions necessarily imply unjust discrimination":

> 1. We admit and welcome to academic equality and even to academic identity of opportunity all colors, creeds, nations, individuals—who measure up to the requirements dictated by sound educational and Catholic principles. 2. In the wider and less well-defined field of social relationships, contacts and activities, we do not

> approve, nor shall we attempt to enforce, identity
> between white and colored students.... Social
> relationships and more specifically race relation-
> ships would be bettered not by revolution but by
> evolution.[85]

Holloran closed the topic by asserting that in this matter he
was in complete conformity with the Archbishop, and that
this twofold policy "is to constitute a norm for those who
would speak or write on this matter in the capacity of representatives of this University."[86]

Holloran was not, however, in conformity with the
Provincial of the Missouri Jesuits; in fact, he did not consult
the Provincial before delivering the address. "Had he done
so," wrote the American Assistant, Maher, the following
month, "Fr. Provincial would have advised him... not make
such public and solemn reference to an extremely delicate
situation." Maher sent an excerpt from the graduation
address along with "the animadversions of Father Heithaus'
[sic] on the same" to LaFarge in order to gain his opinion on
the matter.[87] LaFarge responded that,

> it would be vastly better if he [Holloran] had
> never spoken at all. The phrases he uses: e.g.
> "evolution not revolution," are stock phrases
> which, though they sound well to the inexperi-
> enced, are in fact commonplaces in the propagan-
> da of the advocates of "white supremacy," and
> generally recognized as such by the Negroes....
> They show that somebody has been providing
> him with language. Behind that language and the
> distinctions he tries to make is the same old phi-
> losophy of racialism, which operates by continu-
> ally stirring up the fear of intermarriage.... As for
> what to do now that the milk has been spilt, it
> seems to me the best thing is first, to forget the
> whole thing and act as though he had never said
> it. If queried about it, say that he did not mean it

to be taken too literally; and then show by his conduct that he does not really mean to enforce any rigid plan of segregation.[88]

Maher responded positively to LaFarge's suggestions, and took the liberty "of sending Fr. Zuercher a transcript for his personal guidance."[89]

While this exchange eventually effected the quiet death of Holloran's twofold policy, it occurred after Holloran's first attempts to enforce his policy early in the spring semester of 1945, and after Heithaus's final effort to fully integrate SLU. Holloran abruptly reversed "the informal social integration that had been proceeding quietly since September" when he imposed upon the student council "a resolution excluding African Americans from extracurricular activities."[90]

Dancing with Christian Cannibals

The issue came to a head over a student dance that was to be held at the Jefferson Hotel. Holloran intended the dance to exclude black students, and he wanted it advertised as such in the school paper. Heithaus, still moderator of the *University News*, refused. Here we pick up on the story as told by Dunne. Heithaus "was convinced that to exclude black students upon racial grounds was immoral; by approving the publicity, he would be cooperating in sin, and his conscience forbade it."[91] Fr. Henri Renard met with Holloran to tell him:

> I am Father Heithaus's confessor. You may not agree with him. I may not agree with him. But I must tell you that he is absolutely sincere in his conviction that to do what you want him to do would be to commit a sin. Consequently, if you do this you will be responsible for forcing him to commit a sin.[92]

Dunne claims to have heard this report from Renard himself.

Here Dunne gives a pertinent reflection on the issue of Jesuit obedience. St. Ignatius of Loyola writes in the Jesuit *Constitutions*:

> All should keep their resolution firm to observe obedience and to distinguish themselves in it, not only in the matters of obligation but also in the others, even though nothing else is perceived except the indication of the superior's will without an expressed command.[93]

The complication in this case arises from the fact that Holloran was both the local superior of the St. Louis Jesuit community and the president of the University. If considerations of conscience had led Heithaus merely to disobey the president of the university for which he worked there would not have been complications regarding the obedience a Jesuit owes to his superiors in the Society. Yet Holloran was also his superior, and although Heithaus knew Holloran's will, he felt bound in conscience not to obey. Dunne vehemently defends Heithaus's position, appealing to

> two fundamental principles of Catholic moral doctrine: (1) everyone is obliged to follow the dictates of one's honestly formed conscience, even though erroneous; (2) no one can be obliged to act against one's honestly formed conscience, even though erroneous.[94]

Dunne was incensed by the fact that Heithaus's case was submitted to the Missouri Province's theology school for resolution. "The appeal to the Saint Mary's theologians, implicitly challenging these propositions, in effect tore down the entire system of defense of Jesuit obedience."[95]

Holloran also conflated the issues of obedience and his own roles, and hence he punished Heithaus in his capacity as Heithaus' superior in the order (rather than in the university), although the offense was against the president of the

University. Holloran resolved to impose upon him a public penance—a *dicitur culpa*. The ritual was effected at an evening supper with three hundred Jesuits and scholastics present. Heithaus stood while the charges against him were read—he had ignored "the known wishes of his superiors"—and he was ordered to take a penitential retreat of three days.[96]

The article "Why Not Christian Cannibalism?" with which Heithaus broke his yearlong public silence on the race question, was another deliberate masterpiece directly suited to the current events. Heithaus was encountering opposition from fellow Jesuits who did not deny the truth of his position but held that to move too quickly in the matter of integration would be imprudent in light of the adverse reactions of some parents. They seemed to counsel:

> We must enter quietly into the prejudiced mass and unostentatiously leaven it with the sweetness and light of our unobtrusive tact and circumspection, saying nothing about our inner convictions and conforming "prudently" to the prevailing pattern of discrimination. If we persevere in our "prudence" long enough and practice the virtue of patience, the situation is bound to improve.[97]

Heithaus railed against such notions of "prudence," drawing a comparison between prudently acquiescing to racism and doing the same to cannibalism. He imagined a situation in which Christians establish a school in a cannibal society. There,

> the cannibal visitors to the new school might discover that these Christian teachers may have their private convictions about cannibalism but are much too "shrewd," "sensible" and "realistic" to be dogmatic about them when talking to cannibals.[98]

In classes, "the delicate subject of cannibalism" would be glossed over, and a cannibalistic Christianity would develop which does not offend "[l]ittle cannibal students and big cannibal money," so "bigger and better buildings might go up for the more dignified and commodious accommodation of cannibalistic education."[99] This stinging criticism is obviously aimed at Holloran and others who feared "social" integration on grounds of prudence—which translates into not offending potential donors to the St. Louis University Expansion Program.

Heithaus anticipated the objection that this comparison was too far-fetched:

> But is it? What is the difference between the morality of "Christian" cannibalism and the morality of "Christian" race discrimination? If there is any difference, it must be in favor of cannibalism, for cannibalism only desecrates human corpses, but race discrimination is a profound and relentless assault upon the innate dignity and inalienable rights of millions of living children of God and members of Christ.[100]

The main focus of the religious and moral appeal of Heithaus's indignant article was again the Mystical Body of Christ: "All members of Christ's Mystical Body must imitate Christ themselves and by faith see the Christ who is in all other Christians." The unity of the Body of Christ forbids race discrimination with the force of divine law—it constitutes "a kind of civil war within the Mystical Body," an attack on "the unity of Christendom."[101]

As with his sermon, the career of Heithaus's article extended beyond St. Louis. In the May 1945 issue of *Catholic Digest* a condensed version, with several paragraphs excised, was printed.[102] The article occasioned Heithaus's removal from St. Louis. The tensions were high regarding the events surrounding the integration of the University, and in order to relieve them the American Assistant "advised the Provincial to assign Heithaus to another Jesuit enterprise to ease relations, not as a vindictive measure."[103] Heithaus found himself acting as a chaplain at Fort Riley, Kansas, from April to September of 1945. The next school year he began to teach at Marquette University, where he remained until he returned to SLU in 1958.

Local papers again heralded the results: "Two on St. Louis U. Faculty Out Over Negro Students." Heithaus was the first. Although the Christian cannibalism article was published in March, this late April report from the *St. Louis Post-Dispatch* mentioned only

> the question of admitting Negroes to the annual Student Conclave formal prom, held last Friday [April 13, 1945] at Hotel Jefferson. Father Holloran was said to have opposed admitting them, to have instructed the hotel management not to admit them if they should come, and to have asked for a police detail in case there should be a demonstration.[104]

The *St. Louis Star-Times* also reported the prom as the cause of conflict, quoting Holloran as insisting, "I never said a word to Hotel Jefferson, never, never."[105] "He also instructed Father Heithaus to publicize the event in the University News," the *Post-Dispatch* article continued, "and Father Heithaus said he could not in conscience call this a student dance if the Negro students were excluded. He refused to insert the publicity." Instead, Heithaus "asked to be relieved of his duties."[106]

Dunne was the second. Although the newspaper reports that he was expelled because of his radio addresses on the topics of race relations,[107] he claimed his offense was a long and emotional letter to Zuercher in which he defended Heithaus and attacked Holloran.[108] While this letter is not available to researchers, a gentler rebuke of Holloran's position on the dance written by Laurence Kenny, S.J., is available. This letter demonstrates that there were other Jesuits supporting Heithaus.[109]

Black students did attend the prom, and there was no conflict between them and the white students.[110] This fact indicated the force of Heithaus's moral and theological appeal, expressed again in the Christian cannibalism article that had been published one month before the dance. But students were not the only ones who agreed with Heithaus's positions on both racial justice *and* prudence. Zuercher had called Heithaus to see him in St. Mary's, Kansas, and the latter traveled there on March 22. According to one Jesuit observer, Zuercher also discussed the matter with his provincial advisors, and went on to "order Fr. Holloran to withdraw his orders about the dance."[111] The *Post-Dispatch* corroborated this story, writing that Zuercher "was reported to have...told Father Holloran Negroes must be admitted."[112]

Thus with the student prom of April 13, 1945, St. Louis University in effect achieved—however haltingly—*social* integration alongside *academic* integration. Heithaus's deliberate and timely agitation brought about swift action grounded in Catholic theology and moral principles. This revolution took place in the midst of a radically segregated city, ten years before the integration of American public schools was set into motion by Justice Earl Warren's 1955 decision in Brown v. Board of Education of Topeka.[113] It is rightfully celebrated as a great achievement.[114] Moreover, the move also prepared St. Louis Catholics for the efforts of the bishop who would take over the diocese in 1946. Although encountering some protest from white Catholics, Archbishop Joseph Ritter ended racial segregation in the city's Catholic schools in 1947.[115] The St. Louis crisis also prepared the Jesuits of America for the statement issued soon after by Maher, the American Assistant, that a qualified candidate for admission to the Society of Jesus "ought not to be excluded merely because of his color."[116]

Conclusion

Claude Heithaus intervened at a crucial moment in the history of SLU, when the consideration of integration was being urged by the Jesuit hierarchy and by a handful of zealous local Jesuits. The party opposed to integration was represented by president Holloran, who—whether or not racist himself—exhibited concern that the potential benefactors of the university and students' parents feared integration, likely because of the specter of miscegenation. Concerned above all with his University Expansion Program, Holloran addressed himself to parents and donors rather than to the students. Heithaus, on the other hand, invoked the developing notion of the Mystical Body of Christ in an appeal to Catholic consciences directed primarily towards his student audience, through them to parents, and ultimately to as broad a public as he could reach via the media. Heithaus's actions for the promotion of integration centered on the sermon of February 11, 1944, and on the article entitled "Why Not Christian Cannibalism?" published first in the university newspaper of March 16, 1945. Each composition was brilliantly calculated to address current situations directly by appealing to Catholic consciences with Catholic teachings, particularly the notion of the Mystical Body of Christ.

By addressing the university students and at the same time masterfully using the media to disseminate his appeals, Heithaus forced the University leadership and those higher in the Jesuit hierarchy to stop stalling and to make their decision on the basis of moral rather than financial considerations. This was a brilliant manipulation of Jesuit politics. The sermon, viewed within its historical context, brought about the academic integration of Saint Louis University; the "Cannibalism" article effected a huge step towards social integration. Heithaus's stress throughout was unequivocally on Catholic teachings, above all on the developing understanding of the Church as the Mystical Body of Christ.

Notes

1. Peter McDonough, *Men Astutely Trained: A History of the Jesuits in the American Century* (New York: Free Press, 1992), 183.

2. Daniel T. Kelleher, "St. Louis 1916 Residential Segregation Ordinance," *Bulletin of the Missouri Historical Society* 26, no. 3 (1970): 239-48. Neighborhood groups such as the West Tower Grove Heights Association vigorously promoted residential segregation as a means of preventing instances of "negro invasion of white neighborhoods" which they felt caused depreciation of property values ("2 Improvement Clubs Unanimously Indorse Segregation Ordinance," *St. Louis Republic*, 21 Feb 1916, photocopy of the article in *Segregation*, a scrapbook in the Missouri Historical Society Library, St. Louis, 18).

3. "The United States Supreme Court decision yesterday barring use of courts to enforce real estate title restrictions against Negroes will apply to hundreds of block areas in St. Louis and St. Louis county..." ("417 Block Areas Here Affected By Supreme Court Racial Ruling," *St. Louis Post-Dispatch* 4 May 1948, photocopy of article in *Negro Scrapbook*, vol. 1, Missouri Historical Society Library). "Restrictive covenants" were a common means of enforcing residential segregation in cities of the southern states (Kelleher, 248).

4. On developments concerning Catholic education, see Philip Gleason, *Contending with Modernity: Catholic Higher Education in the Twentieth Century* (New York: Oxford University Press, 1995). In several articles published in *America* (see note 18), William Markoe, S.J., stressed the necessity of Catholic education for blacks by appealing to the teachings of U.S. bishops concerning Catholic education, and decried the lack of institutions to meet this need. "In our day and country really 'to learn the essentials of what is necessary for us to believe and to do in order to attain salvation' requires a Catholic education. Catholic parents, accordingly, are bound by the moral law to give their children a Catholic training in a Catholic school. If this is denied to a colored boy or girl, they have no alternative but to go to one of the many non-Catholic schools that will receive them, which is usually equivalent to a loss of faith."

("Negro Higher Education," *America* 26 [1 Apr 1922]: 558-60).

5. According to a survey conducted in 1940 to which 92 Catholic institutions responded, 222 full-time black students were enrolled in a total of 38 Catholic colleges and universities in the U.S. Eight of the responding institutions had policies of exclusion, 20 had formulated no policy because the question had not come up, 59 had definite policies of accepting blacks, 2 failed to specify a policy, and 3 were in states where by law they were forbidden to mix white and colored students. Only 3 (segregated) institutions provided Catholic higher education to blacks in former slave states: Xavier University of Louisiana, established by the Sisters of the Blessed Sacrament in 1925, the Catholic College of Oklahoma, founded by the Benedictine Sisters of the Congregation of St. Scholastica in 1936, and St. Augustine's Seminary in Bay St. Louis, Mississippi (John T. Gillard, *Colored Catholics in the United States* [Baltimore, MD: The Josephite Press, 1941], 212-5).

6. William Barnaby Faherty, S.J., *Dream by the River: Two Centuries of Saint Louis Catholicism 1766-1980* (St. Louis, MO: River City, 1981), 155. George Dunne, S.J., relates that the Archbishop was rightfully called "an obdurate race bigot" who suffered from "negrophobia" (George H. Dunne, S.J., *King's Pawn: The Memoirs of George H. Dunne, S.J.* [Chicago: Loyola University Press, 1990], 80).

7. *Dream by the River*, 180.

8. Laurence Kenny, S.J., to Joseph King, S.J., 1945, typed letter, Laurence J. Kenny Manuscript Collection, Saint Louis University Archives, St. Louis. The number Dunne gives is 61, but he is writing 45 years later and seems to be relying upon his memory (Dunne, 61). Kenny writes: "I've inquired to learn whether there was any friction anywhere, but strange to say have been unable to learn that there has been even the slightest." The first black student accepted to the university, Sylvester Smith, corroborated Kenny's observation when many years later he recalled: "As an individual, I didn't feel discriminated against. I carried myself in such a way that I respected others and they respected me." However, Anita Lyons Bond, one of the first black women admitted to the university, recalls encountering discrimination frequently in and around the university (Daniel J. Ladd, "History Lessons," *Universitas* 12, no. 2 [1995]: 17).

9. Francis K. Drolet, S.J., "Negro Students in Jesuit Schools and Colleges, 1946-1947: A Statistical Interpretation," *The Woodstock Letters* 76 (1947): 302.

10. Dunne, 86.

11. Claude Herman Heithaus Personnel Record, Heithaus Files, Midwest Jesuit Archives, St. Louis.

12. Steve Francisco, "First Newspaper Remembered by Its Progenitor," *University News*, 13 Oct 1995.

13. Heithaus Personnel Record.

14. Claude Heithaus, "Supplementary sheet on travel of C.H. Heithaus," Heithaus Files, Midwest Jesuit Archives, St. Louis.

15. Handwritten, signed pledge with title "Shrine of Our Lady, Saint Stanislaus Seminary, Feast of the Assumption, 1917," William Markoe files, Midwest Jesuit Archives, St. Louis. For a concise overview of William's career, see William Barnaby Faherty, *Rebels or Reformers? Dissenting Priests in American Life* (Chicago: Loyola University Press, 1987), 65-77.

16. Jeffrey H. Smith, "John Prince Markoe, USMA 1914: A Pioneer of Civil Rights," *Assembly: Association of Graduates of the U.S. Military Academy* 44, no. 4 (March 1991): 9. This article provides a concise overview of John's career.

17. Gillard, 229, 209.

18. W. M. M., "Catholics and the Negro Question," *America* 21 (9 Aug 1919): 451; William M. Markoe, S.J., "Viewing the Negro Supernaturally," *America* 23 (19 Jun 1920): 200-2; "Negro Higher Education," *America* 26 (1 Apr 1922): 558-60; "The Importance of Negro Leadership," *America* 29 (3 Oct 1923): 605-6; "The Negro and Catholicism," *America* 30 (23 Feb 1924): 449-50; "A Great Migration," *America* 30 (9 Feb 1924): 396-7. The first of these was a letter to the editor, whereas the others were brief articles.

19. William Markoe, *The Memoirs of William Markoe, S.J.*, ed. Kenneth P. Feit and Thomas M. Nolan, unpublished typed manuscript, Midwest Jesuit Archives, St. Louis, pp. 11-22.

20. Smith, 9.

21. David W. Southern, *John LaFarge and the Limits of Catholic Interracialism, 1911-1963* (Baton Rouge, LA: Louisiana State University Press, 1996), 114.

22. *Markoe Memoirs*, 125.

23. Donald J. Kemper, "Catholic Integration in St. Louis, 1935-1947," *Missouri Historical Review* 73 (1978): 8; William M. Markoe, Personnel Record Card, William Markoe files, Midwest Jesuit Archives, St. Louis.

24. Kemper, 11-2; Heithaus Personnel Record.

25. Smith, 9.

26. *Markoe Memoirs*, 168.

27. To this end the two Jesuits together visited the parents of Anita Lyons and encouraged them to send her to SLU. She registered in 1946 and graduated in 1950 (Anita Lyons Bond, interview by author, St. Louis, 7 Sept 1999). Concerning the Evans family and Clarence Hunter, see William Barnaby Faherty and Madeline Barni, *The Religious Roots of Black Catholics of Saint Louis* (St. Louis, MO: Saint Louis University, 1977), 54.

28. Southern, xiii.

29. John LaFarge, *Interracial Justice: A Study of the Catholic Doctrine of Race Relations* (New York: America Press, 1937); *The Race Question and the Negro: A Study of the Catholic Doctrine on Interracial Justice* (New York: Longmans and Green, 1944).

30. Robert A. Hecht, *An Unordinary Man: A Life of Father John LaFarge, S.J.* (Lanham: Scarecrow, 1996), 143.

31. Southern, 213, 261. LaFarge also cultivated the authorities of his own order. He informed the American Assistant about a young Negro worthy of and willing to be admitted to the Society of Jesus. LaFarge then went on to express why he communicated this information: "not with the idea of pushing the matter from above, but with the idea of learning what might be your own mind on the matter before I take it up with Father Sweeny [the local Provincial]" (LaFarge to Maher, typed letter, 24 Aug. 1944, LaFarge Papers: Box 17, folder 24, Georgetown University Archives). Maher later wrote an unequivocal statement allowing black novitiates.

32. William Barnaby Faherty, S.J., "Claude Heithaus Funeral Sermon May 15, 1976," Heithaus Files, Midwest Jesuit Archives, St. Louis.

33. "Minutes of the Meeting of the Special Committee on the Admission of Negroes to the University February 2, 1943," typed,

Heithaus Files, Midwest Jesuit Archives, St. Louis.

34. William Barbey Faherty, *Better the Dream: St. Louis University and Community 1818-1968* (St. Louis: St. Louis University Press, 1968), 339-340.

35. *Markoe Memoirs*, 168; C. Denny Holland, "The St. Louis Story Retold," pamphlet, Heithaus Files, Midwest Jesuit Archives, St. Louis. Here and on the following pages, Markoe quotes Holland's pamphlet at length, supplying some names and details Holland had left out.

36. Holland, "The St. Louis Story Retold"; Jeffrey H. Smith, *From Corps to Core: The Life of John P. Markoe, Soldier, Priest, and Pioneer Activist*, Midwest Jesuit Historical Series, vol. 1 (Florissant, MO: St. Stanislaus Historical Museum, 1977), 90.

37. Patrick J. Holloran, S.J. to [name blotted out], typed letter, 26 Jan 1944, Heithaus Files, Midwest Jesuit Archives, St. Louis. This cautious letter has been criticized for demonstrating that Holloran knew little about the means and abilities of blacks in St. Louis *(Dream by the River*, 155).

38. Susan C. Thomson, "SLU Celebrates Its Pioneering of Integration," *St. Louis Post-Dispatch*, 31 Jan 1995. It is possible that Thomson did not investigate the question at all.

39. Faherty, "Breaking the Color Barrier," *Universitas: The Saint Louis University Magazine* 13, no. 2 (Autumn 1987): 19.

40. When Markoe and his fellow Jesuits Jack White and George Dunne presented their case for admitting blacks before the regents and deans of the university sometime after the letter had gone out, only two of the fifteen attending supported them (Smith, 91). This may indicate that a number of the responses were negative towards integrating the university.

41. "St. Louis U. Inquires on Accepting Negroes," *St. Louis Post-Dispatch*, 27 Jan 1944.

42. *Pittsburgh Courier*, 5 Feb 1944.

43. Holland, "The St. Louis Story Retold."

44. "Breaking the Color Barrier," 18.

45. "President Holloran Makes Annual Report," *Alumni News of St. Louis University*, June 1945, p. 3.

46. Monsignor Jack Maguire, interview by author, St. Louis, 20 Nov 1997.

47. Dunne, 83.

48. Maguire, interview.

49. Paul C. Reinert, S.J. and Paul Shore, *Seasons of Change: Reflections on a Half Century at Saint Louis University* (St. Louis, MO: St. Louis University Press, 1996), 21. This observation is corroborated by the fact that the League of Women Voters of St. Louis invited Heithaus to speak on integration in October 1944. The talk is reproduced in Rev. Claude H. Heithaus, S.J., *An Appeal to American Conscience* (St. Louis, MO: St. Louis Branch NAACP, 1944).

50. Jake McCarthy, "The SLU Segregation," *The St. Louis River Front Times* 22-8 April 1998. McCarthy was the sports editor of the *University News* at the time.

51. "St. Louis University Students Asked to Back Admitting Negroes," *St. Louis Post-Dispatch*, 11 Feb 1944.

52. "St. Louis U. Head Surprised at Priest's Plea on Negroes," *St. Louis Post-Dispatch*, 12 Feb 1944.

53. "Text of Sermon," *University News*, 11 Feb 1944, 1.

54. Ibid.

55. Holloran to [name blotted out].

56. "Text of Sermon," *University News*, 11 Feb 1944.

57. The Mystical Body of Christ is central to all of Heithaus's appeals to fellow Catholics. A long letter he co-authored to the Provincial of Missouri emphasizes the theme again and again: "It cannot be too strongly emphasized that the Mystical Body of Christ is a divinely revealed *reality*. It is a reality of such profound significance and vital importance that integral Christianity becomes impossible when its obvious implications are ignored" (Claude H. Heithaus and John Markoe to Zuercher, typed letter, 23 Nov 1944, Zuercher files, Midwest Jesuit Archives).

58. See, e.g., Yvon Charron, *Encyclique sur le corps mystique du Christ: Analyse et commentaires* (Montreal: Fides, 1945), 7.

59. Emile Mersch, *The Whole Christ: The Historical Development of the Doctrine of the Mystical Body in Scripture and Tradition*, trans. John R. Kelly (Milwaukee, WI: Bruce Publishing Company, 1938); Henri de

Lubac, "*Corpus Mysticum*: Etudes sur l'origine et les premiers sens de l'expression," *Recherches de sciences religieuses* 29 (1940): 257-302, 429-80; 30 (1940): 40-80, 191-226.

60. Pius XII, *Mystici Corporis Christi*, ed. Claudia Carlen (McGrath, 1981), par. 5.

61. Ibid., 74.

62. Nor was he the last. For example, in 1948 William Markoe delivered a series of lectures "on racism in the light of the doctrine of the Mystical Body of Christ" at Marathon, Wisconsin (*Markoe Memoirs*, 166).

63. *The Race Question and the Negro*, 105-6.

64. "Text of Sermon," *University News*, 11 Feb 1944.

65. Ibid.

66. *St. Louis Argus*, 18 Feb 1944.

67. George B. Stafford, "St. Louis University Professor Scores Race Prejudice and Assembly: Father Heithaus Calls for Practical Application of Teachings of Christ Now," *St. Louis American*, 17 Feb 1944.

68. Doris Walsh and Mary Alyce Divis, "What We Are Prepared to Do About the Negro," *University News*, 18 Feb 1944.

69. Mary Jeanne Johnston, Interview with Dr. Robert M. Hutchins, *University News*, 25 Feb 1944; Carl Kisslinger, "What Prejudice Is...," *University News*, 25 Feb 1944.

70. *Pittsburgh Courier*, 19 Feb 1944; *Chicago Defender*, 26 Feb 1944; *Denver Star*, 26 Feb 1944; *Catholic Worker*, March 1944; *Catholic Herald Citizen*, 26 Feb 1944; *St. Louis American*, date unavailable (the clipping can be found in the Heithaus Files, Midwest Jesuit Archives); *Interracial Review* 17, no. 3 (1944): 40-2.

71. *Better the Dream*, 243.

72. *St. Louis Star-Times*, 26 April 1944; also, "St. Louis U. Opens Doors to All when Five Colored Enroll," *St. Louis American*, 27 April 1944; "St. Louis U. Opens Doors: Will Admit Five," *St. Louis Argus*, 28 April 1944.

73. "St. Louis U. Admits Five Negroes," *St. Louis Post-Dispatch*, 26 April 1944.

74. Ibid.

75. Dunne, 83-4.

76. Reinert and Shore, 21-22.

77. *Better the Dream*, 342.

78. Dunne, 84.

79. "The *University News* was fortunate in having as its moderator for the past two years the Rev. Claude H. Heithaus, S.J., whose patience and perseverance never failed" (Jack Maguire, ed., *The Archive*, 1945).

80. "Breaking the Color Barrier," 19-20.

81. *University News*, 10 Nov 1944. Frances Robinson gave a report on the lecture in the following week's paper (*University News*, 17 Nov 1944).

82. *An Appeal to American Conscience*, 2-3.

83. "Breaking the Color Barrier," 20. William Markoe noted this concern among his fellow Jesuits: "We should consider it poor form to express emotional apprehension about miscegenation before a supposedly intelligent Jesuit audience" ("Miscegenation and Jesuit Thinking," *Bulletin of the Institute of Social Order* [January 1947]: 2).

84. "Breaking the Color Barrier," 20.

85. *The Alumni News of St. Louis University*, June 1945, p. 4.

86. Ibid.

87. Maher to LaFarge, typed letter, 3 June 1945, LaFarge Papers: Box 17, folder 24, Georgetown University Archives.

88. LaFarge to Maher, typed letter, 7 June 1945, LaFarge Papers: Box 17, folder 24, Georgetown University Archives.

89. Maher to LaFarge, typed letter, 11 June 1945, LaFarge Papers: Box 17, folder 24, Georgetown University Archives.

90. Gleason, 238. Various members of the university administration saw to it that gym classes and many extracurricular activities remained segregated for several years. This changed when Paul C. Reinert, S.J., replaced Holloran as president of SLU in 1948 (Bond, interview).

91. Dunne, 89-90.

92. Dunne, 90.

93. St. Ignatius of Loyola, *The Constitutions of the Society of Jesus*,

trans. George E. Ganss (St. Louis, MO: The Institute of Jesuit Sources, 1970), 246.

94. Dunne, 90. These are fundamental principles of Catholic moral doctrine. Cf. St. Thomas Aquinas, *Summa Theologiae*, vol. 18: *Principles of Morality*, trans. Thomas Gilby (New York: Blackfriars with McGraw-Hill, 1966), I-II, 19.5.

95. Dunne, 90.

96. Ibid., 92. The ritual infuriated Dunne. Hence he adds; "the thought entered my mind that I should cross the few feet to where [Holloran] sat, pick up the large soup tureen, and dump its contents over his head. I did not do so, but have sometimes regretted it."

97. Claude H. Heithaus, "Why Not Christian Cannibalism? Race Problem Can Only Be Solved by Applying Moral Principles," *University News*, 16 March 1945.

98. Ibid.

99. Ibid.

100. Ibid.

101. Ibid.

102. Claude H. Heithaus, S.J., "Why Not Christian Cannibalism?" *Catholic Digest* 7, no. 9 (May 1945): 83-6.

103. "Breaking the Color Barrier," 18. Maher was sympathetic with Heithaus's intention; he would soon issue "a far-reaching and far-sighted statement for all American Jesuit provinces on the admission of black novices" ("Breaking the Color Barrier," 21).

104. "Two on St. Louis U. Out Over Negro Students," *St. Louis Post-Dispatch*, 20 April 1945.

105. "2 Quit St. L.U. Faculty; Race Issue Denied," *St. Louis Star-Times*, 20 April 1945.

106. "Two on St. Louis U. Out Over Negro Students."

107. Ibid.

108. Dunne, 93-4.

109. Kenny to King. William Markoe noted that Laurence J. Kenny was one of his main sources of encouragement in his work for interracial justice (*Markoe Memoirs*, 65).

110. "Two on St. Louis U. Out Over Negro Students."

111. Kenny to King.

112. "Two on St. Louis U. Out Over Negro Students."

113. Chief Justice Earl Warren, "Brown v. Board of Education of Topeka, Enforcement Decree, 349 U.S. 294 (1955)," in *Let Freedom Ring*, ed. Peter B. Levy (Westport, CT: Praeger, 1992), 40-1.

114. "Breaking the Color Barrier," 18.

115. Cyprian Davis, *The History of Black Catholics in the United States* (New York: Crossroad, 1990), 256. The white population of St. Louis, however, remained committed to segregation. During the 1950s, when segregation could no longer be legally enforced, the white population of the city fell dramatically in areas where blacks moved (Cornelia F. Sexauer, *St. Louis in the 1940-1950s: Historical Overview and Annotated Bibliography*, unpublished typed manuscript, 5 March 1993, Missouri Historical Society Library, St. Louis).

116. "If however because of his color it is judged that he will not be useful in a given Province, then efforts should be made to find a Province in which he will be useful, and he should be accepted for that Province" (Zacheus J. Maher, S.J., to the Provincials of the American Assistancy, typed letter, 3 May 1945, Father Assistant Correspondence [Maher] 1945, Midwest Jesuit Archives).

Part III
THE WORLD OF MEDIATION:
EMBODIED HOLINESS

"Your Face Is My Only Homeland": A Psychological Perspective on Thérèse of Lisieux and Devotion to the Holy Face

Mary Frohlich, HM
Associate Professor of Spirituality
Catholic Theological Union

Introduction

When fifteen-year-old Thérèse Martin entered the Lisieux Carmel on April 9, 1888, she took the title "Thérèse de l'Enfant-Jésus." Only six months later, however, when she received the habit (January 10, 1889), she added the phrase "et de la Sainte Face." Although it is by the first title that she is most popularly known, she is recorded as having said at the end of her life that devotion to the Holy Face was closely linked with the very foundations of her piety.[1] A case can easily be made, then, that the Holy Face is the "root metaphor" of Thérèse's spirituality—that is (in Paul Ricoeur's words) a dominant image that "assembles subordinate images together" and "scatters concepts at a higher level."[2] Clarifying the origins, character, and import of this devotion in Thérèse's life will be essential if we are to understand her spirituality and its potential contribution to ecclesial life in the twenty-first century.

The present paper will explore Thérèse's devotion to the Holy Face as a psychospiritual node where personal history, sociocultural milieu, and mystical transformation creatively reacted with one another in the making of a saint. The largest portion of the paper is concerned with a psychoanalytical reflection on Thérèse's life history.[3] I have used an eclectic approach to this interpretation, drawing upon a variety of psychological concepts that seem especially apt for shedding light on the phenomena we encounter in studying Thérèse's life. We begin, however, by situating her devotion to the Holy Face within its historical and cultural context.

The Devotion to the Holy Face in Historical and Cultural Perspective

Popular devotions often have two major sources of power: first, the deep human need to resolve one's crises of meaning by shaping personal and communal symbols from whatever materials are at hand; second, the concern of institutionalized religion to recruit and control the sentiment of the masses to its own agendas.[4] Thomas Kselman finds both very much at work within nineteenth-century French cultural dynamics.[5] The entire century was a time of crisis, as the nation was repeatedly rent by massive political, philosophical, economic, and ecclesial changes. Devotional activity offered a creative and emotionally sustaining way for individuals to re-establish a personal center when disorder and insecurity reigned in so many areas of social experience. At the same time, throughout the century there was a sustained effort on the part of the ecclesiastical hierarchy to suppress the local and "wild" character of popular religious activity, harnessing it instead to the agendas of the national and international Church. In this way the intense energy of personal meaning-making was directed into the construction of a shared identity rather than functioning to send individuals and groups off on centripetal trajectories.

An explicit spirituality of reparation was central to the devotion to the Holy Face as it was practiced in nineteenth-century France. The center of the revival of the devotion was at the Carmel of Tours, where in 1845 the nun Marie de Saint-Pierre consecrated herself to the reparative cult of the Holy Face.[6] The link between a spirituality of reparation and devotion to the Face of Jesus goes back at least to 1694, when the French Dominican Antonin Thomas published a tract on this topic. During Marie de Saint-Pierre's time it was taking on fresh impetus from the aftermath of the French Revolution. In 1846 the Virgin Mary appeared at LaSalette calling the devout to acts of reparation, and in 1847 Bishop Parisis of Langres founded a new archconfraternity, the "Society of Reparation for Blasphemies and the Violation of Sunday." A major movement, arising from the grassroots but quickly taken up and underwritten by the ecclesiastical hierarchy, was underway. The cult of the Holy Face, then, developed in close conjunction with this intense reaction of many French Catholics, both clerical and lay, against the threatening tide of secularization and anticlericalism that they saw rising on all sides.

Heinz Kohut's psychoanalytic theory is helpful in showing how the therapeutic and the political dimensions of the devotion work together. Kohut's idea of the "group self" proposes that groups, like individuals, have a life history with moments of crystallization of "self" in relation to "self-objects."[7] Selfobjects, in Kohut's understanding, are those persons, environments, etc., that one experiences as so important to one's psychological survival as to be essentially a part of oneself. Leaders, artists, or "stars" of popular culture often function as selfobjects for groups. When the group experiences a severe threat and potential fragmentation, it is in need of selfobjects who enable it to move through the crisis to a renewed sense of coherence. This is usually accomplished by the charismatic presentation of a set of symbols and myths that are compelling because they are drawn from the depths of that group's particular psyche.

The reparative cult of the Holy Face was one important facet of a set of symbols and myths that sustained and repaired the deeply threatened sense of identity of the cultural subgroup to which Thérèse belonged. One of the ways in which these extremely devout Catholics responded to the changing political reality was by withdrawing from others and forming an intense "we-they" mentality. Encouraged by their ecclesiastical leaders, these French "ultramontanes" long clung to fading hopes for a society in which the Church would be central and the Pope would be chief hero and leader. By participating in the cult of reparation together, they gave a communal name to the experienced threat: it was a result of the sacrilegious evils of blasphemy, desecration of the blessed sacrament, and profanation of the Sabbath. And, together with each other and God, they acted to repair it: by their devotion, God's anger would be deflected and the longed-for utopia of an ecclesially centered society would return. The popularity and power of the cult of the Holy Face may have been due to the way it met profound needs both for individuals and for the cultural subgroup of ultramontane Catholics, for whom it functioned transformatively in relation to their urgent need for a myth of the "repair" of their wounded social world.

In this context, Marie de Saint-Pierre creatively synthesized three elements: the burgeoning concern with reparation; devotion to the Infant God (a tradition that had also bloomed in the seventeenth century, and was promoted especially by the Carmel of Beaune); and devotion to the Holy Face. Thus, the link among these elements was not original with Thérèse. Years later, Thérèse's debt to Marie de Saint-Pierre's synthesis would be acknowledged in the fact that throughout her religious life she always carried on her person both a photograph of Marie and a lock of the nun's hair.

The visual image of the Holy Face that accompanied the

devotion usually showed Jesus' weeping, bleeding face imprinted on the veil of Veronica.[8] The model for this image was the one installed at St. Peter's Basilica in Rome. The layman Léon Dupont became known as "The Holy Man of Tours" for his widespread promotion of the spirituality of Marie of Saint-Pierre and of devotion to this image.[9] Many miracles were attributed to the copy of the image that he placed in his salon in Tours, which became a pilgrimage site drawing crowds second only to those flocking to the confessional of the Curé of Ars. Isidore Guérin, Thérèse's maternal uncle, paid for a copy of the image to be installed and maintained in Saint-Pierre cathedral in Lisieux. Thérèse was exposed to this image, then, from childhood. Indeed, on April 26, 1885, twelve-year-old Thérèse, her father, and her three sisters not yet in the cloister were officially enrolled in "The Atoning Confraternity of the Holy Face."

Looking at a copy of this image, it is easy to see the inspiration for some of the themes that developed in the cult. These themes include: a spirituality of suffering with Christ as a reparative act; compassion for Christ's suffering in imitation of Veronica's compassionate gesture of wiping his face during the Passion; and hiddenness with Christ, as behind a veil. Later in the paper we will see the particular twist that Thérèse gave to these themes.

The Divine Face in Biblical and Mystical Traditions

Much of this paper deals with psychological themes, but it is important to keep in mind that Thérèse is not just a psychological "case." She is, more importantly, a saint, a renowned spiritual teacher, and a Doctor of the Church. Without attempting to do a complete survey of the mystical theme of the "Divine Face," this section places the subsequent, more psychologically focused reflections in the context within which Thérèse herself would have understood her experience—namely, that of Christian mystical traditions.[10]

The scriptural theme of the Divine Face offers an entree to

the paradoxical character of the symbol in mystical literature. The key topus is the story of Moses, which much of the
patristic tradition took as the prototype of the mystical journey. Exodus 33:11 says that "The Lord used to speak to
Moses face to face, as one person speaks to another." But in
verse 20 Moses is told by the Lord, "My face you cannot see,
for no one sees me and still lives." This seeming antinomy of
the impossibility of seeing and yet of seeing, of radical
incommunicability combined with intimate presence, characterizes many mystical references to the Face of God.

In the New Testament a related idea occurs in 1
Corinthians 13:12: "Now we see indistinctly, as in a mirror;
then we shall see face to face. My knowledge is imperfect
now; then I shall know even as I am known." Here the antinomy of the face is placed in an eschatological context; the
mutual intimacy of face-to-face knowledge is not available
now, but will come to pass in the time of fulfillment. Another
interesting passage in relation to Thérèse's attraction to "lit-
tleness" is Matthew 18:10: "See that you never despise one of
these little ones. I assure you, their angels in heaven constantly behold my heavenly Father's face." Here, the antinomy operates by displacing the pole of "seeing" to the angels,
while the "little ones" evidently do not share directly in the
capacity to see. As we will see, for Thérèse also the Holy Face
is as much a veiled absence as it is a radiant presence.

From the vast riches of the Christian mystical tradition we
will only mention two examples that may be fruitful for reference in our reflections on Thérèse. The first is the tradition
of female mysticism that flourished in many parts of Europe
during the late middle ages. Although Thérèse would not
have had direct contact with the writings or imagery of these
women, in a very broad sense she can be said to be their heir.
An antinomy of radical abandonment and ecstatic fulfillment converging in the experience of union with God
appears in the writings of many of these women. In at least
one case—that of the Flemish mystic Hadewijch—this is

directly linked to the image of the Divine Face. In her Vision 13, Hadewijch sees the Countenance of God in the shape of a six-winged seraph.[11] Among the many facets of divine truth that are revealed to her there, she sees first how those "wholly annihilated in humility" are raised to inexpressible beauty. But further on she sees that others—those who have gone as far as "Unfaith" and the "denial of Love"—are the ones who are most fully "adorned with Love." Thus Hadewijch's vision illustrates in the most "excessive"[12] form the radically paradoxical character of mystical language expressing encounter with the Divine Face.

The Carmelite tradition, within which Thérèse was explicitly formed, has its own development of the theme. John of the Cross, of whom Thérèse stated, "At the ages of seventeen and eighteen, I had no other spiritual nourishment,"[13] wrote frequently of both the awesome glory and the essential ineffability of the Face of God. In one place John quoted Job 4:16, "...there stood before me one whose countenance I knew not, an image before my eyes," adding, "he says that he did not know his countenance, to signify that in such a communication and vision, even though most sublime, the countenance and essence of God is neither known nor seen."[14] Once when John quoted Psalm 30:21 (Vulgate), "You will hide them in the secret of Your face from the disturbance of people," he added the comment: "To be hidden in the face of God from the disturbance of people refers to the fortification this dark contemplation provides against all occasions that may arise because of others."[15] These are just two of numerous examples that indicate how, as she nourished her spirit on the writings of John of the Cross, Thérèse was introduced to the mystical traditions that link hiddenness and presence in the image of the Face of God.

The Human Face and Infant Development

The significance of the human face in infant development is well established. Foundational research on this topic was done by René Spitz, who found that a series of "organizers" mark the child's psychological growth through substages of infancy.[16] The first organizer of experience for the child is the action of sucking, which begins at birth. The second organizer, typically emerging around two to three months, is the human face. Spitz found that babies of this age clearly turn their attention to faces—and even to cardboard circles inscribed with key facial features, such as eyes, nose, and mouth. The third organizer, coming to the fore at six to eight months, is the attachment to the mother that manifests as "stranger anxiety." Finally, the fourth organizer, marking the end of infancy at about fourteen months, is the capacity to say "No."

Spitz's theory, then, is that the discovery of the human face is central to the infant's emergence from the relative autism of its first few weeks of life into rudimentary participation in human social intercourse. The fact that even caricatures of the face draw the baby's attention suggests that there may be an instinctual or archetypal character to this attraction; it may not be driven *only* by the fact that adoring gazes, interesting sounds, etc. come forth from human faces. Nevertheless, presumably the actual character of the faces the child encounters does make a difference. A baby who is exposed to conflicted, angry, or blank faces has a different foundation for future relationships than does a child who primarily sees joyful, inviting faces.

Thérèse's Infancy

In the six years immediately preceding Thérèse's birth on January 2, 1873, her parents experienced the death of four of their own children and the stillbirth of a nephew.[17] It is hard to imagine the level of trauma that this drumbeat of child death would inflict upon parents. Yet Thérèse's older sister Céline later reported that "When our little sisters died, people said: 'There is no need to try to console Madame Martin; she does not suffer at all from the loss of her children!'"[18] Zélie Martin evidently rigorously practiced a spirituality that refused to allow human feeling to impinge upon the conviction of faith that God's providence cannot be questioned and that her dead children are fortunate to be innocent angels in heaven.

Yet human feeling is not so easily disposed of. In a recent book French psychoanalyst Denis Vasse suggests that Zélie Martin's fear for the infant Thérèse's possible death was "inscribed in her flesh and in her eyes. She was afraid—and fear is not welcoming."[19] At age ten weeks, Vasse proposes, Thérèse was driven into anorexia (the refusal of the breast) and radical distancing from her mother by her desperate need to escape the visage of anguish in her mother's face. Zélie, acknowledging that she had "death in her soul,"[20] walked six miles to fetch Rose Taillé, a peasant wetnurse. As soon as Rose arrived, the previously inconsolable baby fed voraciously and immediately fell into a deep sleep. Taken to Rose's sunny farm, Thérèse thrived. For the remainder of the year that she stayed there, she showed relatively little interest in her mother or her mother's world.

Vasse makes a number of fascinating suggestions about the effect of this period of Thérèse's life. First, he proposes that the bitterness of her initial experience of mother-love planted in her soul a core memory of the unsatisfactoriness of libidinal attachments. Yet this would have literally killed her, if not for the appearance of Rose Taillé and her (apparently) welcoming, uncomplicated face and breast. Vasse also notes the significance of Rose's name: "Thérèse had received and was going to give life in Rose."[21] Throughout Thérèse's writings "rose," "flower," and "sun" (i.e., the memory of living in the sun with Rose) are constant signifiers of life and vitality. On the other hand, Thérèse images the suffering of giving oneself without apparent response from the loved one as "unpetaling the rose." Vasse observes that the name "Rose Taillé" translates as "pruned (or cut) rose"—perhaps a premonition of the antinomy of presence and absence already contained in Thérèse's initial experience of psychological salvation.

The Face as "Transformational Object"

Indeed, Thérèse never explicitly speaks of Rose Taillé; Rose remains for her "the unconscious figure of the compassion of God…. What Thérèse understands of God, of Life…she *does not know* or, better, she is not conscious."[22] Vasse's insights correlate remarkably well with the insights of two other psychoanalytic interpreters of infant development, D.W. Winnicott and Christopher Bollas. Winnicott developed the idea of the "True Self" as a self that rests in its own body and feelings and spontaneously acts from that basis. The "False Self," on the other hand, is a compliant self that is cut off from its own primal resources and instead acts primarily in reaction to others' demands and expectations.[23] Taking on some degree of False Self is probably universal in human development, but Winnicott probes how this dynamic can be reduced and/or healed. What an infant needs, he observes, is someone who can be an embracing, affirming presence without impinging upon the baby's formless quiescence. When a caretaker is unable to allow the baby to rest in that "formless state" of unintegration, the baby "becomes prematurely and compulsively attuned to the claims and requests of others…. He loses touch with his own spontaneous needs and gestures, as these bear no relation to the way his mother experiences him and what she offers him."[24]

Christopher Bollas's idea of the "transformational object" takes Winnicott's earlier notion of the "transitional object" a step further back in development.[25] Winnicott had proposed that, especially at the critical turning point of around six to eight months when the child manifests "stranger anxiety" because she or he is developing awareness of the mother as an individual who can go away, the child will begin to invest the meaning of the mother's presence into an object, such as a blanket, teddy bear, or thumb. The transitional object helps the child to control anxiety, and it also is a foundational step in the spreading out of personal meaning over a cultural field structured by symbols.[26]

Bollas took the roots of object relations back even earlier, to the stage at which the "face" is a key organizer. The "transformational object" is the trace of a core experience of transformation from despair to hope. For example, the baby wakes up at night, wet, hungry, and lonely; the mother swoops in to remedy the situation in an aroma of her favorite perfume. The odor of that particular perfume might be imprinted as a "transformational object" that would henceforward mysteriously evoke a shift from emptiness to joy. Bollas notes that the transformational object, unlike the transitional object, is not fundamentally something that the child creates and thus controls. Rather, it is available only as a "happening"; it exists only in the actual moment when a transformation is being experienced. While the transitional object deals with manageable anxiety by creating an internalized fantasy of security, the transformational object addresses radical despair by turning it inside out in what is experienced affectively as a "death-resurrection" dynamic. Edward Shafranske observes, "The trace of the transformational object can be gleaned in all later-developed object representations that the subject imbues with the power to evoke transformation."[27]

Thérèse, it seems, had an extreme experience of potential annihilation by the death-obsessed face of the mother, whose panicked demand that her child not be sick deeply infringed upon the child's need simply to rest "formlessly" in welcoming arms. The transformational object, the face of Rose Taillé, appeared in the nick of time. The image of the face, then, was planted at the core of Thérèse's sense of hope. Yet the earliest experience of radical dissatisfaction could not simply be wiped out. It too had to be included, even in the image of the face. The Holy Face that became the "foundation of her piety" was a face that was bleeding, anguished—and veiled.

Many years later Thérèse would write: "Our Lord, willing for Himself alone my first glance, saw fit to ask my heart in the cradle, if I can so express myself."[28] Vasse suggests, indeed, that in some sense Thérèse's earliest bitterness in human relations was a key factor that helped to catapult her to the heights of mystical fidelity to God. The deep suffering of her life as "naked, referred to the impossibility of attaining to the presence of the one who is desired."[29] Her vocation—imprinted in the cradle—was to learn to love without any attachment whatsoever to the *feeling* of love.

Thérèse's Childhood

At age fifteen months, little Thérèse left the peasant cottage of her wetnurse and returned to her family's comfortable middle-class home. She apparently made an adequate adjustment; within a few months, Zélie reported that "The dear little thing does not want to leave me."[30] When Thérèse was only four years old, however, Zélie died of breast cancer. On the day of her mother's funeral, Thérèse threw herself into the arms of her sixteen-year-old sister Pauline and took her as her new "Mamma." This immediate substitution apparently satisfied Thérèse sufficiently that, at least on the surface, she did not manifest any other major symptoms of grief. Yet with hindsight, the adult Thérèse recognized that it actually took her ten years to come to terms with the loss that she experienced at her mother's death; she referred to this as the most "painful" period of her life.[31]

Jesuit psychoanalyst William Meissner, writing about Ignatius Loyola—another saint who lost his mother in early childhood—notes that children do not mourn as adults do. "Typically, at the time of the loss, there is little crying or expression of sadness; the child seems to go about his activities relatively unperturbed."[32] While adults will struggle with the process of detachment from the lost loved one, children instinctively seek "to avoid the acceptance of the reality and emotional meaning of the death and to maintain in some internal form the relationship that has ended in external reality."[33] Meissner notes two patterns that may result: an attachment to a highly idealized parent-figure (perhaps a hero or heroine, or a noble cause) or identification with the dead parent and with the state of death itself as a way to be reunited with the parent. All of these reactions—substitution, idealization, and identification with death—can perhaps be seen in Thérèse's way of coping with early mother-loss.

In Vasse's interpretation, another dynamic at work in Thérèse's reaction of seeming indifference was the reality of ambivalence toward her mother. According to his thesis of the initial bitterness of the relationship with Zélie, it was Rose Taillé who had first successfully established an affectionate maternal bond with Thérèse. The return to her blood family was already a "loss" for Thérèse. The transition seems to have been negotiated successfully enough, and Thérèse apparently did bond with Zélie. Yet Zélie was already in some ways a "substitute"—and one whose face evoked unconscious memories of annihilating fear. When Zélie died, two reactions were thus evoked in Thérèse: first, a repetition of the primal pattern of loss; and second, guilt for her ambivalent feelings. The immediate substitution of Pauline as a new "Mamma" was, says Vasse, like an "hysterical symptom that manifests two contradictory tendencies—that of changing the object, the mother, in order not to lose her, proving thus non-culpability, while, nevertheless, she proves herself guilty."[34]

It is also worth noting that her mother's death occurred when Thérèse was at the prime age of oedipal dynamics. According to classical Freudian theory, the death of the same-sex parent at this age is unconsciously a "dream come true" that can induce terrifying guilt. In any case, Thérèse clearly developed an intense, perhaps even inordinate, attachment to her father. She became his "little Queen," and emotional investment in him remained pivotal throughout her life. Indeed, an incident occurred about two or three years after Zélie's death that shows how Thérèse had already unconsciously linked her father with the image of the Holy Face. Louis was away on a trip, and Thérèse was gazing out upon the sunny garden. Suddenly she saw a man who looked just like her father, but more stooped and with "a sort of apron of indistinct color" veiling his face. Her soul was invaded by "a feeling of supernatural fright" as she called out to him; but he walked away and disappeared.[35]

This "vision" has been referred to as "prophetic," since Louis later would suffer from the "veiling" of his mental capacities. Indeed, even apart from prediction of the future in the strict sense, Thérèse may have had a deep sensitivity to factors that were already at work in her father—both the physical condition that would eventually incapacitate him, and the cumulative emotional effects of grief at the loss of four children and his beloved wife. What is most fascinating, however, is how this coalesced for young Thérèse (six or seven years old at this time) with the image of the suffering, veiled Holy Face.

By this time Thérèse had surely been introduced to this devotion, even if only by observing the devotional activities of adults at the Cathedral of Lisieux. Her psyche performed the work of merging the image from the sociocultural cult, the experience of her father's incipient suffering, and her own deepest transformative longings centered around the "face." Years later she named the meaning of the vision in terms of her adult spirituality: "Just as the adorable Face of Jesus was veiled during His Passion, so the face of His faithful servant [Louis Martin] had to be veiled in the days of his suffering in order that it might shine in the heavenly Fatherland near its Lord, the Eternal Word!"[36] For the child, however, the meaning was more primordial, more "raw": she was simply terrified as she saw the veil of absence slip over the beloved face of her only surviving parent.

Yet another shock came into Thérèse's life in October 1882, when her "second Mamma" Pauline departed to become a Carmelite postulant. Deprived almost totally of contact with Pauline by the customs of the cloister, within a few months nine-year-old Thérèse began to suffer from constant headaches. By Easter, she was being stricken with strange bouts of paralysis, trembling, and hallucinations. Although she revived sufficiently to attend Pauline's reception of the habit two weeks later, she then became so ill that her family feared for her life. Then on Pentecost a "miracle" happened: while two of her sisters were weeping and praying for her in the sickroom before an image of the Blessed Virgin, Thérèse saw the Virgin's face "suffused with an ineffable benevolence and tenderness." What penetrated to the depths of her soul, she later said, was the "ravishing smile of the Blessed Virgin."[37] She was immediately cured of her strange illness.

Awareness of psychological factors contributing to the specific character of this transformative event need not detract from recognizing its character as a core event of grace, in the strict theological sense of that term. At the psychological level it is not difficult to see that Thérèse's illness has the character of a hysterical reaction to the loss of yet another "mother." Nor, considering Thérèse's history, is it difficult to understand how the face of the Mother of God—specifically, her "ravishing smile"—is the form in which healing grace manifests for her. Here we see in remarkably pure form the manifestation of the "transformational object" which, as Shafranske noted, has the power to evoke transformation from the deepest unconscious levels of the psyche.[38]

The ambiguous part of this transformative event for Thérèse was the fact that it troubled her that her experience became known to others. Here we can gain insight by returning to Winnicott's further discussion of the dynamic of True and False Selves. The positive function of the False Self, says Winnicott, is to hide and protect the True Self, which is "safe" only when it does not have to "have it all together" but can simply rest in formlessness and, when ready, emerge into relationship in a playful spirit. Thus, Winnicott finds at the core of human life a sense of solitude, inviolability, and ineffability that is essential and positive.[39] Trouble comes when the split between True and False Selves widens into a terrifying sense of isolation and alienation. Paradoxically, the chief cause of this is caretakers who demand *too much* sociability, on their own terms; for then the incommunicable core must build intense primitive defenses to protect itself from being dismembered.

Asked to speak about her "miracle," Thérèse recognized immediately that this most intimate transformative moment was something not to be shared with anyone. And yet, under the pressure of her sister Marie's "tender and pressing questions," she acknowledged it—only to have it then broadcast in the speakroom of Carmel, where the nuns pressed her further for details of the "vision." Thérèse was subsequently burdened for years with scruples about whether she had claimed to see something that she had not really seen.[40] The "transformational object," after all, is not something seen; rather, an experience is evoked by a "trace" while the evoking object often remains largely unconscious.

In this vignette of Thérèse being forced to share what could not (and should not) be shared, we see quite clearly the intrusive and enmeshed character of the familial (and religious community) relations to which Thérèse was subjected. Despite their extreme expressions of affection, these women are far from providing for one another the welcoming, freeing presence that Winnicott spoke of as necessary for the emergence of the spontaneity and vitality of the "True Self."

The End of Thérèse's Childhood

The event that Thérèse herself identified as the end of her childhood took place on Christmas Eve, 1886, when she was nearly fourteen. Her father, tired out by attendance at Midnight Mass, reacted peevishly to the fact that Thérèse was still practicing the childish custom of receiving gifts in her slippers after Mass. Thérèse, who according to her own testimony was a spoiled and over-sensitive child who normally would have made a major scene even over such a small slight, unexpectedly found the strength to respond graciously. She attributed this to the fact that "Jesus had changed my heart."[41]

The incident seems tiny, and yet it looms large in Thérèse's life story. She later stated that on this "night of light," "Thérèse had discovered once again the strength of soul which she had lost at age four and a half [when her mother died], and she was to preserve it forever!"[42] Indeed, the evidence is there that henceforward Thérèse manifested both a determination and a clarity of purpose that are rare even in much older persons. Before another year had passed, Thérèse would not only conceive the conviction of her call to enter Carmel immediately, but would carry her petition all the way to the Pope himself.

In this "Christmas conversion," the event of grace seems to predominate over psychological factors. Nevertheless, it is not inappropriate to ask how the "transformational object" functions in this remarkable turnaround. Perhaps it is seen in the unhappy face of her father, to which she responds with a desire to give him joy. The radical transformation is that she no longer seeks the face only to receive life, but to give life. She states, "I felt charity enter my soul, and the need to forget myself and to please others; since then I've been happy!"[43] Shortly thereafter, before a picture of Jesus on the Cross, she discovered the vocation both to receive the "divine dew" and to quench Jesus' thirst by assisting in the salvation of sinners. As she prepares to enter Carmel, Thérèse is ready to launch full-sail upon the mystical vocation of love.

Early Years in Carmel

Mother Geneviève, foundress of the Lisieux Carmel, instilled in all her novices a love for the devotion to the Holy Face as taught by Marie de Saint-Pierre.[44] Shortly after Thérèse entered on April 9, 1888, with the title "de l'Enfant Jésus," her sister Pauline (now Sr. Agnès of Jésus) took her before the statue of the Child Jesus of the Carmel of Beaune and explained "how wonderful it would be if she added the title of the Holy Face to her religious name."[45] Thus the link between the two devotions was initially a received one for Thérèse. We can see the link between crib and cross depicted in many holy cards of the time, which show the infant Jesus in the cradle dreaming of the cross, lance, etc.[46] Thérèse, however, seems to have made a creative step when, in an 1894 painting for Mother Agnès,[47] she modified one of these pictures to show the infant Jesus dreaming of his future sorrowful, bleeding face. In her commentary she wrote: "His infant face is so beautiful. He sees it disfigured, covered with blood!…unrecognizable!…Jesus knows that His spouse will always recognize Him…Then He will lower His divine Face to her, radiant with glory, and He will allow His spouse to taste eternally the ineffable sweetness of His divine kiss!"[48]

From the beginning of her life at Carmel, Thérèse's devotion to the Holy Face was intensely linked with her anxiety over a humiliating and frightening illness that was afflicting her father.[49] She later declared, "Until my coming to Carmel, I had never fathomed the depths of the treasures hidden in the Holy Face…";[50] and her coming to Carmel coincided exactly with the onset of Louis Martin's public decline. Even before Thérèse received the habit (nine months after her entrance), he had begun to manifest disturbing signs of dementia. Some such signs had been present even earlier, but they were kept well repressed or hidden by family members. In February 1889 Louis, hallucinating and reacting violently, had to be hospitalized. He would not return home again until May of 1892, by which time he was so debilitated that family members could manage him. Thérèse and her sisters were deeply upset by these events, especially since in those days mental illness was regarded as shameful, indeed quite possibly a manifestation of hidden sin; hence it was a blight upon the entire family. Her father's quite literal "veiling" and public humiliation—as well as her own resultant shame and sorrow—were quickly assimilated by Thérèse into her developing devotion to the veiled, sorrowing, rejected Holy Face.

The theme of the "hiddenness" of the Holy Face was particularly significant for Thérèse's developing spirituality. This was greatly amplified by her July 1890 discovery of the text from the suffering servant song in Isaiah 53, "His face was as though hidden." Reference to this topus will surface repeatedly in Thérèse's letters, prayers, and plays from this time until the end of her life.[51] A typical example of how she employed this theme is in a letter written on her profession day, September 8, 1890: "Now His Face is as though hidden... Soon His resplendent Face will be shown us in the fatherland and then this will be the ecstasy of the eternal union of glory with our Spouse."[52]

Even at this early date it is evident that Thérèse finds in this image a way of coping with the disconcerting non-availability of her beloved Jesus. In another letter written only a few days before her profession she spoke of the spiritual experience of being in a "subterranean passage where it is neither cold nor hot, where the sun does not shine, and in which the rain or the wind does not visit, a subterranean passage where I see nothing but a half-veiled light, the light which was diffused by the lowered eyes of my Fiancé's Face!"[53] Gazing on the image of the veiled and abused Holy Face, the young Carmelite Thérèse saw a Beloved whose presence also encompassed invisibility and absence. Identifying with Him, she could find ultimate meaning in her own experience of being unknown, misunderstood, and even scorned by those around her.

It is also noteworthy that at this early stage the link between "face" and "flower" was already significant. Once again the link was not original with Thérèse. In April 1890, Sr. Agnès gave Céline (another Martin sister, who was not yet in the convent) a parchment with a drawing of the Holy Face imprinted on Veronica's veil atop a thorny stem.[54] She also composed a prayer in which she compared each of Jesus' features to a different flower. Thérèse commented on this prayer in a subsequent letter.[55] Later, shortly after their father's death in 1894, Thérèse painted a chasuble based on that drawing. The Holy Face on its veil is the central "flower" presiding at the center of a thorny branch in the shape of a cross, with two roses (the Martin parents) at the base, five lilies (the five surviving daughters) surrounding the face, and four buds (the dead Martin children) at the top.[56]

Thus we see Thérèse as a young Carmelite working at deep levels of psyche and spirit with the imagery of the Holy Face. Her infantile experience of the maternal face as anguished and disappearing, but finally as supremely vitalizing, combined with popular devotional ideas of the coalescence of "crib and cross," went into the crucible with her present experiences of familial and personal suffering, of dryness in prayer, and of deep longing for the total presence of the Beloved. Also present in the crucible, again from several sources, is the imagery of "flowers." From all this the familiar themes of her spirituality came forth: spiritual childhood, "the Little Flower," and hiddenness for the sake of mission.

The End of Thérèse's Life

The scope of this paper prohibits detailing the numerous references to the Holy Face throughout Thérèse's career.[57] Of particular importance for a complete study would be examination of her poems (written between February, 1893 and May, 1897), many of which prominently feature the imagery of the "face" and the correlative fascination with receiving "glances" from Jesus. In this final section I will only briefly review a few key texts that reveal the particular character of the spirituality of Thérèse's final years.

Verses three and five of PN 20, "Mon Ciel Ici-Bas!," written on August 12, 1895, and dedicated to the Holy Face, sum up much of Thérèse's attitude in the period prior to her "trial of faith."[58]

> Your Face is my only Homeland.
> It's my Kingdom of love.
> .....
> Your Face is my only wealth.
> I ask for nothing More.
> Hiding myself in it unceasingly,
> I will resemble you, Jesus...
> Leave in me the Divine impress
> Of your Features filled with sweetness,
> And soon I'll become holy.
> I shall draw hearts to you.

In this poem we see a joyful expression of Thérèse's matur-
ing spirituality. Although she clearly seeks the Face of Jesus
for her own solace and fulfillment, she also identifies with it.
Hiding herself in the Face of the Hidden One, she will share
in His mission of drawing others to the ineffable mystery of
life with God.

The final episode of Thérèse's life, which has been termed
the "trial of Faith," would put this tender spirituality to the
supreme test. It began at Easter, 1896—eight months after the
composition of the above poem, and only days after she
coughed up blood and realized that her remaining days on
earth would be few. During her "night of nothingness" her
faith was challenged to its very roots. As she struggled
intensely with this, we find that many of her most original
expressions deal with the theme of "heaven." Very often,
"face," "gazes," "smiles," and "glances" are prominently
featured.

Three months into the trial, in June 1896, she wrote PN 32,
"Mon Ciel à Moi," which includes the following verses:[59]

> My God's Glance, his ravishing Smile,
> That is Heaven for me!
> .....
> Heaven for me is smiling at this God whom I adore
> When he wants to hide to try my faith.
> To suffer while waiting for him to look at me again,

That is Heaven for me!

On August 6, 1896—the feast of the Transfiguration, which was a special day of celebration for the Confraternity of the Holy Face—Thérèse invited two other sisters to join her in making a solemn consecration to the "adorable face of Jesus."[60] Later that month she wrote PN 36, "Jésus Seul," of which the last part of verse 4 reads:[61]

> After this exile, I'll go to see you in Heaven...
> When in my heart the storm arises,
> To you, Jesus, I lift my head.
> In your merciful look,
> I read: "Child, for you I made the Heavens."

Then in September she wrote in Manuscript B (the second part of *Story of a Soul*):[62]

> I am but a poor little thing who would return to nothingness if your divine glance did not give me life from one moment to the next.... [Your little bird] will always stay with its gaze fixed upon You. It wants to be fascinated by your divine glance.... I beg you to cast Your Divine Glance upon a great number of little souls.

The end finally came a year later. On August 5, in preparation for her last feast of the Transfiguration, the sisters placed in her infirmary room the large image of the Holy Face from the choir. The *Last Conversations* record a number of comments that Thérèse made as she lay gazing at the image. One of the most significant—called by Guy Gaucher a kind of "last will and testament"[63]—is the following:[64]

> These words of Isaias, "Who has believed our report?.... There is no beauty in him, no comeliness, etc.," have made the whole foundation of my devotion to the Holy Face, or, to express it bet-

> ter, the foundation of all my piety. I, too, have
> desired to be without beauty, alone in treading
> the winepress, unknown to everyone.

Thérèse died, after terrible agony, on September 30, 1897. Later, at the beatification process, Mother Agnès would testify that "As tender as was her devotion to the Child Jesus, it cannot be compared to her devotion to the Holy Face."[65]

Concluding Reflections

That Thérèse is much better known by her title "of the Child Jesus," and for her doctrine of "spiritual childhood," than for her devotion to the Holy Face is not entirely unjustified. Thérèse did have a kind of fixation on infancy and childhood, which (according to the present interpretation) probably had roots in the deeply traumatic character of some of her foundational early experiences. No doubt, the most powerful symbol is one that is at one and the same time intensely "regressive" and intensely "progressive"—that is, it evokes in us our earliest and most foundational experiences in the same moment that it beckons us to our ultimate, eschatological fulfillment. This seems to have been Thérèse's genius: to evoke and enfold, not only for herself but for millions of others, both the earliest psychological wound of absence and the highest, most "divine" embrace. For her, the transforming movement in relation to this root wound was focused around the "face." As we have seen, there is a deep psychological logic in this. By the face of Rose Taillé, three-month-old Thérèse was saved from psychological disintegration and physical death. Twenty-four years later, the dying Thérèse gazed on the Holy Face of Jesus and knew that she was "saved" for all eternity.

One of the ironies of Thérèse's heritage is that it is not the Holy Face, but her own face, that has become established globally in popular devotion. After Thérèse's death, her sisters attempted to promote the devotion to the Holy Face as the appropriate response to the *Story of a Soul*.[66] They were not particularly successful. In France the ultramontanes, who had formed the bulwark of the devotion's popularity, were being called by Pope Leo XIII himself to accept reconciliation with the secular government through the *ralliement*. As the political and ecclesial function of the cult of the Holy Face faded, the devotion became increasingly marginalized.

Instead, it is Thérèse herself who has become the focus of an intensifying groundswell of popular devotion. One of the interesting aspects of this is that fascination with Thérèse crosses boundaries of ecclesial and secular politics. She has been claimed as an unofficial "patron saint" by very conservative movements within Catholicism as well as by the movement for women's ordination.[67] While the hierarchy has staked its claim on her by naming her first a saint (1923) and then a Doctor of the Church (1997), much of the devotion to her has spread outside of official control. All this public attention and fervor seems quite contradictory to her repeatedly stated desire to be hidden and unknown with the hidden Christ. On the other hand, this sort of antinomy of absence and presence, abandonment and exaltation, is not an uncommon theme in the history of mysticism.

A particularly difficult aspect of Thérèse's spirituality for many is that she seemed almost eager to suffer and to die. Even though this attitude was common among the fervent in her time, it still does not seem like a sign of full mental health. The neurotic dimension of this can perhaps be explained as a compulsion to repeat the trauma of early loss, or as an identification with the absent or dead parent.[68] Yet even more significant are the ways in which Thérèse did *not* remain fixated in an immature position of desperate and destructive neediness, but instead transmuted these core psychological themes into foundation-stones for a mature spirituality. Her fullest expression of her sense of vocation, the "Act of Oblation to Merciful Love" which she made on Trinity Sunday, 1895, profoundly re-envisions the cultural theme of desire to be a suffering (and therefore reparatory) victim of divine justice into a desire to be a "victim of holocaust to [God's] merciful love."[69] In Thérèse's mature spirituality, the core focus is clearly shifted from desire for suffering to desire for participation in divine love.

Psychologically speaking, what is it that makes Thérèse more than simply another struggling neurotic? Denis Vasse suggests that Thérèse is a saint because her desire, in search of the Other, continually transcends fulfillment in any particular object. Rather than resting in enjoyment of loving and being loved, Thérèse rests in radical loving without any feeling of loving.[70]

As mentioned earlier, Vasse sees the roots of this in the initial failure to find libidinal satisfaction in her Mother. Yet that failure is *also* the root of neurosis. As Jacky Bodelin observes in the Preface to Vasse's book, above all we must not split Thérèse as "neurotic" from Thérèse as "saint." Rather, Thérèse demonstrates for us "an anthropology that places the encounter with God at the most intimate core of ourselves, the same place where, in our personal histories, we were blocked by the greatest of refusals."[71]

Notes

1. *St. Thérèse of Lisieux: Her Last Conversations*, trans. John Clarke (Washington, DC: Institute of Carmelite Studies, 1977), 135.

2. Paul Ricoeur, *Interpretation Theory: Discourse and the Surplus of Meaning* (Fort Worth, TX: Texas Christian University Press, 1976), 64.

3. I acknowledge indebtedness to two Carmelites who have covered this ground, with somewhat different emphases, before me: Constance FitzGerald, "The Mission of Thérèse of Lisieux," *Way Supplement* 89 (1997): 74-96; Marc Foley, "The Psychology of Thérèse of Lisieux," lecture given at Catholic Theological Union, Chicago, Winter 1996 and available in cassette form by ICS Publications Cassettes, Washington, DC, under the title "St. Therese: Psychological and Spiritual Perspectives on Her Childhood Illness."

4. See Mark R. Francis, "Building Bridges between Liturgy, Devotionalism, and Popular Religion," *Assembly* 20 (1994): 636-638, for

a brief review of these two emphases.

5. Thomas A. Kselman, *Miracles and Prophecies in Nineteenth-Century France* (New Brunswick, NJ: Rutgers University Press, 1983). Cf. especially the summary on p. 200.

6. See J. A. Robilliard, "Sainte Thérèse de l'Enfant-Jésus et de la Sainte Face, Sainte de Lumière et de Clarté," *Révue des Sciences Philosophiques et Théologiques* 40 (1956): 670-679; also idem, "Face (Dévotion à la sainte Face)," *Dictionnaire de Spiritualité Ascétique et Mystique, Doctrine et Histoire*, ed. M. Viller (Paris: Beauschesne, 1937-1995), 5: 26-34; "Marie de Saint-Pierre," 10: 528- 530.

7. Heinz Kohut, *Self Psychology and the Humanities: Reflections on a New Psychoanalytical Approach*, ed. Charles Strozier (New York: W.W. Norton, 1985). For summary and specific references see Mary Frohlich, *The Intersubjectivity of the Mystic: A Study of Teresa of Avila's Interior Castle* (Atlanta, GA: Scholar's, 1994), 383-395.

8. For a variety of examples, see Pierre Descouvemont, *Thérèse and Lisieux* (Grand Rapids, MI: Eerdmans, 1996), 136-141 and elsewhere. For a historical survey of the development of the legend of Veronica's veil, see Robilliard, *Dictionnaire de Spiritualité* 5: 26f.

9. Louis-Marie Danviray, "Léon Papin-Dupont," *Dictionnaire de Spiritualité* 3: 1831-1833.

10. See Bernard McGinn, *The Flowering of Mysticism: Men and Women in the New Mysticism, 1200-1350* , vol. 3 of *The Presence of God: A History of Western Christian Mysticism* (New York: Crossroad, 1998), 208, 420-421, for some resources on the theme of the "divine countenance" in Jewish and Christian mystical literature.

11. *Hadewijch: The Complete Works*, trans. and intro. by Columba Hart (New York: Paulist, 1980), 297-305. For discussion, see McGinn, 207-211.

12. Bernard McGinn uses the term "excessive" to refer to the extravagant, often corporeal, manifestations of mysticism that began to occur after 1200, especially among women. See McGinn, 25 and elsewhere.

13. *Story of a Soul: The Autobiography of St. Thérèse of Lisieux*, trans. John Clarke, 3d ed. (Washington, DC: Institute of Carmelite Studies, 1996), 179.

14. "The Spiritual Canticle" 14-15:20, in *The Collected Works of St. John of the Cross*, trans. Kieran Kavanaugh and Otilio Rodriguez, rev. ed. (Washington, DC: Institute of Carmelite Studies, 1991), 534.

15. "The Dark Night," II, 16:13 (*Collected Works*, 434-5); cf. also "The Living Flame of Love" 2:17 (*Collected Works*, 664).

16. René Spitz, *The First Year of Life: A Psychoanalytical Study of Normal and Deviant Development of Object* (New York: International Universities Press, 1965).

17. February 1867, Joseph-Louis Martin, age 6 months. August 1868, Joseph-Jean-Baptiste Martin, age 8 months. February 1870, Hélène Martin, age 5 years. October 1870, Melanie-Thérèse Martin, age 2 months. October 1871, Paul Guérin (son of Zélie Martin's brother Isidore), stillborn.

18. Quoted in Ida F. Gorres, *The Hidden Face: A Study of St. Thérèse of Lisieux* (New York: Pantheon, 1959), 34.

19. Denis Vasse, *La Souffrance sans Jouissance ou le Martyre de l'Amour: Thérèse de l'Enfant Jésus de la Sainte Face* (Paris: Seuil, 1998), 35. (All translations from this text are my own.)

20. *Letters of St. Thérèse of Lisieux*, Vol. II, trans. John Clarke (Washington, DC: Institute of Carmelite Studies, 1988), 1204.

21. Vasse, 43.

22. Vasse, 51.

23. Cf. D.W. Winnicott, "Ego Distortion in Terms of True and False Self," *The Maturational Process and the Facilitating Environment* (London: Hogarth, 1965).

24. Jay R. Greenberg and Stephen A. Mitchell, *Object Relations in Psychoanalytic Theory* (Cambridge, MA: Harvard University Press, 1983), 194. I also acknowledge with gratitude the contribution of an unpublished paper by one of my students, John Kim, to this discussion. The title is "Winnicott's Formless State as a Basis for Self-Possession and Authentic Freedom: A Theological Appraisal."

25. Christopher Bollas, "The Transformational Object," *International Journal of Psychoanalysis* 60 (1979): 97-107. Cf. also Edward P. Shafranske, "God-Representation as Transformational Object," in Mark Finn and John Gartner, eds., *Object Relations Theory and Religion: Clinical Applications* (Westport, CT: Praeger, 1992).

26. D. W. Winnicott, "Transitional Objects and Transitional Phenomena," *Playing and Reality* (London: Tavistock, 1971) 1-25.

27. Shafranske, 66.

28. *Letters* II, 1016.

29. Vasse, 14.

30. *Letters* II, 1211. We may note that the "adequacy" of Thérèse's adjustment is questioned by Jean-Francois Six, who presents evidence that the relationship with her mother continued to be troubled. See *La*

Véritable Enfance de Thérèse de Lisieux: Névrose et Sainteté (Paris: Éditions de Seuil, 1971).

31. *Story of a Soul*, 34.

32. William Meissner, *Ignatius of Loyola: The Psychology of a Saint* (New Haven, CT: Yale University Press, 1992), 10.

33. J. B. M. Miller, "Children's Reactions to the Death of a Parent: A Review of the Psychoanalytic Literature," *Journal of the American Psychoanalytic Association* 19 (1971), quoted in Meissner, 9-10.

34. Vasse, 48.

35. *Story of a Soul*, 45-47.

36. *Story of a Soul*, 47.

37. *Story of a Soul*, 65-66.

38. Shafranske, 66.

39. D. W. Winnicott, "Communicating and Not Communicating Leading to a Study of Certain Opposites" in *The Maturational Processes and the Facilitating Environment* (London: Hogarth, 1965).

40. *Story of a Soul*, 66-67.

41. *Story of a Soul*, 98.

42. *Story of a Soul*, 98.

43. *Story of a Soul*, 99.

44. Mother Geneviève of Saint Teresa was already 83 years old at the time of Thérèse's entrance, and she had handed over her duties as prioress and novicemistress to Mother Marie de Gonzague. Mother Geneviève died on December 5, 1891.

45. Descouvemont, 161.

46. Descouvemont, 158. Descouvemont notes that this depiction expresses the Bérullian spirituality of Christ's primordial "yes" that accepts from the very first instant of his human existence the full implications of his incarnational mission.

47. Agnès of Jésus had been elected prioress on February 20, 1893.

48. *Letters*, LT 156, 838-9. See Descouvemont, 157-159.

49. Currently, scholars believe that his disease was cerebral arteriosclerosis. At the time, however, it was regarded as a case of insanity. See Descouvemont, 146.

50. *Story of a Soul*, 152.

51. Cf. Guy Gaucher, *The Passion of Thérèse of Lisieux* (New York: Crossroad, 1998), 225 for a list of her references to this text.

52. *Letters*, Vol. I (1982), LT 117, 675.

53. *Letters*, LT 110, 652.

54. Descouvemont, 149.

55. *Letters*, LT 103, 613.

56. Descouvemont, 206-207.

57. For a listing of most of these references, see: Marie Baudouin Croix, "La Dévotion de la 'Sainte Face' au 19e Siècle et dans les Écrits de Thérèse," *Vie Thérèsienne* 109 (1988): 33-41.

58. *The Poetry of Saint Thérèse of Lisieux*, trans. Donald Kinney (Washington, DC: Institute of Carmelite Studies, 1996), 108-110. French text, 272-273.

59. *Poetry*, 153-154 (French text, 294-295).

60. Descouvemont, 270-271. The other two sisters were her sister Celine (now Sr. Geneviève) and Sr. Marie of the Trinity—the same two who had, one year earlier, joined Thérèse in her "Offering to Merciful Love."

61. *Poetry*, 165 (French text, 299).

62. *Story of a Soul*, 199-200.

63. Gaucher, 226.

64. *Last Conversations*, 135.

65. Quoted in Gaucher, 226.

66. Cf. Descouvemont, 312.

67. Thérèse on several occasions indicated her desire to be a priest. See *Story of a Soul*, 192; *Letters*, 1014; *Last Conversations*, 161; also the testimony of Geneviève of Saint Teresa in *St. Thérèse of Lisieux by Those Who Knew Her*, ed. and trans. Christopher O'Mahony (Dublin: Veritas, 1975), 155-156.

68. See the reference above to William Meissner's discussion of St. Ignatius of Loyola.

69. *Story of a Soul*, 277.

70. Vasse, 13-17.

71. Jacky Bodelin, "Préface," in Vasse, 7-8.

Caravaggio, Theologian: Baroque Piety and Poiesis in a Forgotten Chapter of the History of Catholic Theology

Anthony J. Godzieba
Associate Professor of Religious Studies
Villanova University

Introduction

The evidence shows that Counter-Reformation theology along with the culture and piety of the Baroque period (thus the time period from roughly the mid-sixteenth century to 1750) holds little interest for contemporary Roman Catholic systematic theology, and no interest at all for specifically English-language Catholic theology. Baroque Catholicism, which followed the gradual tapering-off of the militancy of the Counter-Reformation and represented the post-Tridentine church's new burst of confidence in the particularly Catholic way of construing reality and God's saving relationship to it, seems to be considered theologically useless and irretrievable. In fact, whenever "baroque" is mentioned in connection with theology it is usually combined with "scholasticism" to denote a style of theology which became the paradigm for stale, rigorist, repetitive theological system-building completely divorced from the vibrant affective life of Catholic practice. Unfortunately, the various styles of Baroque Catholic life thereby get reduced to a stereotype.

In the thirty-plus years since the close of Vatican II, American Catholic systematic theology has developed a greater sophistication in dealing with its immediate past and has come a long way from what appeared in the late 1960s and 1970s to be its fundamental working narrative of theological history. That narrative ran from the Hebrew Scriptures up through the fourth gospel, then jumped to the Rahner essays of the 1950s, with a smattering of Augustine, Aquinas, and Newman thrown in to demonstrate that Catholic systematics certainly was not an exercise in bad faith. This truncated narrative differed noticeably from the publicly professed scope of theology's new historical consciousness (which was held to be wider than anything offered by Neo-Scholastic theology).

The situation has never been quite this bad in continental Catholic theological circles. Theologians there have been working for decades with a different narrative of theological history, one which recognized that the particular forms of Vatican II's *aggiornamento* had deep roots in the Catholic practices and theological reflections of the previous two hundred years. Thus, in order to grasp the complexity of the wide range of issues facing contemporary theology, one needs to practice a wide-ranging hermeneutical "backward glance" and consider the *ressourcement* promoted especially by French and German theologians during the first half of the twentieth century, the period between the run-up to Vatican I and the sloppy denouement to the Modernist controversy, back farther still to the vibrant theology constructed by the Tübingen theologians in their dialogue with modern philosophy and modern Protestant theology, and back even farther to Catholicism's internal and external struggles with Enlightenment thought during the last half of the eighteenth century.[1]

Despite this greater sensitivity to the complexities of the history of Catholic theology, it is clear that Catholic theologies and practices between the close of the Council of Trent and the beginning of the nineteenth century, except for the attention paid to certain movements of spirituality, have dropped out of the theological conversation—and this despite claims such as Thomas O'Meara's that "the metamorphoses of Catholicism in recent decades show that it is Baroque Catholicism (not the Counter-Reformation or Modernity) that is challenged by developments after Vatican II."[2] From my point of view, this lack of attention to the Baroque is a tragic deficiency and exhibits a theological attitude that is fundamentally un-Catholic. And so, in the spirit of an authentic hermeneutical systematic theology, I want to examine some of the religious paintings of Caravaggio in a modest attempt to retrieve and redeem one crucial part of the Catholic tradition.

Michelangelo Merisi da Caravaggio lived from 1573 to 1610. His Roman paintings of both secular and religious subjects were lionized by ecclesial and secular connoisseurs and his turbulent life story reads like a police report. He was involved in multiple scrapes and clashes with the authorities; he once killed a man during an argument, supposedly after a tennis game; he became a Knight of Malta who fled the island's prison after insulting a superior, then was pursued by thugs who caught up with him in a tavern in Naples and disfigured him; finally, he died of a malignant fever in a small port town on the west coast of Italy while the ship taking him to Rome and a papal pardon sailed off with his belongings. His contemporaries considered him to be brilliant and innovative in his realism, but also the one who "had come to earth to destroy painting"[3] and who "lacked *invenzione*, decorum...or any knowledge of the science of painting."[4] His contemporary biographers testify to his fame and his extraordinary popularity among elites such as Cardinal Francesco Del Monte and the Marchese Vincenzo

Giustiniani, two of the most important patrons of the arts in Counter-Reformation Rome. But they also point to his unsociable, arrogant, and belligerent personality, and to his all-too-ready tendency to settle arguments with his sword. His secular art could be invitingly erotic and his religious art could be seductively ordinary and spiritual, and his dramatic use of color and light, called *chiaroscuro*, became one of the primary influences in painting from Italy all the way into Northern Europe. In the standard histories of art, Caravaggio is a prime example of the naturalism that served as a critique of and the successor to the waning dominance of the late Renaissance Mannerists and heralded the birth of the Baroque in Italian painting.

The truth about Caravaggio and his religious paintings is more complex than any biographical report about a turbulent young man with creative passions, a brilliant artistic technique, and an attitude that flouted convention. In order to see this truth, particularly that aspect whereby one recognizes the painter to be involved in a theological reflection which articulated quite precisely some Catholic reformist principles of his time, one must set Caravaggio's work within its immediate context of Counter-Reformation and early Baroque spirituality and theological reflection. Within this context, both the meaning of Caravaggio's religious paintings and the necessity of retrieving this meaning for our contemporary understanding of Catholic identity and practice will become clear.

Counter-Reform Views of Art and the Spiritual Life

Caravaggio's religious paintings include commissioned altarpieces (such as *The Entombment of Christ*, 1603-04, see Plate 1) and chapel decorations (such as *The Calling of St. Matthew*, 1599-1600, see Plate 2) as well as pictures whose destinations are now unknown but which were probably executed for private collectors. Their dates span the period from 1598 until his death in 1610. They are thus set squarely within the period after the close of the Council of Trent in 1563, during which the reforms advocated by the council were being consolidated and put into practice at local levels. One can begin to understand Caravaggio's theology and the meaning of his religious works only when they are placed in their immediate post-Tridentine context and seen over and against that particular horizon of religious expectations. One important contribution to that horizon was a topic widely discussed in Catholic circles in the wake of the Reformation, namely the meaning and means of religious art. Whether or not the treatises directly influenced Caravaggio and official statements generated by this discussion has been a point of controversy among Caravaggio scholars. But there is no denying that the official Catholic stance and the various theological discussions which responded to Trent's decree on sacred images had a direct effect on the overall religious climate in Rome while Caravaggio worked there, affecting both his own artistic intentions and the expectations of those who commissioned his works, some of whom were the most discriminating patrons and well-connected ecclesiastical personages in post-Tridentine Rome.

The central document of this discussion was Trent's decree *De invocatione, veneratione et reliquiis sanctorum, et de sacris imaginibus (On Invocation, Veneration and Relics of the Saints, and on Sacred Images)* promulgated at the final session of the council in December 1563. The intention of the decree was threefold: first, to answer long-standing critiques made by Protestant reformers and others such as Erasmus regarding the popular use and abuse of religious images (some Protestant theologians went so far as to attack the validity of art and representation altogether); next, to blunt the spreading iconoclastic violence which had spread from Zurich to parts of Germany and Italy and was threatening the existence of religious art in France; finally, to encourage local bishops to eliminate the obvious abuses which were at the root of these critiques and had provided an impetus for the growing iconoclastic frenzy.[5] The Council admonished bishops "to instruct the faithful carefully about the intercession of the saints, invocation of them, reverence for their relics and the legitimate use of images of them."[6] As to what this "legitimate use" was, the Council did not present a complex theological justification or a theory of theological aesthetics. Instead, in response to the common Protestant criticism that the veneration of images was idolatry, the official Catholic position announced at Trent defended the use of religious images by having recourse to arguments first formulated against iconoclasm at the Second Council of Nicaea (787) and used repeatedly over the centuries:

> Images of Christ, the virgin mother of God and the other saints should be set up and kept, particularly in churches, and…due honor and reverence is owed to them, not because some divinity or power is believed to lie in them as reason for the cult, or because anything is to be expected from them, or because confidence should be placed in images as was done by the pagans of old; but because the honor showed to them is referred to the original [*prototypa*] which they represent: thus, through the images we kiss and before which we uncover our heads and go down on our knees, we give adoration to Christ and veneration to the saints, whose likeness they bear.[7]

Thus, the Council's response makes a distinction between the image and the one depicted by the image: reverence which is paid to the image does not adhere to the inanimate object itself which has no life or power of its own, rather, it is passed on to the "original" subject who is depicted by the image and gives the image its representational power. The decree is careful to deny any kind of equivalence between the finite image and the supernatural subject to which it refers: "So if accounts and stories from Holy Scripture are

sometimes etched and pictured, which is a help to uneducated people, they must be taught that the Godhead is not
pictured because [i.e., even though] it can be seen with
human eyes or expressed in figures and colors."[8]

The Council also described the important roles which religious images play in the life of the faithful: they teach the
essentials of the faith and they edify. They serve not only as
reminders of the gift of God's saving grace, but help the
faithful to recall the articles of faith "through the expression
in pictures or other likenesses of the stories of the mysteries
of our redemption." Images likewise offer examples of true
Christian behavior which inspire the faithful: "the miracles
of God through the saints and their salutary example are put
before the eyes of the faithful, who can thank God for them,
shape their own lives and conduct in imitation of the saints,
and be aroused to adore and love God and to practice devotion."[9] The decree concludes by admonishing bishops to
strictly supervise the use of religious images and relics in
their dioceses, to be on guard against the communication of
false doctrine, to eliminate superstition, and to curb the
abuses connected with the veneration of relics and the celebrations of feast days. But the Council decree stops short of
specifying in any detail exactly how the artist is to carry out
the twofold responsibility to teach and to edify.

Others writing after the close of the Council expanded on
the decree's recommendations and fashioned more specific
applications in line with its demands. A number of works
appeared, all by clerics or theologians rather than artists,
offering detailed prescriptions for the creation of religiously
meaningful works of art. Even the great reformer Cardinal
Carlo Borromeo of Milan penned a small treatise on church
art and architecture (*Instructiones fabricae et supellectilis eccle-
siasticae*, 1577). The various recommendations proposed by
these treatises can be reduced to three major issues which cut
across all of them: (1) the work of art was to be simple and
intelligible to all; (2) the artist was to offer realistic interpre-

tations of events in the life of Christ and the saints, for truth demanded absolute accuracy of detail, even if this involved the horror and brutality of martyrdom; (3) the work of art was to provide an emotional stimulus which moved the viewer to devotion.[10]

Cardinal Gabriele Paleotti of Bologna, who like his friend Borromeo was committed to implementing the Tridentine reforms, also authored a treatise. His *Discorso intorno alle immagini sacre e profane* (first published in 1582, projected in five volumes of which only the first two appeared) presented a detailed analysis of religious art as well as specific practical recommendations for carrying out the Council's desires. The *Discorso* was well known in Roman circles; it is important because it gives us a clear sense of the demands which Counter-Reformation and Baroque Catholicism made upon the artist.[11]

Paleotti argues that the function of all religious art (and "profane" art as well) is to serve the Church and the truths of faith and to mediate between supernatural reality and the viewer. The artist can be compared to a preacher and has the task of both teaching the articles of faith and exhorting people to live virtuous lives: "in the manner of orators, a painter is directed to persuade the people and, by means of painting, to bring them to embrace whatever is pertinent to religion."[12] Painting addresses the widest possible audience because images, unlike books, are universally accessible to learned and unlearned alike; indeed, "painting replaces the word or supplements it."[13] But beyond the painter's tasks to instruct and to edify, a work of art must also please and move the spectator emotionally, actively persuading the viewer by means of vivid images and colors to experience the picture's deeper content of religious truth and the invitation to meditation and the practice of virtue. Paleotti argues that "seeing an event in front of him in almost tangible forms and colours makes a much deeper impression on the average person than reading a description, however vivid the use of

language may be." Thus, while narrations of events of martyrdom or of the sufferings of Christ have an impact, the
painted record of such events is more moving still.[14] But
these desired effects can only occur when the painter faithfully imitates visible reality and correctly depicts the reality
of biblical or historical scenes. It is here, regarding the truthfulness of religious art, that Paleotti places the weight of his
argument. Only by means of *imitazione* can paintings strongly appeal to the viewer and thus teach, edify, and persuade
the viewer to embrace the truths of faith. Incorrect depictions
are similar to the preaching of questionable dogma, in that
they produce confusion and can lead ultimately to heresy. In
his discussions of *il verisimile*, Paleotti warns artists to avoid
allegory, novelty, unrestrained invention, incorrect proportions, and genre scenes without biblical foundation or edify-
ing value (e.g., a rich chamber for the Annunciation, Mary
with curls or in uncontrollable grief at the foot of the cross,
the Christ Child and St. John the Baptist playing together, St.
Philip sleeping). The artist has a serious responsibility to create works that are clear, simple, and true to life.

> Paleotti is aware that the spectator only lets him-
> self be convinced by a picture when he can feel
> personally involved in the events which are
> depicted. He must be able to believe in the people
> he sees before him in order to feel what they are
> experiencing in the flesh, as it were. Such identifi-
> cation is possible especially when the spectator
> can discover something of himself or his world in
> what is depicted. For this reason Paleotti indicates
> to the painter that, in portraying the virtues, he
> can best glorify [them] by painting portraits of
> well-known people who have distinguished
> themselves in those qualities.[15]

Paleotti's conservative views are obvious in his pointed
criticisms of novelty, unbridled artistic imagination, and
ambiguous allegorical interpretation. On these points he can

be seen to be extending in a practical way the Council's criticism of abuses and its exhortation to bishops to remedy them. But his fundamental argument has a positive thrust, indirectly drawing upon the heart of the Catholic understanding of the sacraments that the Council had defended against Protestant criticisms. The core belief of that sacramental understanding, that there is "an *intrinsic relationship* between God's grace in redemption and the life of God given in creation,"[16] that finite materiality can mediate transcendent divinity, informs both Trent's decree on images and Paleotti's understanding of religious art. Trent's decree asserts that material depictions of Christ and the saints mediate our devotion: our reverence "is referred to" the supernatural subjects themselves (*refertur ad prototypa*).[17] For Paleotti, art's quality of *imitazione* brings the viewer into contact with the truths of revelation; the artist, like the preacher, employs material means in creating a work that makes available to the believer the possibility of experiencing and being moved by divine grace. All of this presupposes an ontology of creation which claims that created effects can and do mediate the divine cause. It is clear, then, that religious art can be considered a moment in the mediation of grace. Thus the artwork itself and the imaginative process which leads up to that work can be understood as aspects of a "poietic" process (*poiesis* here understood as "inventive making") which participates in an overall state of affairs that can be loosely termed "sacramental,"[18] a state of affairs which Caravaggio's religious works share and reflect.

Caravaggio's Work and Popular Movements of Spirituality

Caravaggio's religious canvases represent a decisive critical break with the late Renaissance Mannerism of the previous generation.[19] The theory of *maniera* held that each artist has a right to a personal interpretation of the rules of art and to a self-conscious style which involved complexity, caprice, elegance, and extraordinary virtuosity. Mannerist art (such as Parmigianino's *Madonna with the Long Neck* [c. 1535] or Agnolo Bronzino's portraits, or any of El Greco's work) disdained the Renaissance aesthetic of the imitation and idealization of nature and instead was concerned with formal beauty for its own sake. Mannerist paintings "often exhibited irrational spatial development and figures with elongated proportions, exaggerated poses, and enigmatic gestures and facial expressions."[20] Caravaggio's fundamental style, on the other hand, consists of a naturalism—almost a hyperrealism—focused on representing the ordinary everydayness of situations and objects in the full intensity of the way they show themselves. He insisted on painting from life and used posed models; one early biographer cites Caravaggio's claim "that he imitated his models so closely that he never made a single brushstroke that he called his own, but said rather that it was Nature's."[21] The earliest biographical account of Caravaggio, written during his life, reports that "his belief is that all art is nothing but a bagatelle or children's work…unless it is done after life, and that we can do no better than to follow Nature. Therefore he will not make a single brushstroke without the close study of life, which he copies and paints."[22] Such attitudes led to Caravaggio being branded an iconoclast by his contemporaries because of his failure to adhere to the idealizing standard of Renaissance aesthetics. His realism at times seemed so coarse or brutal that paintings were sometimes rejected by the very patrons who commissioned them because of their lack of "decorum."[23]

Many of his canvases after his early period illustrate the tenebrism or *chiaroscuro* for which he became famous throughout Europe. These works present carefully composed, intensely dramatic scenes with figures emerging from dark interior backgrounds into a strong light whose source lies outside the painting, usually to the left, as in *Judith Beheading Holofernes* (c. 1598, see Plate 3).

Caravaggio's commentators have remarked how closely the sensibilities of his religious works seem to mirror Catholic reform principles of his day, particularly those derived from movements of popular spirituality. Scholars have tried to use these specific principles to discern both Caravaggio's own religious intentions and those of his patrons, since direct reports about his personal religious beliefs are almost non-existent.[24] However, what those precise influences were has been a highly controverted point in Caravaggio studies.

For example, it has been argued that the return to gospel piety and the simplicity of devotion preached by both the Oratorians and the Jesuits—spiritualities which eschewed contemplative withdrawal for a life of discipleship in the world—form a necessary background for unlocking the secrets of Caravaggio's revolutionary "realistic mysticism."[25] The Oratorian movement, extraordinarily popular throughout Rome, reflected the remarkable charismatic personality of its celebrated founder, St. Philip Neri.[26] It emphasized a simplicity of faith, a love for the richness of creation, and a type of mystical devotion that directed every follower toward a rich and direct contact with the love of God within the circumstances of ordinary life. Philip, whose intensely affective spiritual life, personal humility, and playful disdain for ecclesiastical pretense won him followers from every level of Roman secular and ecclesiastical society, practiced an informal spirituality which emphasized creation as a grace from God, the natural as a sign of the supernatural, and the availability of sanctity even in the most ordinary of circumstances. Jesuit spirituality, at first glance so different from the loosely structured practices of the Oratorians, shares a number of the same fundamental principles (Philip himself knew Ignatius, made the *Spiritual Exercises*, and at one point early in his career considered joining the Jesuits). Ignatius disregarded visions and ecstasies and instead insisted that one make the mystery of God actual and tangible through the use of one's senses and imagination in the process of meditation. In the *Exercises*, Ignatius stipulated specific meditative practices: the "composition of place," where one makes a mental representation of a particular scene (for example, in the life of Christ) down to the smallest material detail, and the "application of the senses," where one applies each of the five senses to the represented scene, in order to be imaginatively affected by each sense.[27] The intent of the *Exercises*, and of Jesuit spirituality in general, was to create a situation whereby "the Creator [might] deal directly with the creature, and the creature directly with his Creator and Lord."[28]

Another suggested source has been the sixteenth-century revival of Augustinianism, with its emphasis on God's overwhelming and inscrutable grace and the believer's "total dependence on divine grace and mercy." Hints of such an understanding can be found, for example, in *The Call of St. Matthew* which portrays "the haphazard, apodictic nature of God's Divine Grace" and in *The Conversion of St. Paul*, where Paul is blinded by an unprepared-for divine illumination and the scene as a whole communicates "the arbitrariness of God's grace."[29] In the most recent critical monograph, Catherine Puglisi agrees that "essential elements in Caravaggio's religious art can be associated with Augustinianism: the symbolic use of light as embodying divine grace, the visual emphasis on the individual's direct encounter with God, and the implication that salvation is achieved through faith."[30] She has also proposed the influence of Franciscan piety, with its emphasis on submissiveness and humility.[31] Caravaggio did indeed receive commissions from churches connected with the Oratorians and the Augustinians, and from individuals with strong links to the Oratorians and the Franciscans. But, as Puglisi notes, it is difficult to prove the painter's dependence on any one particular spirituality; rather, it is more likely that "Caravaggio evolved the religious attitudes expressed in his paintings from a range of sources."[32]

But we need not tie Caravaggio's imagination to one or another source in order to understand his religious vision. In order to understand what Puglisi calls the essential elements of his religious works, namely "the sensory realism, humble types, and absence of heavenly visions" as well as "the unceremonious presentation of sacred subject matter,"[33] it is enough to place these paintings within the larger Counter-Reformation context where these spiritualities were all considered live options for describing the heart of a Catholic existence. We can understand all these forms of spirituality as a spectrum of differing yet similar responses to one of the central animating values of the Counter-Reformation which will be developed and which will enliven popular Baroque Catholic spirituality, namely a fundamentally *incarnational* and *sacramental* understanding of reality. All of these types cluster around and share in the Catholic sacramental imagination which is rooted in the belief that, especially in the wake of the incarnation of God in Christ, there is an intense, intrinsic relationship between creation and redemption.

The spiritualities we have mentioned here would all agree on the assertion that the experience of God is available within human everydayness—in other words, a life with God can occur within everyday life and not merely in spite of everyday life. Such an attitude holds true even for a more pessimistic Augustinianism, since it presupposes Augustine's theory of signs.[34] A slightly later French spirituality will call this divine availability the "sacrament of the moment."[35] The set of Catholic values, which formed early Baroque Rome's horizon of religious expectation and the possibilities of religious experience shared by Caravaggio's audiences, are closely tied to this Catholic sacramental construal of reality. Even official prescriptions such as Paleotti's and those of other reformers, while conservative, are part of that spectrum of responses to sacramentality and indeed go out of their way to classify religious art as one of the ways of propagating the faith—hence the serious responsibility of the artist as preacher.

One can argue that Caravaggio's religious canvases from around the year 1600 illustrate the painter's own profound Catholic reactions to Christian faith understood sacramentally, true theological reflections on the incarnational link between creation and redemption which visually employ the vocabulary of the popular spiritual movements. Take, for example, *The Conversion of St. Paul*, painted between 1600 and 1601 for one of the sidewalls of the Cerasi Chapel in Santa Maria del Popolo (see Plate 4).[36]

This is almost a textbook study in the essential qualities of Baroque art: illusion, fantasy, the gorgeous excess of materiality, and the manipulation of color, light, and perspective in order to break down the space between the work and the viewer so that the viewer may identify with St. Paul's experience. But it is also a textbook study in the complexity of Caravaggio's art and why his critics accused him of a lack of decorum. *St. Paul* represents his conscious decision to subjugate biblical history painting to the principles of portrait or genre painting, or even still life. Here is his almost defiant portrayal of a religious scene not as a great supernatural event but as an ordinary one, almost perversely ordinary. At first glance, without the context of the chapel and the title, we might think that we are witnessing a stable accident, with the horse as hero. But there are clues so that the believer— that is, one with the Catholic tradition as context, who views the scene with the eyes of faith—may understand that the ordinary and everyday is raw material for transfiguration and for a revelation of the extraordinary and supernatural. This sacramental imagination is the crux of Counter-Reformation spirituality. The scene before us is transformed in two ways. First, we notice the effect, Paul's supine pose: his body at an illusionistically receding angle, arms raised in surrender and supplication, his head so close to the picture plane that his hair seems to spill over the frame. Only afterwards do we recognize the cause, the light coming down from above, symbolic of the force of divine illumination that has struck him blind and powerless. Apart from the horse's raised hoof, the only action (if we can call it that) is the cascading light representing the inscrutable power and revelation of God: for one person (the groom), nothing has changed; for the other, everything. If any of Caravaggio's paintings represent the confluence of Oratorian, Jesuit, and Augustinian understandings of grace, it is this one.

The Supper at Emmaus

An even more informative case study of Caravaggio's theological imagination is *The Supper at Emmaus* (the London version, painted c. 1600-01), precisely because of its subject matter (see Plate 5).[37]

Caravaggio here depicts the climactic moment of recognition in Luke's narrative of the Emmaus disciples meeting the risen Christ on the road (Luke 24:13–35). "And it happened that, while he was with them at table, he took bread, said the blessing, broke it, and gave it to them. With that their eyes were opened and they recognized him, but he vanished from their sight" (Luke 24:30–31 NAB). Again, Caravaggio has chosen to portray the extraordinary within the ordinary, the supernatural within the everyday, but this time by means of heightened concentration upon the ordinariness of the scene and its elements, with almost the precise observational skills of a natural scientist.

The work is as luminous as it is virtuosic. Christ is seated at the center, as is usual in Italian tradition. But there is nothing usual about the rest of the composition, whose iconographical richness almost defies description. Its visual immediacy involves the viewer directly in the experience. Its drama is achieved through the contrast of deep dark colors and brilliant highlights, by the sensuous fullness of the figures, and by a dazzling use of perspective. The table is set close to the viewer, but with enough room so that the disciple on the left can be seated before it. That disciple grasps the arms of his chair as if he is about to leap out of it in utter amazement at the dramatic revelation of Christ and push it through the picture plane. The basket of fruit perched precariously on the edge of the table looks as if it will drop into our laps at any moment. The disciple on the right, wearing the pilgrim's shell, throws out his arms in a gesture of unforgettable amazement (perhaps symbolizing the crucifixion), expressing "a recognition that is already complete."[38] His left arm, extended toward the viewer and also seeming to break the picture plane, unites the disciples with us, who also stand amazed. Caravaggio has thus caught the suspense and the excitement that are woven into Luke's account.[39]

All attention is focused on Christ, whose beardless face is perhaps Caravaggio's solution to the problem of why the disciples "were prevented from recognizing him" (Luke 24:16) on the road; the painter echoes the brief reference to the appearance in the longer ending to Mark's gospel: "After this he appeared in another form to two of them walking along on their way to the country" (Mark 16:12).[40] Christ's face is illuminated by light falling from the left; its radiance is highlighted even further by the shadow cast by the uncomprehending innkeeper on the wall behind, almost as a kind of dark halo. Here, as in *The Conversion of St. Paul*, the light is of divine origin and signals God's transfiguration of this ordinary scene and the revelation of the identity of Christ at the moment the meal is blessed and shared. And how that scene is transformed: a delicate light passes through the water pitcher and casts both water-reflected light and shadow on the tablecover in a scene of incredibly eloquent brilliance; the same light is reflected from the tablecover onto the face of the disciple on the left, allowing us to see and know his reaction even though we can only catch the barest glimpse of his face.

The fundamental interpretation of the Emmaus episode, by Luke and by Counter-Reformation theologians as well, is

PLATE 1

Caravaggio, The Entombment of Christ.
Pinacoteca, Vatican Museums, Vatican State.
Alinari/Art Resource, NY

PLATE 2

Caravaggio, The Calling of St. Matthew.
S. Luigi dei Francesi, Rome, Italy.
Alinari/Art Resource, NY

PLATE 3

Caravaggio, Judith Beheading Holofernes.
Galleria Nazionale d'Arte Antica, Rome, Italy.
Nimatallah/Art Resource, NY

PLATE 4

Caravaggio, The Conversion of Saint Paul.
S. Maria del Popolo, Rome, Italy.
Alinari/Art Resource, NY

PLATE 5

eucharistic. Due to its dominical warrants this is a central instance of the Catholic sacramental imagination. That meaning is made plain by the extraordinary quality of every individual figure in the painting, but especially by the glowing presence of the bread, the fish-tail shadow cast by the leaves on the right side of the basket, and Christ's blessing which echoes the blessing before the moment of consecration at Mass. But it is the work *as a whole* that "preaches" the eucharistic meaning of the Emmaus episode and manifests the sacramental imagination and care for ordinary materiality that Caravaggio shared with the popular spiritual reform movements. In a very real sense, the work is a reflection of the painter's deeply considered sacramental theology. His complex composition choreographs our performances as viewers and believers. As our eyes move around the picture, the ordinary, without giving up one bit of its materiality, is slowly revealed to be extraordinary; by means of the natural, the supernatural is revealed—to us as well as to the two disciples. This is the spiritual insight that Caravaggio shares along with the popular spiritual reform movements. We can either be as changed as the disciples or as uncomprehending as the innkeeper. The disciples finally recognize Jesus in the blessing and breaking of the bread—thus in a most common personal relationship, sharing a meal with friends. This shared relationship (a *praxical* relationship, it should be emphasized) becomes, by the sheer incarnational initiative of God, the precondition for the revelation of Christ's identity and the meaning of salvation. At Mass, which Counter-Reformation theologians taught was pre-figured at Emmaus,[41] the Catholic believer also recognizes the real presence of the Lord under the ordinary appearances of bread and wine—yet another revelatory transfiguration of the commonplace.

Thus *The Supper at Emmaus* represents not only a virtuoso *tour de force* of a painter making a tremendous leap in artistic growth, but also the kind of rhetorical propagation of the faith which Paleotti and his reformist contemporaries called upon artists to provide. Caravaggio did not (and probably could never) supply the simplicity of composition that Paleotti demanded, but "he must have believed that his own kind of truthfulness in religious expression was somehow consonant with the spirit of reform"[42] and with those practical spiritualities which swept through Rome and energized the reform from the ground up.

Retrieval

What does Caravaggio the theologian have that we need? His sacramentally voluptuous canvases dripping with flesh and light offer an important testimony to the vitality of Baroque Catholicism, to the earthy, affective, and praxical nature of its spiritualities, and to the fundamental sacramental commitments which characterize the Catholic construal of reality, particularly its optimistic evaluation of materiality. The religious art we have examined here provides an important point of access to the incarnationally-saturated essence of Catholicism. It offers a materially-situated and affectively-laden *locus theologicus* which has contributed to the constitution of the present theological situation but which has been largely ignored by contemporary Catholic theology in its headlong pursuit of meaning primarily in texts. Now, a correlation of Baroque Catholic estimations of the body (using Caravaggio as guide) with contemporary Catholic anthropological concerns is too large a topic to tackle here. Rather, what I want to sketch out is a more general retrieval done in the light of two contemporary circumstances. First, there is the failure of much post-Vatican II systematic theology to offer thick descriptions of the breadth and depth of modern Catholic traditions of practice and reflection as theological resources—thus the truncated narrative mentioned earlier. Next, there is also the recent polemic against modernity and modern Christian traditions offered by the movement of "radical orthodoxy" (John Milbank, Catherine Pickstock, and others) as well as by certain postmodern theologies and philosophies of religion.[43]

These disparate theological approaches all share a presupposition: the culture of modernity drops out as a factor; it is considered bankrupt or at least unretrievable. These discourses display a distaste for and a delegitimation of modernity as a locus of meaning and of theological truth. But in a way similar to the theological critique mounted against Neo-Scholastic extrinsicism earlier in the twentieth century, contemporary Catholic theology must vigorously contest any position which claims an epoch to be devoid of the touch of God and unclaimed by God's salvific will. The incarnation, death, and resurrection of Jesus Christ testify to the absolute initiative of God to enter into history and into solidarity with all humanity. The place and time of God's communion with humanity is every place and time, with no one excluded.

Particularly relevant here is the fundamental theological principle of the "dangerous memory" of the passion and resurrection of Jesus. Johann Baptist Metz has developed and applied this principle to the situation of the forgotten dead who have been victims of the history of suffering, in order to understand how they too are included in the salvation offered by Christ. The *memoria passionis, mortis, et resurrectionis Jesu Christi* which forms the heart of Christian faith provides the basis for the Christian hope in universal eschatological justice, "a hope in a revolution *for all men,* including those who suffer and have suffered unjustly, those who have long been forgotten and even the dead."[44] This principle applies as well to any evaluation of Baroque Catholicism and helps us determine the true status of any historical period which has been judged to be dead and useless: God's power of reversal, made manifest in the cross and resurrection of Jesus Christ, guarantees that *no one* and *no time* get left behind, that all persons and all times have access to eschatological transformation. Therefore, the Catholic understanding of God's incarnation in history demands that

we practice a positive retrieval of the Baroque with its testimonies to complex and varied experiences of God and its
proper signs of grace and redemptive liberation.

Such a retrieval will disclose a multi-layered "modernity"
far more complex than some theological commentators
allow, one composed of a variety of cultural and religious
histories. The types of theology and piety which support
Counter-Reformation religious art and the optimistic forms
of Baroque Catholic spirituality explicitly recall the biblical
narratives of creation and incarnation. Art and spirituality
both sought to translate into modern terms the meaning of
these narratives in a life-affirming fashion. Within Counter-
Reformation and Baroque Catholic life, God's use of history,
materiality, and particularly human bodiliness as the crucial
elements of the grammar of the incarnation was confirmed
in new ways (the sacramentality of everyday life, the dignity of the individual human person as the image of God, the
accessibility of grace, etc.), while a continuity with the original "incarnational impulse" in the life, death, and resurrection of Jesus Christ was maintained. It is precisely this
incarnational impulse in its sacramental manifestation
which Caravaggio probes and brilliantly articulates, discloses, and reveals (rather than merely "portrays") in the religious paintings of his Roman years—*actively* discloses or
reveals, since these works of *poiesis* are indeed authentic *performances* in the full Baroque understanding of the term.

And so, in this context, are we correct in claiming
Caravaggio as a theologian? He is too over the top, too
fleshy, too outrageous, too colorful, too "lacking in decorum"...in short, a perfect model of the Catholic theologian.

Notes

1. Currently there is little in English to acquaint us with the riches of
the history of Catholic theology between Trent and Vatican II, nothing
like the systematic surveys which have appeared in German and
French over the past thirty years, and almost nothing since Ted

Schoof's valuable *Survey of Catholic Theology, 1800-1970*, trans. N. D. Smith (Paramus, NJ: Paulist Newman, 1970; the British edition was entitled *Breakthrough*) now long out of print. The second edition of James C. Livingston's *Modern Christian Thought* (Upper Saddle River, NJ: Prentice Hall, 1997-99), a two-volume set due to be completed this year, should go a long way toward filling some of the gaps in the history of 19th and 20th century Catholic theology.

2. Richard P. McBrien, ed., *Encyclopedia of Catholicism* (San Francisco: HarperCollins, 1995), s.v. "Baroque Catholicism" (Thomas F. O'Meara), 141.

3. Nicholas Poussin's judgment, as recorded by A. Félibien (*Entretiens*, 1688), translated in Howard Hibbard, *Caravaggio* (New York: Harper and Row, 1983), 308; cf. also Giovanni Baglione, one of Caravaggio's rivals, in his *Le vita de' pittori, scultori, et architetti…*(Rome, 1642), translated in Hibbard, 355: "Moreover, some people thought that he had destroyed the art of painting; also, many young artists followed his example and painted heads from life, without studying the rudiments of design and the profundity of art, but were satisfied only with the colors; therefore these painters were not able to put two figures together, nor could they illustrate a history because they did not comprehend the value of so noble an art."

4. Giovanni Pietro Bellori, *Le vite de' pittori, scultori e architetti moderni* (Rome, 1672), translated in Hibbard, 371.

5. See David Freedberg, "The Hidden God: Image and Interdiction in the Netherlands in the Sixteenth Century," *Art History* 5 (1982): 133-53; A. W. A. Boschloo, *Annibale Carracci in Bologna: Visible Reality in Art after the Council of Trent*, vol. 1, trans. R. R. Symonds, Kunsthistorische Studiën van het Nederlands Instituut te Rome, Deel III, Band 1 (The Hague: Government Publishing Office, 1974), 134.

6. *On Invocation, Veneration and Relics of the Saints, and on Sacred Images*, trans. John Coventry, in Norman P. Tanner, ed., *Decrees of the Ecumenical Councils*, 2 vols. (Washington, DC: Georgetown University Press, 1990), 2:774, 774q (Latin original and English translation on facing pages).

7. Ibid., 2:775, 775q; regarding "one of the commonest forms of the . Protestant criticism" see Freedberg, "The Hidden God," 139.

8. *On Invocation*, Tanner, 2:775, 775q.

9. Ibid.

10. Rudolf Wittkower, *Art and Architecture in Italy, 1600-1750*, 3d ed. (Harmondsworth: Penguin, 1973), 1-2.

11. On Paleotti, see Giuseppe Olmi, "Paleotti, Gabriele," in *The*

Dictionary of Art, 34 vols., ed. Jane Turner (New York: Grove's Dictionaries, 1996), 23:839-40. See Boschloo, 121-141 (chapter 7) for a detailed summary of and commentary on the *Discorso*. I rely mainly on Boschloo for my own summary here.

12. *Discorso* I, 21, quoted by Steven F. Ostrow, *Art and Spirituality in Counter-Reformation Rome: The Sistine and Pauline Chapels in S. Maria Maggiore, Monuments of Papal Rome* (Cambridge: Cambridge University Press, 1996), 117. According to Ostrow, the comparison of the painter with the orator became commonplace in the post-Tridentine period.

13. Boschloo, 122.

14. Ibid., 125-26.

15. Ibid., 128.

16. Stephen Happel and David Tracy, *A Catholic Vision* (Philadelphia: Fortress, 1984), 91.

17. *On invocation*, Tanner, 2:775, 775q.

18. "Loosely," because even though the *Catechism of the Council of Trent* (the "Roman Catechism," 1566) stresses the materiality of the sacramental sign in its definition of sacrament ("a visible sign of an invisible grace, instituted for our justification" [143], "a sensible object which possesses, by divine institution, the power not only of signifying but also of accomplishing holiness and righteousness" [146]), it goes on to say that "it follows…that the images of the saints, crosses and the like, although signs of sacred things, cannot be called sacraments" because they are not directly divinely instituted (ibid.). Page numbers refer to the English translation, *Catechism of the Council of Trent for Parish Priests*, trans. John A. McHugh and Charles J. Callan (South Bend, IN: Marian Publications, 1976 [orig. ed. 1923]). Regarding Baroque rhetoric and poetics, see John Milbank, *Theology and Social Theory: Beyond Secular Reason*, Signposts in Theology (Cambridge, MA: Blackwell, 1990), 11 (and the literature cited there).

19. For Mannerism and its relation to other contemporary styles, see standard histories such as Marilyn Stokstad, *Art History* (New York: Harry N. Abrams, 1995) and H. W. Janson and Anthony F. Janson, *History of Art*, 4th ed. (New York: Harry N. Abrams, 1991).

20. Stokstad, *Art History*, 712.

21. Bellori, *Le vite de' pittori*, in Hibbard, 371.

22. Carel van Mander, *Het Schilder-Boeck*, part III (Harlem, 1604), translated in Hibbard, 344.

23. Such as the first version of *The Inspiration of St. Matthew* (1602, commissioned for the Contarelli Chapel in San Luigi dei Francesi) and *The*

Death of the Virgin (c. 1605-06, for the Cherubini Chapel in Santa Maria della Scala in Trastevere). See Hibbard, 138-44, 198-206; Helen Langdon, *Caravaggio: A Life* (London: Chatto and Windus, 1998), 237-41, 248-51.

24. For an anecdote that may have at least a grain of truth, see Francesco Susinno, *Le vita de' pittori messinesi* (1724), who recounts that Caravaggio, on entering a church in Messina, Sicily during the last years of his life, was offered holy water by a friend. "Caravaggio asked him what was the purpose of it, and the answer was that it would erase any venial sin. 'I don't need it,' he replied, 'since all my sins are mortal'" (translated in Hibbard, 386). Hibbard warns us that Susinno's accounts are "not necessarily reliable" and can tend to be "garrulous and credulous" (380). See too Hibbard's ingenious attempts to determine Caravaggio's self-image and particularly his religious convictions (256-67, especially 262-4).

25. Walter Friedlaender, *Caravaggio Studies* (Princeton, NJ: Princeton University Press, 1955), 120-30; quote at 121. Friedlaender's classic work is the starting point for all recent discussions of Caravaggio's religious sentiments.

26. See Paul Türks, *Philip Neri: The Fire of Joy*, trans. Daniel Utrecht (New York: Alba House, 1995), especially 111-27.

27. See *The Spiritual Exercises of St. Ignatius*, trans. Louis J. Puhl, S.J. (Westminster, MD: Newman Press, 1951; reprint: Chicago: Loyola Press, n.d.), §47 (mental representation of the place), §§66-70 (application of the senses in the Fifth Exercise, §65). See also Joseph F. Chorpenning, "Another Look at Caravaggio and Religion," *Artibus et Historiae* 16 (1987): 149-50, 157 n.14.

28. *Spiritual Exercises*, §15.

29. Hibbard, 100-02, 128, 129-31.

30. Catherine Puglisi, *Caravaggio* (London: Phaidon, 1998), 251.

31. Ibid., 248-49.

32. Ibid., 252. See also Troy Thomas, "Caravaggio and the Roman Oratory of Saint Philip Neri," *Studies in Iconography* 12 (1988): 61-89, who also proposes such a "middle course," i.e., understanding Caravaggio to be a serious religious painter, but avoiding "dogmatic interpretations that follow a narrow doctrinal line of thought in discerning the sources of Caravaggio's religious expression" (82). Thomas's entire essay is a valuable survey of recent interpretations of Caravaggio's religious sensibilities.

33. Puglisi, 248, 249.

34. See Augustine, *On Christian Doctrine* [*De doctrina christiana*], trans. D. W. Robertson, Jr., The Library of Liberal Arts (Indianapolis: Bobbs-Merrill, 1958).

35. See Jean-Pierre de Caussade, *Abandonment to Divine Providence*, trans. John Beevers (Garden City, NY: Image/Doubleday, 1975), 24 (on "the moment"); 36 (on the presence of Christ to every moment of time). Francis de Sales subscribes to a very similar "sacramental" under-standing; see his *Introduction to the Devout Life*, trans. John K. Ryan (New York: Doubleday, 1982). For the role of such a spirituality in a contemporary retrieval of early modern Catholicism, see Anthony J. Godzieba, "Prolegomena to a Catholic Theology of God between Heidegger and Postmodernity," *The Heythrop Journal* 40 (1999): 319-39, at 329-30.

36. Hibbard, 121-31; Langdon, 182-90; Alfred Moir, *Caravaggio* (New York: Harry N. Abrams, 1989), 86-87; Richard G. Tansey and Fred S. Kleiner, *Gardner's Art Through the Ages*, 10th ed. (Fort Worth: Harcourt Brace, 1996), 835-36.

37. Hibbard, 73-84; Langdon, 230-33; Moir, 82-83; Mina Gregori, cata-logue entry in *The Age of Caravaggio* (New York: The Metropolitan Museum of Art; Milan: Electa, 1985), 271-76; Charles Scribner III, "*In Alia Effigie*: Caravaggio's London *Supper at Emmaus*," *The Art Bulletin* 59 (1977): 375-82.

38. Gregori, *The Age of Caravaggio*, 271.

39. Joseph A. Fitzmyer, *The Gospel According to Luke (X-XXIV)*, The Anchor Bible, vol. 28A (Garden City, NY: Doubleday, 1985), 1559 ff.

40. Scribner, "*In Alia Effigie*."

41. For example, in Jerome Nadal's *Evangelicae Historiae Imagines* of 1593 (cited by Hibbard, 80).

42. Thomas, "Caravaggio and the Roman Oratory," 82.

43. For a summary of and an alternative to these positions, and for a more detailed version of the argument offered below, see my essay "Prolegomena to a Catholic Theology of God" (n. 35). See also John Milbank, Catherine Pickstock, and Graham Ward, eds., *Radical Orthodoxy: A New Theology* (London and New York: Routledge, 1999).

44. Johann Baptist Metz, *Faith in History and Society: Toward a Practical Fundamental Theology*, trans. David Smith (New York: Seabury/Crossroad, 1980), 76 (my emphasis).

New Age, Environmentalism, and Liturgical Inculturation

Michael F. Steltenkamp, S.J.
Associate Professor of Religious Studies
Wheeling Jesuit University

When learning to do anthropological fieldwork, I was told to be suspicious of what people "say" they believe, and rather look for what they actually "do." This advice echoed what my grandmother always said: "actions speak louder than words!" Both taught the importance of looking at deed over creed, and both made me sensitive to the issue of how behavior or ritual reflect or express an individual's or community's yearnings or ideals. This personal and professional interest is the focus of the reflections that follow.

My observations arise from time spent within different American Indian communities where I observed rituals that offered participants a satisfying religious experience. I eventually came to lead religious ceremonies in my role as a Jesuit pastor, and write about them as an anthropologist within the University setting.[1] This paper is, then, an ethnography based on my participant-observation within religion as a Catholic layman, a Jesuit priest, and an academic.

I show that by de-emphasizing certain traditions, the Church gave rise to devotional forms and religious practices that were spawned in a spiritually convulsed culture and spurned or ignored by mainstream religious groups. I suggest how the Church might prevent this from continuing and how it might implement liturgical and paraliturgical inculturation. Readers are thus offered practical forms to use (instead of just speculation) as they journey through life here to life in the hereafter.

American Religious Trends Since Vatican II

My generation grew into Christian maturity with the *aggiornamento* of Vatican II that brought about many changes within Church practice. We witnessed John XXIII open the window of the Church by convening an ecumenical council, hoping that the Holy Spirit would rush in and provide a breath of fresh air. However, some found the new institutional modes of worship wanting, and so they quested for experiences of the sacred in other forums.

Since Vatican II, many people found that new Church practices could be just as uninspiring or lifeless as the old ones they replaced. While updating was needed, the many forms of religious expression that were altered or abandoned left a spiritual void that people needed to fill (with or without their Church's blessing). Over time, a number of people abandoned their institutional affiliation, and took on new religious identities which *aggiornamento* unintentionally helped fashion.

I used to attend a remote country church whose pastor often presided at Mass in the late night hours. I would accompany him into the sanctuary, and be his "congregation" standing just off to the side of the altar. There I would give responses while watching him look out toward the empty pews and say, without so much as a glance in my direction, "The Lord be with you," "Lift up your hearts," and other proclamations which implied that more than just the two of us were participating in this liturgy.

After witnessing this a number of times, I finally asked why he never turned and addressed me, the only person in attendance. I told him that I did not understand why he would look out at an empty church and tell the pews that the Lord was with them, or that they should lift up their hearts. Although his reply gave me a theology of Eucharist that had some merit, its liturgical expression was always dead on arrival.[2] It was this type of lifeless liturgy that was gradually, and globally, emptying pews.

In recalling those Masses, I think of the many celebrants, tolerated by people of faith, whose liturgical style could be labeled, at best, robotic. Straightfaced and straitlaced, their cultic demeanor could be described as precision without vision. Sadly, the Sunday obligation has regularly reminded people-in-the-pews that rote rubrics and passion-free homilies are very much removed from the Sermon on the Mount and table fellowship with the Lord.

This type of experience became intolerable for many from my generation who went in search of a religious practice that could elicit some sense of the numinous instead of the usual numbness associated with "the Mass." Over time, people adopted other forms of religious expression that they positively asserted was their "spirituality" and not what they would negatively refer to as "organized religion."[3] Culture industries capitalized on the interests of rock and film stars like the Beatles, Cat Stevens, Bruce Lee, and David Carradine, and domesticated what were formerly exotic Hindu and Buddhist traditions.

"Alternative" religious practices have grown fast and have gained adherents who, free from the constraints of an "institutional Church," believe that they can bring about a new consciousness.[4] "New Age" became the catch-all term for a plethora of self-help programs, non-Western philosophies, and behaviors that claimed independence from the practices or disciplines associated with Judeo-Christian tradition. Unfortunately, the Church has largely ignored the valid concerns expressed by this movement's many devotees. Instead, these people were drawn to the writings of people like John Collier.

This one-time Commissioner of Indian Affairs (and others like him) magnetized many questers into the American Indian world when he reported:

> They had what the world has lost. They have it now. What the world has lost, the world must have again, lest it die. Not many years are left to have or have not, to recapture the lost ingredient.[5]

Non-Indians wanted to know what had been lost, what the Native world still possessed, and what must be "recaptured" in order to survive. Collier's words were timely, as were those of Carlos Castaneda, since the period was fraught with different types of death associated with Vietnam, nuclear weaponry, environmental pollution, and racial strife. These writers showed it was possible to gain access to the "separate reality" sought by their readers.[6]

I joined others in thinking that perhaps American Indians (the "*in dios*" or "in God" people) might have some insight revealed uniquely to them by the Creator whose "real presence" was difficult to experience at many Masses. Our curiosity and agnosticism were aided by the "Keep America Clean" spokesman, Iron Eyes Cody, who was everywhere pictured on billboards and television spots. His distinctive Indian garb and tearful visage beckoned many into an ecology movement that had not, as yet, gathered much steam. Portrayed as an Indian from yesteryear who could recall when the world was cleaner than it had now become, Cody represented a Native perspective on life that seemed more insightful, at least in terms of the environment, than Western tradition.

Alternative religion appealed to people because its "spirituality" seemed "more natural" than fossilized Judeo-Christian traditions. Mainstream denominations had evolved within a synthetic urban milieu (regarded as "spiritually bankrupt") and were generating spiritual ennui among growing numbers of disaffected churchgoers. By contrast, tribal groups from all the continents were often referred to as "natural peoples" and this designation implied some kind of pristine relationship, still intact, with a sacred entity that was more appealing than the punishing deity associated with an urban scene's storefront or concrete churches. People of good will turned to ritual forms practiced by pre-Christian European or Indian ancestors in the hope of restoring balance to their lives.

An important moment of insight came to me when I was the substitute for a pastor stationed at one of the country's largest reservations. There occurred a "paradigm shift" which has, since that time, challenged me to learn about the everyday world of a given faith community so that I understand how a sacramental ministry can best address its needs. Implications of this approach will be spelled out in the rest of this paper.

Finding the Christian God in All Things

Mass drew two dozen adults and children who were not entranced by the sacramentary prayers I dutifully recited. In looking up from the book and scanning their faces, I was aware as never before that the theological idiom I read aloud was miles removed from the religious or secular vocabulary which people used in everyday life or traditional Indian prayer-forms. I thus chose to conduct what Canon Law refers to as a "valid" but "illicit" Mass.

Instead of reading what the sacramentary prescribed, I followed the lead of local medicine men (and common sense) by composing prayers that reflected the reservation milieu. People then seemed to connect with the ritual action that faith alone had moved them earlier to accept passively and without wonder. I did not eliminate the Eucharistic Prayer but rather inserted phraseology that I had heard numerous times within Native gatherings. Carefully preserving the "essentials" of a Eucharistic Prayer, I made references that were more meaningful to people than the theologically precise, English translations of the official Latin texts.[7]

In good conscience, I was doing what Vatican II had instructed:

> ...even in the liturgy the Church has no wish to impose a rigid uniformity in matters which do not involve the faith or the good of the whole community. Rather she respects and fosters the spiritual adornments and gifts of the various races and peoples. Anything in their way of life that is not indissolubly bound up with superstition and error, she studies with sympathy and if possible preserves intact. Sometimes, in fact, the church admits such things into the liturgy itself as long as they harmonize with its true and authentic spirit.[8]

With this text in mind, I continued to preside in the fashion described above at reservation and off-reservation liturgies. I did so because I saw many who had "fallen away" from the Church "return" to a sacramental medium whose message of hope had become comprehensible. Unfortunately, since most clergy regard the canonical Eucharistic Prayers as sacrosanct utterances that must be recited verbatim, Church attendance has suffered. Many have listened to these official texts over and over, and eventually concluded that they had heard enough.

While in graduate school, I would hear my anthropology colleagues evaluate religious ritual as simply the means whereby people sought supernatural affirmation of their very natural and ordinary lives. A "community of affliction" was drawn together at Mass, and this sacrament provided a moment of respite for people who needed some type of refuge from life's storms. Unlike me, my analytical colleagues were not charged with fostering a flock's faith-life within the sacred context, or calling the people of God to new understandings of how they should address the "real world" outside ritual occasions.[9] Their understanding did not correspond to my experience as a disciple struggling to make faith incarnate within the limbs and minds and relationships of those in the pews.

Because it should occur as a "given," it is discouraging to assert that the creative orchestration of sacraments should be a pastoral imperative adapted to the persons and circumstances of every parish community. Sadly, however, because this is more the exception than the rule, a steady stream of young people quest for a spiritual home outside the gospel fold. It is, then, a poor commentary on the quality of *aggiornamento* and inculturation to observe that canonically authorized prayers might just as well be said in Latin since their present form bears little resemblance to the people's "vernacular." Similarly, and surprisingly, it is simply self-defeating when sacraments communicate sterility instead of the tangible presence and action of God in the world.

When different Indian people express dissatisfaction with Christianity, their perspective is not unlike that of many within the non-Indian world. That is, media portrayals of missionary interaction with Indians are most often in caricature form, and a complex history is reduced to the stereotypical misperception that Christianity was responsible for every social ill that struck the Native population.[10] The gospel was, then, "bad news" for Indians.

Unlike their elders, the younger generation has become more and more removed from Church involvement, and today each denomination holds a fairly precarious position within the Native world. Moreover, young people have sought to reclaim a "traditional" Native religious identity, and this includes forsaking what some characterize as "white man's religion" (i.e., Christianity). The special history of Indian people makes this socio-religious trend quite understandable, but Indian sentiments toward Christianity are not unique, and are shared by non-Indians within the larger population.

While Native America's religious revitalization has a momentum of its own, it has not been isolated from a larger trend which this paper addresses. That is, while Native people have turned to their religious roots for a spiritual succor that speaks to their experience, so have many non-Indians. Some, for example, have tapped what they consider to be a kind of primal European religious identity which they call "Wicca" (Old English for "witch"). On a religious plane, this questing demonstrates the biological principle that "nature abhors a vacuum." Namely, Church practices have not met the needs of people who, as a result, have looked elsewhere to be filled.

Now recognized by the Army as a legitimate expression of "religion," Wicca has formal "services" and "chaplains." Claiming to be a reconstruction of European druidism, it presents itself as a benign form of witchcraft that reverences the creative power of women and Mother Earth. "Flower children" and "hippies" might seem a cultural aberration that came and went, but Wicca's core rule (known as the "Wiccan Rede") shows the legacy of Haight-Ashbury to be alive and well. Taking the place of a lengthy catechism, the Rede seems a mantra of the situation ethics which so earmarked the seventies. It simply states that if "it harm none, do what you will." As with others within the New Age fold, Wicca drew its following from different denominations, the human potential and women's movements, holistic health, ecology, and a variety of counter-culture groups.[11] As the new millennium begins, nothing suggests that this alluring trend will diminish.

Where Have All The Angels, Medals, and Devotional Aids Gone?

The changes brought by Vatican II were part of a larger cultural trend that saw an exodus of Church membership into the individual-oriented, smorgasbord world of pick-and-choose religious practice. To the surprise of more literate people of faith, many who went elsewhere took with them the traditional belief in angels![12] The staying power of this tradition may owe itself to something very old and very primal within human makeup since such beings are found within tribal religions worldwide. Benevolent or malevolent, they are supernatural intermediaries often referred to in the literature as "spirit-helpers," and they require no denominational allegiance.[13]

Although post-Vatican reformers had little use for the long-standing folk-belief in angels, experience has shown that such smugness was not productive. As it has done for centuries, Church tradition can certainly accommodate this "spirituality" for those who appreciate it (and at the same time not elevate it to undeserved prominence). This traditional piety spoke to the everyday experience of people whose formal knowledge of theology was limited. Angels went hand-in-hand with tales told about saintly souls from the past, and the people of God found solace in these secondary beliefs.

Catholicism's rich array of devotional aids also included benedictions, rosaries, genuflections, scapulars, medals, and a host of other spiritual artifacts that eventually became identified with persons whose religious practice was considered "pre-conciliar." Resisting innovations suggested by the "liberal element" (i.e., those favoring *aggiornamento*), this group became the resident reactionaries waging internecine conflict within every parish. Since Church life was so monochromatic before Vatican II, it was not easy to label clergy or laity as "conservative" or "liberal." Now, however, these new labels could be applied to each member of a given congregation, and devotional modes unnecessarily became the divisive markers that polarized parishioners and moved others to quest elsewhere for an experience of the sacred.

Particularly noteworthy within the panorama of post-Vatican II Catholicism, the ecology movement touched religious sensibilities that the Church failed to appreciate.

Encompassing back-to-nature behaviors in all areas of life, natural phenomena like rocks, claws, feathers and sticks became the new "holy medals" and power-objects that people wore around their necks. These were now the sacred reminders of a powerful Creator who was their author. As with traditional devotions, these eco-fetishes and the environmental consciousness that spawned them deserve a pastoral affirmation that the Church has been too slow in dispensing. After all, when Jesus spoke about many rooms being within his Father's house, he was perhaps referring to, among other possibilities, the Church having numerous and diverse devotional forms for its many diverse worshipers. This, after all, is what "catholic" means: the faith locally incarnate.

During my tenure in high school campus ministry from 1985 to 1990, I was forcefully reminded that popular religious trends perhaps reflected a longing whose expression could simply be varied. For example, I occasionally distributed crosses, medals, or rosaries after a liturgy that was very much tailored to the experience of "Generation X." Invariably a large crowd of contemporary teens would remove whatever was being handed out. A rush of young people (normally quite wedded to the transitory fads of the time) would eagerly reach for these tangible reminders of the supernatural. Whether popular or fringe, these students were youthful illustrations of a religious hunger for a "material" spirituality that has existed through time and across cultures.

Lineages, Saints, and Natural Phenomena

When anthropologists record ancient lineages which tribal peoples recite with pride, they argue that such lineages are actually "fictive kin" whose apotheosis affirms heirs who are living today. Matthew's genealogy for Jesus might sedate American listeners of the Word, but it is just such a lineage that is well understood and appreciated by tribal peoples who still preserve the tradition of acknowledging one's special "kin." These relatives are, in some way, able to guide, inspire, or protect the living ("ancestor worship" is a misnomer), and savvy anthropologists do not tell tribal people to adopt a more empirical approach to history and genetics. Rather, they try to learn, among other things, what beneficial function is served by so widespread and so long-standing a phenomenon as "the lineage."[14]

Perhaps buoyed by Vatican II, Catholic change-agents did not realize the extent to which Christian identity and piety relied on a "lives of the saints" tradition. As a result, demythologizing the Church's folk tradition moved many to look elsewhere for inspiration because a once-esteemed genealogy (and the faith it nourished) had become either suspect or dismissed. An enormous lacuna was created that gave rise to a contemporary form of pantheism that re-mythologized natural phenomena. Nourished by the ecology movement, flora, fauna, and the elements took on qualities that were previously accorded the Christian luminaries of old. This new pantheon was not in books or CCD class lectures, but was right outdoors and as close as the air one breathed. The appeal of earth's elements seemed a timely focus for all who considered themselves a "child of the universe."

The strength of St. Christopher could now become the bear spirit since this special creature could endure harsh winters, cold waters, and any sort of corporeal assault the wilderness (of life) might inflict. Similarly, praying for help from such patrons and patronesses as Gerard, Dymphna, Jude, Lucy, and numerous others was replaced by invoking the spirit-power who was resident in a quartz crystal, wolf claw, owl feather, or stick that a needy supplicant could hold in hand. Since the relics of saints seemed more associated with barbarism than religious inspiration, they gave way to rocks, stones and other naturally abundant purveyors of power that were sought by growing numbers of ecology-sensitive persons.

Anthropomorphizing natural phenomena is, of course, second nature to persons who have known the devotion of a pet dog, and owners regularly say they receive "unconditional love" from their canine companions. When docile dogs fight viciously with one another and, just moments later, frolic together quite forgetful of their earlier, snarling duel, owners often comment that they wish human behavior was as noble as that of their pets (in this case, "forgiving" or "letting bygones be bygones"). Millions of people have these experiences with their dogs who hold a special place within the home.

Some churches are well aware that most of their members have a "pet" they would very much like to have "protected" by means of a blessing. On the feast of St. Francis of Assisi, families are invited to bring their pets to these churches for a blessing. However, besides this one, extremely modest "outreach" to the natural world, institutional Christianity has made little accommodation to the many ecological sensitivities that have become so significant a part of secular and religious consciousness. The Church's oversight in this regard has been costly for all who live in a world that daily sees one species after another disappear forever. Left unchallenged by the Church, humanity will once again reveal the wisdom of Genesis and this time banish itself altogether from an Eden we know as planet Earth.

While global catastrophes can certainly occur with the improper stewardship of creation, there occurs a smaller, but very real pastoral problem that periodically arises which is tangential to this very broad and important issue. Namely, when parishioners ask to have their marriage ceremony take place in the open air, sparks will often fly. This happens because the couple learns that their diocese prohibits marriages from taking place outside the confines of a church. Their pastor teaches them a theology of the sacrament that equates membership in the faith-community with attendance at services held within a building's worship space. Moreover, they are instructed that the sacrament is not a private event that just involves two people, but is an event of the faith community at large, and so is celebrated, acknowledged, and ratified where the community gathers.

While there is merit in this position, the prevailing Church practice need not be so pastorally restrictive. After all, why should God's natural creation be denied as a setting for the sacramental commitment of a new Adam and a new Eve in marriage? Forests and fields, mountains and moors, lakes and lagoons all certainly reflect the majesty of the Creator more than any edifice constructed by humans.

Architects have modeled shopping malls after cathedrals, and now the Church can learn from developers who wisely include trees and ponds that provide secular souls with a more holistic shopping experience. Few parishes have been as circumspect as these entrepreneurs and practically none have addressed the theological role their properties play within the natural environment of their neighborhood.[15] The re-design of baptismal fonts occasionally mimics a stream, but there is nothing at typical parish churches to suggest that nature's bounty is a significant partner in the community's relationship with God. When "church environment" is addressed, people think of the color of carpeting, or the sandblasting of exterior walls instead of the church's relationship to the ground on which it sits or the neighborhood trees, soil, plants, and animals. As a result, lifeless concrete and desert asphalt define urban and suburban Church property, and parishioners must make a mighty mental stretch to imagine they have arrived at their spiritual oasis.

Increasing numbers within the fold do not regard Earth Day as a yearly, secular event sponsored by aging hippies. Rather, a growing *sensus fidelium* is that this might just as well be a "holy day" that calls the people of God to acknowledge their reverence for all creation. Some who still practice the faith take solace in belonging to a Church that has at least given its verbal commitment to a vision of seeing God's grandeur in nature. With the institution issuing pastoral letters that have called countries and corporations to account for actions that affect the environment, many hope this expression leads to greater ritual fruition within the worship space. Clergy will then be able to bestow many blessings upon their flock by adverting to the diverse voices and faces of the natural world that exist outside the walls of churches.[16]

In recent times, the luster of Christian sacraments has appeared tarnished while within the Indian world native rituals have glistened anew and poignantly personalized supernatural presence. Unfortunately, this has resulted in both Indians and non-Indians—all former Church members—leaving to find other channels of religious expression.[17] Their exodus particularly couples with today's ecological consciousness and calls the institution to be more liturgically responsive in stewarding the garden into which our Creator has placed us.

The Liturgical and Paraliturgical Imperative

In his opening address to the North American Conference on Cultural Awareness in Liturgy (November 14, 1990), Francis Cardinal Arinze addressed how the gospel should be made relevant to people's experience. Using *Lumen Gentium* as the basis for his remarks, he said that the gospel can incarnate itself in every culture, and that all peoples can come to Christ bringing their unique gifts. A candidate for the next pope, Arinze said that since the Church is Catholic, each part of her contributes to the good of the entire Church, and that the pastoral challenge is clear. At local or national levels, people's experience should be addressed through practices and professions of faith which are uniquely tailored to their circumstances.

The Cardinal addressed Vatican II's liturgical updating which, like the demythologizing of saints, related to a pastoral need. Since the laity's religious education was not great, and since the Mass was still able to draw a fair number of worshipers, "Mass in the vernacular" was an expedient concession to modernization. People could at least hear the faith's central truths read to them when fulfilling their "Sunday obligation." With many parochial school systems no longer in operation, the prayers and homily at Mass were, for most people, the only Christian pedagogy they would ever receive.

To his credit, Cardinal Arinze (an African quite familiar with tribal practices) was suggesting that Vatican II had not been fully implemented. While some might argue that a decline in attendance at Mass can be attributed to a "sense of majesty" lost with the prayers now in English, the core issue remains the same as when the Mass was in Latin. That is, the people are listening as they always have been listening, but they are not hearing much that speaks to their experience. Hence, the Mass might just as well be said in Latin since the English texts are in too abstract an idiom for vast numbers of people to appreciate in a personally meaningful way.

Commonplace within different American Indian religious practices, but often absent within the Church, is a personalizing of prayers and ritual involvement for those in attendance. Although easier to pull off within the small assemblage permitted by most Native rituals, an accommodation to all present, young and old, prevails. Tradition-bound rubrics are observed as vigorously as in a Mass, perhaps more so, but participants seem to have more of a proprietary or participatory interest in what occurs.

When anthropologists study a culture's religious practitioners, be they priests or ministers, "medicine men" or shamans, they often refer to such persons as "ritual specialists." However, describing the mechanistic liturgical style of Christianity's "high Church" clergy as being that of a "specialist" is flattering, just as it would be for "low Church" ministers who rely upon Scripture alone for feeding their flock. By contrast, the term really is apropos for many who conduct Native ceremonies.

Such people often orchestrate entrancing ritual that captures in prayer and action the attention of people who, within a typical eucharistic context, would only be physically present. The daily celebration of the Mass certainly can be valuable, but perhaps its repetitiveness, day in and day out, ultimately causes celebrants to develop a kind of cruise control in which the liturgy becomes lackluster and its drama becomes dreary. What we commonly refer to as a "priest shortage" just may be the Spirit's call for us to either refine our ritual or democratize our shamanism. By doing so, communities might be better served by more skilled practitioners than presently exist within the liturgical and paraliturgical context.

Many Indian ritual specialists execute their roles in a manner that usually addresses the needs of their clientele quite satisfactorily. This may be attributable to Native ceremonialism directly addressing individuals, seasons, and community events. In the same way, sacraments can still be encounters with God, but can only be so if parishes make sure they speak to the experience of younger and older members. Moreover, priests (and others) need to realize that sacramental and paraliturgical practices do not automatically spring to life and communicate anything of substance to the assembly. Rather, codified rubrics should be regarded as the skeletal form over which the flesh of faith is draped. In this way, parish personnel can help people see, know, and feel that a living God is in their midst.[18]

Native America does not have some special access to the supernatural but Native America does emphasize certain elements within its religious repertoire that Christianity could re-enliven for communities today. Non-Indian peoples can take a prophetic cue from this tradition that has survived so well against odds that were so great.

In Native ritual, for example, fire and smoke are commonly employed with American-grown sweet grass (or cedar) that is used as a kind of incense. Sweet grass is twisted into a cord and lit by a ritual specialist who then goes around the assembly and sees that each person is touched by the rivulet of smoke that rises from the barely burning tips. Participants say the smoke cleanses them and, just as within the Christian incense tradition, they say their prayer rises up to God in the same fashion as the smoke.

Although Catholic and Orthodox traditions have long had an incensing ritual, its foreign fragrance frequently elicits choking (young children especially like to react) that detracts from the symbolism associated with its use. Moreover, the metal instruments containing the smoky substance are usually swung in mysterious motions some distance from the congregation, and whatever is said by the celebrant is probably most often heard only by him and his assistants. Instead of being touched by its sensuously suffusing reality, parishioners assume that all of this strangeness must have some meaning to the priest and servers because it carries very little meaning for them!

Meanwhile, Indian and New Age others conduct "smudging" ceremonies with much awe and devotion.[19] Moreover, instead of being exotic, the fragrance is familiar to participants since it is one that evokes other experiences such as campfires, home fireplaces, or even marshmallow roasts. Smudging is, then, an American form of incensing. In light of its popularity within Native and New Age religious practice, such smudging could easily replace the Mediterranean accoutrements which unnecessarily give the ritual an exotic strangeness.

Common to both Old and New World religious practice, this prayer-ritual demonstrates how common beliefs are reinforced by sensory experience, or physical involvement. With Indian smudging, one's hand gestures motion the cleansing smoke over their entire body in a kind of washing movement. Prayers rise with the smoke while the "homespun" fragrance reminds all that their entreaties should be pleasing to God.

Curiously, this type of ceremonialism that appeals to contemporary groups is not at all foreign to Church tradition. Upon their first contact with missionaries, Native peoples were impressed with the ritualism brought by Catholic priests, and it elicited a positive response. Over time, however, a meaningful incensing ceremony is scarcely found within Christian practice while Native practitioners still adroitly conduct their smudging. Widely used in counterculture circles, incense became a marketable product, and is now commonly used and appreciated by everyone except those who bring their choking children to church.

Watching the predictable pattern unfold within Catholic services, I followed the example of Indian practitioners. Using homegrown sweet grass and sage, I personalized an incensing rite for non-Native services, and very positive results occurred. Eventually, I successfully restored incensing as a periodic feature of liturgical and paraliturgical gatherings.

If done well, ritual can nourish faith by enacting or dramatizing its theological content, and by involving those who verbally profess it. Catholic tradition acknowledges this, at least in principle, by its preservation and practice of seven sacraments. For the sake of brevity, the reflections offered here will avoid getting bogged down with a discussion of denominational positions regarding the nature of sacrament, and instead simply give some pragmatic suggestions which different groups might operationalize.

Since the rituals conducted by priests, deacons, or other clergy require little skill, creativity, or intelligence if done simply by "following the book," there may exist non-ordained others within a community who have special abilities for leading different types of ceremony. In the course of trial and error, a community will discover what "works" since good ritual will draw a crowd, and weak ritual will play to an empty house. Such is how Christians have seen the Spirit move and bring life to religious education classes, marriage preparation courses, healing ceremonies, baptisms, first communions, and numerous other parish activities. Rather than rely completely on the sacramentary, or simply allow the liturgical season to follow an unaltered script, faith communities need to fashion paraliturgical observances which somehow touch upon, or speak to, the social and personal issues which are part of the local community's experience.

Parishes have varieties of people with varieties of religious tastes. What some people might regard as "old Church" or passé, strange or even bizarre devotional forms or rituals, others might truly consider inspiring. Some might have a degree in theology, and some have no instruction whatsoever. Others, meanwhile, might vocally consider themselves the true bearers of Church tradition. It is precisely within this diverse lot that there exists a need to tap the creative resources which are no doubt present. Rather than define one's parish community as rife with generational and theological divisions, a more contemporary paradigm for understanding its religious predispositions is that of the "multi-cultural community" or "global village."

Parish boundaries, like Christianity as a whole, encircle persons who profess the same faith, but they do so in the form of multiple expressions. This translates into communities having persons who might be able to serve for a given interest group, where appropriate, as leader or ritual specialist. Just as tribal cultures had varied types of religious practitioners who "ministered" to the different needs within a given group, so can faith communities follow this model by more vigorously delegating pastoral responsibilities. Minimally, and supplemental to what exists sacramentally, parishes can benefit from concerned, skilled, and sensitive persons who can structure what really amount to diverse services of simplicity.

Native rituals basically deal with such things as the simple but profound symbolic gathering of persons in a circle. The circle demonstrates that from God's point of view all people are equal, and the circle reflects God by having no beginning and no end. All are bound to one another—like links in a chain—as each person has a unique strength that is necessary for the circle of the community to exist. As participant within the circle, each person feels an important role to play for the welfare of the group.

Native rituals are services of simplicity which also orient those present to the four directions (as a cross might do if set down in the middle of a group). Different categories of people might be positioned in each direction, e.g., young people (or girls) in one direction, single people (or boys) in another, parents in a third, and grandparents in the last (different groupings can be designed for different occasions). With the whole community assembled within the four directions, sacred responsibilities are cited. Some special Power is said to reside in each direction and that Power is invoked to touch the lives of those who turn that way.

A prayer leader might be in each of the four groups, or might oversee the entire proceeding. The person saying a prayer (or someone from each group) might go around to each child or young person in the east, and perhaps touch or incense them as the prayer is recited.[20] One then moves to another direction, and again prays for those who are assembled there.

The person who leads the ceremony might move in each direction, and incense it in the manner described earlier.[21] This use of the circle, the directions, the prayer words, fire, and perhaps the sprinkling of water, can be variously and artfully accomplished. Since these elements are what sustain existence, they can play a very important role within such services of simplicity.

Native peoples sometimes have a little leather pouch slung through their belt, somewhere present within their car, a purse, or placed anywhere readily accessible. A pouch might contain a number of items considered by the bearer to have special, sacred meaning, or it might simply contain tobacco or corn meal. In either form, these pouches are used when a person ritually entreats, or offers their thoughts or prayers to, the Sacred.[22]

These pouches are the modern equivalent of what ethnographic literature refers to as "medicine bundles," and what Catholics might consider to be a kind of portable tabernacle wherein the Sacred resides.[23] Appreciating this form within tribal culture, non-Indians have created their own culturally and personally relevant medicine bundle which they carry as a kind of special wallet. Accessible in moments of need throughout a given day, they contain whatever sacred reminders the person chooses to select, e.g., a photograph of a special person or place, a coin, a leaf, stone, a twig, or anything that reminds them of some experience they considered sacred. Pouches or wallets or bundles can vary in size or content since they are one's personalizing of the Sacred.

An Indian friend told me that he had a better sense of well being by just touching his medicine bundle (a little leather pouch that hung from his belt). In hearing what he said, I was reminded of the many drivers who no doubt felt a bit more secure with some representation of St. Christopher on their dashboard or visor. Just as modern day medicine bundles are not intentionally worn for all to see and wonder about, so medals or scapulars have been worn inconspicuously by persons for the divine assurance they represent. Both are private, tangible reminders of God's presence anywhere and anytime for the person carrying them. They communicate the intangible to incarnate beings who do not just utter *cogito ergo sum*, but also *sentio* and *video ergo sum*.

Theological and Pastoral Implications

The preceding pages have called for the creative adaptation of prayer to its cultural context, re-affirmation of the role played by sacred artifacts and persons in fostering Christian asceticism, the delegation of ritual roles to specialists, and the enlivening of paraliturgical experiences by whatever means are needed within diverse communities. The doctrinal foundation for what I suggest might be challenged since *ad lib* rituals or practices, admittedly, can lead people into error. However, what I have written arises from a trend over several decades that shows people have acquired very little theological instruction of any sort via conventional means. Out of felt-need, people have looked elsewhere for a spiritual sustenance they have found wanting in mainstream religious institutions.

This exodus need not be so widespread if the Church tapped its centuries-old reservoir of experience and offered people the varied forms of religious expression that have long been known to its members. Fuller theological instruction can certainly take place within the pastoral practices suggested here, but it can only do so once people have been shown that the Church offers something that speaks to their contemporary experience. Drawn from the Church's missionary experience in the Far East, "rice Christians" has been a derogatory phrase applied to people whose decision to accept conversion was based more on a decision to avoid starvation, for within the fold such people would be fed. A contention of this paper is that the Church must create "ritual Christians" who are drawn to the prayerfully articulate enactment of human longing. By practicing deftly depicted religious ritual rooted in a historical tradition sanctioned by the Spirit, more and more Christians will be able to preach a gospel creed that issues forth more and more in deeds that are life for the world.

An Indian woman once told me that "God made our people to be thunderbirds. But too many of our young are ending up in ditches. Too many of our young are thunderbirds with broken wings." Native thunderbirds are now mending those broken wings because through their religious reawakening, they have discovered what the ancestors had and what the world must have again lest it die. These pages are drawn from watching religious ritual help Native thunderbirds take flight, motioning for Christian soulmates to join them in rising toward the Son.

Notes

1. Michael F. Steltenkamp, *The Sacred Vision: Native American Religion and Its Practice Today* (Mahwah, New Jersey: Paulist Press, 1982); *Black Elk: Holy Man of the Oglala* (Norman, Oklahoma: University of Oklahoma Press, 1993).

2. The pastor stated that we were not simply two people celebrating the Eucharist but were, rather, the entire Church in prayer at the Holy Sacrifice of the Mass. I was only one among many and other hearts were also being "lifted up" in prayer. He explained that the celebrant's task was to ask that the Lord be with all the unseen members of the Church whose mystical presence was with us each night there in the otherwise empty and quiet house of worship.

3. Although altruism is associated with being "spiritual" and with not formally belonging to any religious institution, a not-so-noble byproduct of this new "commitment" is that one has no obligation to invest their time or money in any sort of larger community.

4. M. Ferguson, *The Aquarian Conspiracy* (Los Angeles: J.B. Tarcher, 1980).

5. This is the introductory paragraph for John Collier, *Indians of the Americas* (New York: Mentor Books, 1947).

6. *A Separate Reality* (1973) was published after the success of Castaneda's bestseller, *The Teachings of Don Juan* (1970). Saying that his mentor was a wise, old, Mexican Indian, Castaneda convinced a large readership that the ritual use of hallucinogenic plants produced a mystical awareness mainstream religions no longer provided. Long after his works cast their spell, it was revealed that Castaneda's "fieldwork" never occurred and that what the author wrote was fiction!

7. In adapting the sacramentary to my congregation, the following prayer was used: "Grandfather, Great Spirit, Father of our Lord Jesus Christ, we send our voices to you. Often, our world is in a pitiful condition, and so we cry to you for help. We, the two-leggeds you have lovingly made—as ever, we are in need of your help. We thank you, Grandfather, Great Spirit, Father of Jesus, for

all creation around us—the trees which give us shade on a hot summer day, the little ones whose fresh young faces bring smiles to our hearts, the winged creatures of the air who call our attention heavenward, and the four-leggeds who remind us of your creative power and artistry." Relevant to this point is Carol Zaleski, "Worship and American Cultural Spirituality," which shows that the official English translation of the Exsultet actually omits parts of the normative Latin text that make grateful reference to the bees who made the Paschal candle wax. See *Antiphon: A Journal for Liturgical Renewal* 4, no. 1 (1999): 5-13.

8. See paragraph 37 of *The Constitution on the Sacred Liturgy* in Walter M. Abbott, editor *The Documents of Vatican II* (New York: The America Press, 1966). Proposals in this essay are in keeping with C. J. McNaspy's observation in his preface to this document. There he stated that the Constitution's "reforms are by no means final or fixed…. They mark only a beginning, and are part of a dynamic, ongoing process of renewal inspired by God and directed by our spiritual shepherds."

9. Victor Turner was often cited since his work was held in such high regard, and his proposition sounded reasonable, viz., ritual addresses the liminal identities of people who constitute a "community of affliction." See *The Ritual Process: Structure and Anti-Structure* (Ithaca, NY: Cornell Paperbacks, Cornell University Press, 1969).

10. A typical example of pop culture's understanding of this relationship is evident in the 1999 television series "The Magnificent Seven." The heroic lead character solemnly declared in one episode that "the only thing missionaries do is make money off the Indians." Although inane, a similar charge is also often made in regard to the Church's dealings with non-Indians.

11. See J. Gordon Melton, Jerome Clark, and Aidan A. Kelly, *New Age Almanac* (Detroit, MI: Visible Ink Press, 1991).

12. The television series "Touched By an Angel" partially owes its high popularity rating to scripts which carefully avoid naming any deity or associating any religious tradition with the angel-protagonists.

13. In recent years, some have equated these entities with extraterrestrials (another example of how pop culture trends outside the religious world affect thinking within it).

14. One of my South African students stated: "When I meet someone here, we simply shake hands or nod and say hello. When meet-

ing someone back home, it takes me fifteen minutes to recite my ancestry in order to tell people who I am. It sounds like I am reciting a poem." The last "relative" he recites during such an introduction is a sky deity.

15. When attending Mass at Mary, Help of Christians parish in southern Florida, I found an exception to the rule. Its "Grounds Committee" has created prayer walks, grottoes, and assembly places for diverse kinds of worship experiences. The committee also publishes a bulletin entitled "Green Leaf" that keeps parishioners abreast of the natural world around them. Their web site is www.mhocrc.org.

16. A layman's experience is reflective of many as he publicly stated that he felt closer to God when watching a mother fox play with her young on his lawn than he did when watching most priests preside or homilize at Mass. Besides serving on the archdiocesan marriage tribunal, this layman also held a Master's degree in theology. Unfortunately, institutional Christianity has been blind to this growing perception of its members. Correctives can occur if parishes creatively include "nature" as a worshiping member of the faith community.

17. Institutional religion's irrelevance to people is dramatically evident when funeral directors see within and outside the Indian world a trend away from mourning families even asking for clergy to be present.

18. Since few Christians consider the phrase "ritual specialist" synonymous with their clergy, and since this is a reality across the denominations, seminaries need to prepare clergy who truly fit the designation.

19. "Smudging" or "to smudge" is the term employed today by Indians and others when referring to their practice of incensing.

20. This is the type of praying done on such occasions: "Creator of all, Our Father in heaven, we have gathered the young children here in the east. They represent new and vital life. Just as the sun rises in the east and brings us new light each day, so do these young people represent new light, new leadership, and new hope for us. We ask you, Lord Jesus, our Brother, to make the power of the rising sun glow in the hearts of our young people here. Give them eyes of light which can see through any darkness which might trap them."

21. Other prayers follow the model already described: "Creator of all, Father in heaven, we have gathered our elders here at the north

point of our circle. From the north you send strong winds which clean our world and which give power to the eagle's flight. We ask you, God of the Cleansing Wind, to continue to give our elders the power of eagle flight and eagle vision that they may lead us with a wisdom learned from the heights of heaven."

22. Besides having these pouches, persons often will elevate a pinch of tobacco or corn meal in prayer to the four directions (sacred stories relate to the use of tobacco and corn meal in this fashion).

23. The medicine bundle phenomenon has been re-enlivened within some Native circles, and New Agers have embraced the form in recent times, but Robert A. Orsi has described a similar devotional enthusiasm related to St. Jude among daughters of immigrants that started early in the twentieth century. See *Thank You, St. Jude: Women's Devotions to the Patron Saint of Hopeless Causes* (New Haven: Yale University Press, 1996).

Eucharist as Basic Training: The Body as Nexus of Liturgy and Ethics[1]

M. Therese Lysaught
Assistant Professor of Religious Studies
University of Dayton

What does it mean to "live Christianity"? One might suggest that "lived Christianity" refers to particular things that only Christians do, that to examine "lived Christianity" means to study Christian practices. One aspect of lived Christianity to which scholars might attend, then, would be liturgical practices such as the Eucharist. Alternatively, one might suggest that "lived Christianity" refers to how Christians live, that to examine "lived Christianity" means to study if or how being Christian makes a difference in the kinds of choices one makes, the values one holds, the virtues one embodies, and so on. In short, lived Christianity, then, would be about ethics. A third approach, however, suggests that neither Eucharist nor ethics can be examined in isolation from the other, but rather that Christianity truly lives in lives shaped by Christian practices. Thus, we are challenged to explore the relationship between the Eucharist and the Church as a community of discipleship and moral formation.[2]

This latter claim serves as the starting point for this article. How might one describe the relationship between the

Eucharist and the Church as a community of discipleship and moral formation? More generally, how do Christian practices shape practitioners' lives? I will argue that any consideration of the relationship between Christian practices and the Christian life must necessarily attend to the ways in which bodies are engaged and produced.

Before proceeding, however, two initial caveats are in order, for in speaking of Eucharist and ethics, two dangers present themselves. First, to posit a relationship between Eucharist and "moral" formation risks construing "morality" as somehow separable from, and perhaps more important than, other dimensions of the Christian life, such as politics or truth or worship or prayer. In the Eucharist, however, these are always inextricably integrated. In fact, in resisting the analytic reduction of the Christian life to morality, the Eucharist points to a wider reality—that in naming the moral, one signals both one's political commitments as well as the God or gods one worships. In the Eucharist, God does not call us to be "moral" people; God calls us to be much more—to be disciples who live in and toward the Kingdom. Clearly, "morality" resonates through the Christian life of politics and praise, but care must be taken not to abstract the "moral" from the story.

Relatedly, in speaking of Eucharist and ethics, a second danger lies in the tendency to allow the terms following the conjunction—ethics, moral formation, social justice—to become the controlling terms in the relationship. Certainly, whether worshipers or scholars, we cannot help but come to the Eucharist with a particular hermeneutic or set of questions. We must take care, however, that the Eucharist not simply be read through the lens of the particular issue or interest of the day, not be used simply as a resource, mined so as to warrant ends defined *a priori* and driven by alien agendas. Instead, re-read through the prism of the Eucharist, such issues and interests will often be significantly recast. As the Eucharist challenges and reshapes our lives, so it must always be allowed to challenge and reshape our agendas, however noble, as well.

For the Eucharist, and attendant Christian practices, are not primarily concerned with ethics or social justice or individual moral formation but rather with the worship of God and the formation of the Church as a community of discipleship. In Henri de Lubac's classic phrase, the Eucharist makes, or produces, the Church.[3] The Eucharist produces Church as the Body of Christ. It is this Body—and only this Body—which is both charged with the task of discipleship and truly capable of following Jesus, of performatively embodying the Kingdom of God in the world. Adapting the Foucaultian claim that the body is the site at which power is contested, it is likewise this Body that is called to and capable of resisting the powers that would otherwise determine God's creation. Discipleship then, as a mode of performance and resistance, is principally a mark of the Church and is rooted in the Eucharist.

However, for the Church to fulfill its call to discipleship, to be active in the world concretely and materially, the Body of Christ must literally be embodied. Such embodiment comes in the shape of Christians. In producing the Church as the Body of Christ, the Eucharist simultaneously, through the breaking of the bread, produces us "individually as members of it."[4] The nature of this production is what I wish to explore in this article. More specifically, I will argue that discipleship—that is, authentic, lived Christianity—requires the production of Christian bodies. Through a matrix of practices, central to which is the communal celebration of the Eucharist, the Church seeks to reconfigure bodies precisely as Christian. So reconfigured, the bodies of Christians, like the Church, become the site at which power is contested, capable of performatively living the kingdom in the world and of resisting the powers that would otherwise determine our lives.[5]

In the following, I will sketch the broad outlines of this

claim. A brief overview of recent reflections on liturgy and ethics demonstrates that the body has been overlooked within the contemporary academic debate. Two analogies—the military and athletics—and one example from the early Church then display how bodies are "produced" in different contexts. These examples highlight seven key aspects of such production: (1) that bodies are produced, over time, through a consistent regimen of bodily practices; (2) that different sets of practices produce different sorts of bodies; (3) that a key dimension of such production is tacit or implicit; (4) that such practices produce bodies capable of distinctive actions; (5) that over time such actions become "natural" or instinctive; (6) that performance is often also resistance; and (7) that performance and resistance have a dual locus, simultaneously deployed by individual bodies as well as by a *corps*, for the sake of whose purposes such bodies have been produced in the first place. As will become clear, these seven points are far from exhaustive but rather are offered as suggestive starting points for reflecting on how we might understand the Eucharist and other related practices as producing Christian bodies and thereby fostering the Christian life.

Liturgy and Ethics: The Erasure of the Body

The relationship between Eucharist and moral formation— or at least its broader configuration as the relationship between "liturgy" and ethics—has received considerable attention from liturgical theologians and theological ethicists.[6] Within this growing corpus, the link between liturgy and ethics is generally described in one of four ways: cognitively, affectively, communally, or dramaturgically.

First, liturgy is seen as effecting ethical behavior at the cognitive level. By conveying particular conceptual beliefs, communicating knowledge, or changing consciousness, liturgy "opens [the] minds" of the participants and "underscore[s] the[ir] awareness" of God.[7] A number of cognitive motifs are employed. Some describe liturgy as a model, pattern, mirror, or "paradigm" for living and acting. As Geoffrey Wainwright notes:

> The Eucharist provides enabling paradigms for our ethical engagement in the world: [it] allows us to learn, absorb, and extend the values of God's kingdom.... In terms of ethical theory, the eucharistic paradigm points us in the right direction: it sets the vector within which the difficult concrete decisions and actions of everyday life have to be taken and performed if they are to be authentically Christian.[8]

Others use the metaphor of "vision." Liturgy is described as shaping the vision, perceptions, and imaginations of participants, providing participants with an alternative construal of the world. Through liturgy, we come to "see ourselves" differently; we are given a "worldview."[9] Still others draw on the notion of narrative, arguing that liturgy shapes vision by providing a narrative context into which participants enter and locate themselves, a universe of discourse into which we become situated.[10] In entering into the narratives of the Christian life, the stories become the "grammar" of our lives, as we learn "the language of God"; they thereby help us to "read the world."[11]

A second approach holds that the link between liturgy and ethics is not primarily cognitive but rather emotional or affective. Kathleen Hughes maintains, for example: "We do not celebrate the liturgy in order to think about ideas, however worthy.... Liturgy is less a matter of the head than of the heart...."[12] Liturgy is seen to shape participants' affections, sensitivities, virtues, character, personality, motivation, and dispositions, as well as change their hearts. Liturgy, then, enters the ethical equation at the point of intention, motive, or will.

A third approach holds that liturgy becomes translated into ethics *vis à vis* its social and communal dimension.

Liturgy constitutes the unity of those who participate by putting us into "proper relationships with ourselves, others in
the community, and God."[13] In doing so, it simultaneously
challenges autonomous individualism and constitutes the
self: "An individual becomes a person in and through
engagement with a community."[14] Given that ethics is about
relationships between persons, and that the essence of justice
is right-relationship, only selves communally constituted
will be capable of ethical engagement in the world.

Finally, others locate liturgy's effectiveness in its essential
nature as dramatization or dramatic reenactment. For Paul
Ramsey, the Christian narrative is dramatically presented in
liturgy:

> It could be asserted that the story of the Christian
> Story that is the *principium* of both *credendi* and
> *bene operandi* can best be told by the dramaturgy,
> the rehearsal, the reenactment, the repetition that
> belongs to the nature of liturgy.[15]

As participants again and again act out the script of the
Christian story, the dramaturgical nature of liturgy provides
a nexus through which the cognitive, affective, and communal coalesce into one grand synthesis.

Each of these approaches highlights an important aspect
of liturgical practice. One crucial dimension, however, seems
consistently to be overlooked. Consider, for example, the
marvelous Orthodox rite of Chrismation, cited by Vigen
Guroian in his article "Seeing Worship as Ethics":

> Sweet ointment in the name of Jesus Christ is
> poured upon thee as a seal of incorruptible heav-
> enly gifts.
>
> *The eyes [are then anointed]:*
> This seal in the name of Jesus Christ enlighten
> thine eyes, that thou mayest never sleep unto
> death.

The ears:

This holy anointing be unto thee for the hearing of the divine commandments.

The nostrils:

This seal in the name of Jesus Christ be to thee a sweet smell from life unto life.

The mouth:

This seal in the name of Jesus Christ be to thee a guard for thy mouth and strong door for thy lips.

The hands:

This seal in the name of Jesus Christ be to thee a cause for good works and for all virtuous deeds and conduct.

The heart:

This seal establish in thee a pure heart and renew within thee an upright spirit.

The back:

This seal in the name of Jesus Christ be to thee a shield of strength thereby to quench all the fiery darts of the Evil One.

The feet:

This divine seal direct thy goings upon life everlasting that thou mayest not be shaken.[16]

Guroian cites this rite to display an ethical imperative that derives in part from the rite's ontological effect but also in its "call...to [conscientiously] cultivate a certain disposition and character."[17] In doing so, however, he does not mention the fact that in this rite, the candidate's body is anointed...again and again and again—the eyes, the ears, the nostrils, the mouth, the hands, the heart, the back, the feet. As the candidate is anointed, the words of the rite—the theological concepts it conveys, the dispositions it invokes—are physically inscribed onto the body by the community (in whose midst the candidate stands as their representative anoints). The internal wisdom of the rite is intrinsically embodied. In

Guroian's account of worship as ethics, however, this bodily dimension is not addressed.

On this point, Guroian is not alone. Neither Ramsey nor Saliers, for example, include the bodies of participants in their analysis of the dramaturgical dynamic of liturgy. As quickly becomes evident, nowhere in the methodological literature on the relationship between liturgy and ethics is the human body mentioned, discussed, or taken into account.[18] This might be unremarkable except for the fact that liturgy, as one liturgical theologian notes, is "not a matter of 'ideas' but of 'bodies' or, better, of 'corporeality.'"[19] Liturgy, Eucharist, and the broader matrix of Christian practices that texture the Christian life are intrinsically corporeal.

Thus, liturgical practices, such as the Eucharist, inherently impact and engage bodies. But not only this. Return for a moment to the text of the Orthodox rite of Chrismation outlined above. Not only is the body richly and excessively anointed again and again; the words of the rite themselves seek to shape and direct the candidate's body in a particular way: the ears are guided toward God's commandments; the mouth becomes "guarded"; the hands are steered toward good works and virtuous conduct; the feet are grounded on the path toward everlasting life; and the back is fortified as a shield. Chrismation, then, intends that the bodies—and thereby lives—of those anointed become distinctively reconfigured. Through chrismation and the lush matrix of rites and practices in which it is embedded, Orthodox Christianity seeks to produce particular Christian sorts of bodies. Only insofar as such bodies are produced will they be capable of the types of performance and resistance required to sustain the Church as a community of discipleship.[20]

Corpus/Corps: Soldiers, Athletes, and Martyrs

The Orthodox, of course, are not alone in employing practices so as to reconfigure distinctive bodies capable of specific actions. This same dynamic appears in a myriad of contexts. Two analogies and an example from the early Church may assist in displaying the particulars. These three realms of practice which aim at the production of particular sorts of bodies are the military, athletics, and martyrial ascesis.[21]

The military, for example, knows that "catechesis" is far from enough to turn an average, ordinary citizen into a soldier. Instead, what is required is a physical and physically grueling program of drills, penalties, uniforms, and communal living designed not only to deconstructively break recruits of any vestiges of individuality but also to constructively produce military bodies.[22] Only bodies so produced will be able to kill systematically and efficiently, whether on command or by instinct, unquestioningly obey orders, or kill or even die to protect one's comrades. These are not actions that come "naturally," but through embodied practices they become so. Bodies so produced often are so for the duration; military bodies are easy to pick out of a crowd—standing, sitting, walking, speaking in a particular way—even if the person left the military long ago. Moreover, the military seeks not only to produce military bodies but a "corps" as well—a confederation of soldiers who, functioning as a unit at the service of the powers of the State, will be capable of embodying the will of those who rule, dominating or resisting other powers as required.[23]

Likewise, one might consider athletics. Even more explicitly than the military, athletics aims to produce particular types of bodies. Clearly, the type of body produced differs with the sport: football, weight-lifting, basketball, gymnastics, baseball, track, hockey, all shape bodies differently. Again, physical and physically grueling programs of training, drills, practice, and competition produce bodies that are powerful, fast, agile, precise, can hit, catch, shoot, throw, bend, balance with significant levels of endurance and toleration of pain. So produced, athletic bodies are capable of doing things both that they formerly could not do and that most average, ordinary bodies cannot. And generally, athletic training seeks to produce a team, a coalition of athletic bodies that together are capable of performing specific actions (playing the sport) better than any other team while resisting the power that others bring.[24]

One need not, however, look only to a secular context to find examples of this dynamic in action; instances of this process are replete within the Christian tradition as well. Nothing displays this as well as the practices of asceticism and martyrdom by which the early Church produced bodies capable of resisting Imperial torture. As Maureen A. Tilley persuasively argues, ascetic practices of the early Church provided training and preparation for the possibility of martyrdom. Specific practices of fasting, sleep deprivation, physical mortification, sexual continence, and simple repetitive prayer served to reconfigure Christian bodies to withstand the tortures of martyrdom. As Tilley notes:

> ...the torture victim cannot control either the intensity or the duration of the torture, but the martyrs could and did simulate both in their practice of asceticism. The type of ascetic preparation for martyrdom was tied to the sorts of tortures the martyrs would undergo, especially deprivation of food and water. Christian communities would begin fasting as soon as they realized police action was imminent.... Such pre-torture practices actually helped change their metabolism so that they survived longer under torture.... Tertullian exhorted his readers to prepare for prison.... What they would suffer there would not be any penalty but the *continuation of their discipline*. One trained for prison...In undergoing pain, the confessors engaged in a cosmic battle in which the torturers did not merely attack the bodies of the martyrs; they even strove against God. Ascetic training brought the power of God to bear on the battlefield of the body. Christians taught

> their martyrs to endure pain either by escaping it
> or by reconfiguring its meaning.... Correspondence
> between Cyprian and the confessors at Carthage
> shows him teaching them to turn each instrument
> of torture and pain in each part of the body into a
> means of uniting themselves to the passion of
> Christ and training them in the skill of reconfig-
> uring their own bodies.[25]

Bodies so produced, then, were capable of what seemed to be superhuman endurance and of, more astoundingly, glorifying God and rejoicing in their salvation in the midst of agonizing torment. Under great duress, they could almost unconsciously utter over and over, "I am a Christian," "Thank you, God," and "Christ have mercy."[26] In so doing, they not only thwarted the objectives of their torturers individually, i.e., they neither recanted their faith nor would make sacrifice to the Imperium. They also enabled the Church to withstand the intended annihilation, as their examples and stories taught the faithful to be strong in persecution and prepared the victims to be victors. Their bodies became battlegrounds between God and the demonic; Caesar would not determine their salvation or the meaning of their deaths. For this reason, not just anyone could be a martyr—"voluntary" martyrdom was strongly discouraged. True ascesis took time.[27] Those not properly produced would not only not be able to withstand the torture, their failure would both empower the enemy and undermine the morale of the persecuted community, threatening it with dissolution.

Eucharistic Bodies, Practically Produced

These examples illustrate at least seven features of practical bodily production relevant to consideration of the relationship between the Eucharist, Christian bodies, and the Christian life, namely, that: (1) bodies are produced, over time, through a consistent regimen of bodily practices; (2)

different sets of practices produce different sorts of bodies;
(3) a key dimension of such production is tacit or implicit; (4)
such practices produce bodies capable of distinctive actions;
(5) over time such actions become "natural" or instinctive;
and (6) performance is also resistance; and (7) performance
and resistance have a dual locus, simultaneously deployed
by individual bodies as well as by a *corps*, for the sake of
whose purposes such bodies have been produced in the first
place.[28]

First, bodies are produced, over time, through a consistent
regimen of bodily practices. The two points of emphasis here
are "over time" and "consistent regimen." The sort of reconfiguration witnessed in the case of martyrs or athletes does
not happen overnight but rather over months, if not years, of
training. As is most evident with the military analogy, it is
often first necessary to deconstruct a body's initial form before
it can be reconfigured. Progress may initially be made quickly; then, as anyone who has exercised or tried to develop a
regimen of prayer knows well, one hits a plateau. The body
resists. Daily practice is an effort, a chore; one seems to be
regressing rather than progressing. Such obstacles can be
worked through, but only with disciplined consistent attention to practice. And once a desired state is achieved, it must
be vigilantly maintained through both practice and performance. It is a case of "use it or lose it."

Thus, the production of "Eucharistic" bodies requires, at
minimum, the sustained discipline of regular participation
in the Eucharist over a lifetime. De Lubac observes that such
is the case even for the Church, that "The Church and the
Eucharist make each other, every day, each by the other."[29] If
such is the case for the Church, for the Body of Christ, how
much more so for its individual members? The *Constitution
on the Sacred Liturgy* signals this continuous, recursive
dynamic when it notes: "The liturgy daily builds up those
who are in the Church, making of them a holy temple of the
Lord, a dwelling-place for God in the Spirit."[30]

However, throughout the Christian tradition, the Eucharist—the summit toward which the activity of the Church is directed and the fount from which all her power flows[31]—has never stood alone as sufficient. To be properly productive, eucharistic practice must be located within a *regimen* of practices that shape various aspects of the body on a consistent basis. Especially for contemporary Catholic communities, where the communal celebration is a weekly event, or for Protestant communities where celebration is less frequent, daily auxiliary practices are required to both get one "in shape" and to maintain the body's configuration. Thus, throughout the tradition, a variety of practices have developed—the praying of the Office and the Liturgy of the Hours, fasting, hospitality, group Bible study, the sacrament of reconciliation, contemplation, the Spiritual Exercises, praying of the rosary, the corporal works of mercy, devotions to Mary and the saints, and so on. Oriented toward the communal celebration of the Eucharist in the Mass as their norm, these practices are likewise productive.

However, as the second point above notes, different sets of practices will produce different sorts of bodies. Clearly, practices as diverse as contemplation, singing in the choir, or giving testimony inform the body with different capabilities. This effect is multiplied through different configurations of practices. Thus, Dorothy Day, shaped by daily Mass, the use of the breviary and Little Office, and the corporal works of mercy (among other things) embodies the Christian life quite differently from Thomas Merton, shaped similarly through the daily Mass, the breviary and the Liturgy of the Hours, and the practice of contemplation.[32] Moreover, what looks like the same practice ostensibly—for example, the practice of fasting—may differ in its perfomative productivity depending on context. In the context of persecution, fasting helped the martyrs withstand starvation as a means of torture; in contemporary U.S. culture, fasting alternatively may serve to produce bodies that can withstand the seductions of a culture of consumption and desire.

Third, a key dimension of the production of bodies is tacit or implicit. Catherine Bell notes that practices like the Eucharist invest the body with a "sense [which] exists as an implicit variety of schemes whose deployment works to produce sociocultural situations that the ritual body can dominate in some way."[33] This concise phrase encompasses three important claims. Chiefly, embodied practices produce a "sense"—not a "feeling" but rather a faculty, a capacity or capability analogous to taste or sight or smell or hearing or touch—a faculty whereby we encounter, perceive, and interpret the world and which is crucial for facilitating action. Thus, just as a seasoned batter can sense whether it will be a fastball or a slider, low and away, before the ball leaves the pitcher's hand, so someone formed by the practice of contemplation can sense God's presence even in the most unlikely of places.

Moreover, both the production of this "sense" and its deployment operate tacitly. Bell describes ritual practice as "a particularly 'mute' form of activity," reconfiguring bodies in such a way that they neither perceive that they are being reconfigured nor the substance of that reconfiguration.[34] Thus, bodies are produced not primarily through "messages" communicated during a practice but rather implicitly through the various activities in which participants engage. These activities, repeated again and again over time, slowly and subtly reconfigure participant bodies.

Two examples illustrate this point. Consider the act of kneeling, an act in which any attendant at worship may engage. As Bell notes:

> The act of kneeling does not so much communicate a message about subordination as it generates a body identified with subordination. In other words, the molding of the body within a highly structured environment does not simply express inner states. Rather, it primarily acts to

> restructure bodies in the very doing of the acts
> themselves. Hence, required kneeling does not
> merely *communicate* subordination to the kneeler.
> For all intents and purposes, kneeling produces a
> subordinated kneeler in and through the act
> itself.... [W]hat we see in ritualization is not the
> mere display of subjective states or corporate val-
> ues. Rather, we see an act of production—the pro-
> duction of a ritualized agent able to wield
> physically a scheme of subordination and insub-
> ordination.[35]

Thus, while few communicants may consciously articulate the thought "I am subordinate to God," anyone raised in a Catholic context knows how hard it is to approach the altar without genuflecting. Even lapsed Catholics or those who consciously resist hierarchical, austere images of God and wish to approach the altar as Jesus' friend, may find their bodies resisting their wills, bending them toward their knees.

Likewise consider the contemporary Rite of Christian Initiation of Adults in the Roman Catholic Church. Here catechumens and candidates join the congregation for the Liturgy of the Word. Before the Offertory, however, they are asked to stand, week after week, addressed by the celebrant, and then, as the congregation stands and sings, ritually and ceremoniously *marched* out of the sanctuary, marshaled by their catechists. This process does not merely *communicate* a message of exclusion; rather, the catechumens and candidates are constructed as bodies that are valued (they merit special attention within the Mass) but not yet fully incorporated into the Body of Christ, not yet ready to stand in the presence of the holy mysteries, not ready to share in the Eucharist. The rites reconfigure their bodies as desirous of the sacraments and full communion, whose lack will only be fulfilled—and then joyously—by re-creative incorporation into Christ and the Church on Easter Sunday. As such, although they might powerfully wish or resolve to return to the congregation for the Eucharist, their bodies would resist.[36]

Clearly, careful attention to each particular component of the Eucharist could multiply examples.[37] This brings us to our fourth point, that such practices produce bodies capable of distinctive actions. Following Bell's definition above, a practice as complex as the Eucharist is capable of producing bodies invested with a variety of schemes. In addition to becoming subordinated kneelers, they are likewise produced as: "other" from the world, as communal, as living in and toward the kingdom, as repentant sinners condemned yet mercifully forgiven, as attentive to and desirous of God's Word, as Psalm-speakers, as witnesses, as offerers of their goods and selves to God and others, as forgivers, reconcilers, and peace-givers, as open to and dependent upon God, as "become Christ," as praise-singers, as constituted by and constitutive of others in the community, as sent into the world bearing God's peace, as blessed, all at once, and more.

Invested with these schemes cultivated over time, such bodies will deploy them distinctively in the world. Examples worth exploring include the kiss of peace and the practice of testimony.[38] Although theologically rich, the kiss of peace in Caucasian Catholic services has, admittedly, become rather rote. Prior to the Offertory or Communion, congregants turn to those within arm's length to "offer each other a sign of peace." Usually a handshake, family members and friends may be treated to a hug or even an actual kiss. Even in its most minimalist incarnation in the most homogeneous of congregations, however, such a gesture can counter cultural-ly inscribed individualistic tendencies, reconfiguring us as those who turn to the neighbor, to the "other," reaching out to them, speaking peace to them, touching them, reconciling with them, and receiving from them their hand and their blessing. In more diverse urban congregations, however, the power of this simple gesture is more profound, as the face of the neighbor becomes truly "other"—the elderly, the poor, the homeless, the disabled, the mentally handicapped, those of different ethnicity or race. Through this simple gesture, we become capable of seeing, touching, speaking, and reaching out to—and being touched by—those who are often invisible or from whom we have been taught to recoil.

The practice of giving testimony likewise reconfigures the practitioner. In giving testimony, one is called to stand before the congregation to give witness to "how I have seen God working in my life." This action shapes the one testifying in at least two ways. First, through giving testimony, one engages in a culturally difficult task—of speaking of God out loud and of giving witness to God's presence and power in particular situations. Second, she who gives testimony becomes configured as one who gives witness to God out loud *in public*. Clearly, hearing the testimonies of others is important for learning the language of witness and for learning how to see God's presence in one's life. But only in stepping up to the lectern and saying the words do we become those capable of speaking publicly of God.

Such deployment, though, is largely implicit as well. As the fifth point notes, over time characteristic actions practically incorporated become "natural," that is, instinctive, intuitive, or unreflective. In short, practices and the characteristics they incorporate become habit. Stephen Buckland elaborates this dynamic:

> Habits are, by definition, not reflectively conscious.... There may, of course, be initial instruction...and subsequent explanation or commentary; but postures and gestures are learnt principally by imitation and soon become "natural" and unreflective...appropriated by repetition over time. Bodies are shaped, "memory" incorporated, by familiarization through time with movements in space, of eye or hand, lip or limb; in time and over time, instruction, explanation, commentary

> become unnecessary. With the habitual skills are
> incorporated human values and dispositions
> which, in time and over time, come to be "natu-
> ral." Such knowledge is largely unspoken: literal-
> ly embodied, profoundly, secretly effective...the
> power of bodily practices to constitute "memo-
> ries" of past experiences depends, paradoxically,
> on their remaining unreflected upon and, appar-
> ently, "natural."

To suggest a mundane example, my body has been "produced" to drive a car with manual transmission. To first
learn, of course, required quite a bit of instruction, appren-
ticeship at the hand of one who had mastered the skill, education as to the "theory" behind the process (i.e., how the
clutch works, what is going on within the engine during
acceleration) as well as error and trial (mostly for the truck).
Now, however, I generally do not "think" about what to
do—when to push the clutch, when to shift; my body simply
does it naturally. While this is clearly useful on a day-to-day
basis, it might prove particularly valuable in an emergency
situation when I do not have time to think; my body will
simply do the right thing. The extent of this embodiment
becomes apparent when I, on occasion, drive an automatic.
My foot "naturally" goes for the clutch, my hand to the stick,
even though they are not there. Eucharistic practices likewise have the power to so habituate. By practicing the kiss of
peace week after week, literally extending a hand to the
stranger becomes natural. As one gives testimony again and
again, it becomes increasingly natural, increasingly instinctive to speak of God in public.

The habituated character of such schemes becomes quickly apparent when it confounds us: when the context changes
and/or they conflict with alien agendas. I recognize how
profoundly I am configured as a manual driver only when
my context changes and I drive someone else's car. The dis-
tinctiveness of Amish embodiment only becomes strikingly

apparent when members of an Amish community travel public roads or sojourn into town. This aspect of bodily configuration signals both that such production is context-dependent and that the twin face of performance is resistance. As the example of martyrial ascesis cited earlier attests, practical production of bodies necessarily occurs within a larger sociocultural situation. As such, however, and as the persecuted Church illustrates explicitly, the performance of schemes in any sociocultural context inevitably entails, as part of its productive negotiation, resistance.

This mention of resistance brings us to the seventh and final point, namely, that performance and resistance, as achievements of specifically configured bodies, have a dual locus, simultaneously deployed by individual bodies but more importantly by a *corps* for the sake of whose purposes such bodies have been produced in the first place. The production of bodies is linked, recursively, with the production of a social body, a *corps*. Three implications of this claim merit brief elaboration. First, practices, by definition, cannot simply be individually generated modes of personal formation. Practical production is necessarily communally mediated. While individual martyrs themselves both resisted their torturers and performed acts of witness and glorification, it is doubtful that they could have done so if not located within a particular community. The local Church communities trained its members for the battle. To maintain such rigorous training required tutelage, exhortation, the company of comrades both as co-trainers (e.g., during periods of fasting) as well as conscience (e.g., to keep one from abandoning continence). Moreover, the local Church communities attended the apprehended in prison with material support and spiritual encouragement, prayed for them unceasingly, and refused to disband their communal practices, i.e., to dissolve under the threat.

Second, as bodies navigate the matrix of practices that comprises any *corps*, they incorporate an identity; one might say that they become "traditioned." As Chauvet notes:

> To be initiated is not to have learned "truths to believe" but to have received a tradition, in a way through all the pores of one's skin. Initiation comes about through a process of education which is like life: it is not the end of a simple intellectual course (indispensable though such courses may be today) but originally an identity.[39]

Clearly, practical formation is not formulaic; practices are appropriated by particular bodies, located within very particular socio-historical and personal circumstances. As such each appropriation is singularly negotiated, resulting in slight variations each time. However, in spite of this creativity in appropriation, authentic practices resist individuation and individualism. In becoming so traditioned, in assuming such an identity, bodies incorporate historied schemes of performance and resistance. In this way, practices both produce and sustain a particular *corps*.

Moreover, and thirdly, in the end, although the process of production is recursive, it is primarily for the sake of such a *corps* that bodies are produced and schemes of performance and resistance are wielded. One is produced as a Marine primarily for the sake of the Corps and for the defense of the nation; to learn to kill for one's own sake would rather be regarded as a socio-pathology. One is produced as an athlete solely for the sake of a team; one cannot play football alone. While individual martyrs certainly understood their deaths as benefiting their souls personally, their deaths effectively strengthened the Church itself; the truth and faith it witnessed and preached emerged publicly before its pagan detractors as something worth dying for.

Conclusion

Thus, the vector that connects the Eucharist and attendant practices with the Christian life necessarily runs through bodies—the bodies of Christians and the Body of Christ. Hopefully, the preceding account dispels any naive notion that eucharistic reconfiguration is facile or instantaneous,[40] and demonstrates rather that it is a gradual process of "incubation" or habituation over time dependent upon an arduous, complex, and lengthy regimen of physically mediated practices. Eucharistic reconfiguration requires a tapestry of practices beyond the liturgy itself, although ultimately such practices must be normed by and oriented toward the Eucharist. Nor does this process find a terminus; just as discipleship is a lifelong journey, the process of reconfiguration is an ongoing activity, requiring vigilance to resist the atrophy that comes with disuse as well as to resist those powers which would reconfigure us differently.

While the preceding account provides a first step toward a fuller articulation of these relationships, it also points toward a number of issues that merit further exploration. Clearly, an important next step will be to broaden the perspective provided here and to display the interconnections between practices, discourses, and the institutions that sustain them, for discourses and institutions are equally crucial for bodily production.

Moreover, while practiced bodies become capable of distinctive modes of performance and resistance, neither configuration nor deployment is univocal. A broader account of Christian practices will also take into consideration a concomitant to any process of bodily production, namely, the cultivation of resistance to that very production and the authority behind it. Even apparent global uniformity and therefore consensus among practitioners may belie more deeply rooted disagreements or conflicts. Many women in the Roman Catholic Church, for example, faithfully and joyfully participate in the practices of the Church—from daily or weekly Mass, to corporal works of mercy through service, to the practice of theology, to private devotions such as praying the rosary and daily reading of the lectionary or breviary.

Many of these very practitioners, however, may simultaneously find deeply problematic the Church's position on ordination. Within this context, practices that embody consent
may also serve as practices of critique and resistance. As Bell
notes, "ritual *can* be a strategic way to 'traditionalize'...but
in so doing it can also challenge and renegotiate the very
basis of tradition to the point of upending what had been
seen as fixed previously or by other groups."[41]

Moreover, a fuller account will likewise explore the rich
diversity that has characterized the Christian life from the
beginning. Just as configuration resists univocity, so does
deployment. Different sets of schemes are wielded by individuals, whose particular negotiation of appropriation finds
an even wider context of play at the point of engagement.
Schemes incorporated are enacted in an infinite variety of
socio-historical contexts. Thus Bell notes that practical
knowledge "is not an inflexible set of assumptions, beliefs,
or body postures; rather it is the ability to deploy, play, and
manipulate basic schemes in ways that appropriate and condition experience effectively."[42]

This perspective likewise provides those interested in
articulating the connection between liturgy and the
Christian life a critical starting point from which to analyze
what sorts of bodies current liturgical practices are producing, to critique liturgical practices which produce bodies
inconsistent with Christian norms, and to suggest what
types of bodies liturgical practices ought to seek to produce.
By paying particular attention to the sorts of bodies our practices produce, we can ask whether our liturgies simply rein-
force the bodies of worshipers as they have already been
produced by culture, what sorts of culturally produced bodily configurations need first to be deconstructed, and what
sorts of resistance need to be cultivated in diverse cultural
settings. Finally, it may lead to a critique of the lack of
embodiment in our current liturgical practices.

It is indisputable that liturgy in contemporary Western,

white churches has become rather static and minimally embodied.[43] It may be the case that the liturgies of Western Christianity will become more bodily, following the example of the far more embodied liturgical celebrations of African-American and Hispanic churches. In these churches, where embodied participation is not suppressed, one often finds a greater linkage between worship and life. Absent this revision, it may be unlikely that Eucharist will have any significant impact on the lives of parishioners or, therefore, on ethics.

In the end, however, this account provides an alternative way of envisioning the link between Eucharist and ethics. Only bodies reconfigured through Christian practices will be capable of reproducing, through their actions and their lives, the substance of the kingdom and of facilitating the Church's call to discipleship. Only as one participates in the Body does participation in the life of discipleship become possible.

Notes

1. The genesis of this article was a session at the College Theology Society, Forty-Fifth Annual Convention, in June 1999. I am grateful to Elizabeth Newman, Ken Homan, and Paul LeMasters for organizing the CTS/NABPR Joint Session on "Eucharist and Ethics: A Roundtable Discussion." I would also like to thank my co-panelists, Gary Macy, Barry Harvey, and Gaile Pohlhaus, for engendering a lively and substantive discussion, and my colleagues Terry Tilley, Dennis Doyle, and Curtis Freeman who read and helpfully commented on earlier drafts of this paper.

2. This phrasing comes from the discussions of the panelists prior to the convention, as we sought to determine a good starting point for the session's conversation.

3. Henri de Lubac, *The Splendour of the Church* (New York: Sheed and Ward, 1956), 92; translation of *Meditation sur l'Eglise* (Paris: Aubier, 1953). See also de Lubac, *Corpus Mysticum* (Paris: Aubier, 1949). In his classic double formula, de Lubac uses the term "fait," as in "fait l'Eucharistie" and "fait l'Eglise." "Fait" can be translated either as

"makes" or "produces"; in the following, I will take the liberty of using "produces." For further explication of de Lubac's claim, in dialogue with the ecclesiology of John Zizioulas, see Paul McPartlan, *The Eucharist Makes the Church* (Edinburgh: T&T Clark, 1993). I am grateful to Dennis Doyle for introducing me to McPartlan's work.

4. 1 Corinthians 10:16; 12:27.

5. I am indebted to Curtis W. Freeman for helping me to articulate this more precisely.

6. The beginning of serious efforts to attend to the relationship between liturgy and ethics among theological ethicists is marked by a plenary at the annual meeting of the Society of Christian Ethics in 1979, which featured papers by Paul Ramsey and Donald Saliers and a response by Margaret Farley (see *JRE* 7/2 [1979]). However, liturgical theologians staked out this territory much earlier and more extensively than the ethicists, due to the influence of the work of Virgil Michel and the Catholic Liturgical Movement as well as the initiative for liturgical renewal following the Second Vatican Council. These influences, combined with the Catholic Social Encyclical tradition, have resulted in a heavy—indeed, almost exclusive—focus in this literature on the topic of social justice and the transformation of society.

7. Marva Dawn, "Worship and Ethics," *Dialog* 32 (1993): 300; see also John T. Pawlikowski, "Worship after the Holocaust: An Ethician's Reflections," *Worship* 58 (1984): 321, and Rembert G. Weakland, "Liturgy and Social Justice," in *Shaping English Liturgy*, ed. Peter C. Finn and James M. Schellman (Washington, DC: Pastoral Press, 1990), 347. Dawn further notes, "various elements of worship create certain perspectives and understandings about God and specific attitudes and habits of being which affect how we think, speak, and act" (297). R. Kevin Seasoltz in "Liturgy and Social Consciousness," in *To Do Justice and Right Upon the Earth*, ed. Mary E. Stamps (Collegeville, MN: Liturgical Press, 1993), 54, suggests that "the liturgy as ritual behavior is itself a way of coming to know theologically." That is, liturgy assists people in developing "a right understanding of theology." Less specifically, some see the function of liturgy as "raising consciousness" (see Pawlikowski, 321 and John A. Gurrieri, "Catholic Liturgical Sources of Social Commitment," in *Liturgical Foundations of Social Policy in the Catholic and Jewish Traditions*, ed. Daniel F. Polish and Eugene J. Fisher (Notre Dame, IN: University of Notre Dame Press, 1983), 31.

8. Geoffrey Wainwright, "Eucharist and/as Ethics," *Worship* 62 (1988): 134, 136; see also Geoffrey Wainwright, "Between God and World: Worship and Mission," in Kenneth Stevenson, ed., *Liturgy Reshaped* (London: SPCK, 1982), 107, and Seasoltz, 56.

9. Seasoltz, 55. Paul Wadell, "What Do All These Masses Do For Us? Reflections on the Christian Moral Life and the Eucharist," in *Living No Longer for Ourselves,* ed. Kathleen Hughes and Mark R. Francis (Collegeville, MN: Liturgical Press, 1991), 163, for example, describes "the Eucharist as a training in moral vision...as the ritual activity through which a people's vision is cleansed and healed. More strongly put, through worshiping together in Eucharist, we should gradually take on God's view of things." Vigen Guroian concurs: "The church must strive to transform perception and understanding of what is morally at stake in the lives people lead." "Tradition and Ethics: Prospects in a Liberal Society," *Modern Theology* 7 (1991): 223. Guroian further suggests, 221, that liturgy be understood as iconic: "Liberal agency models almost never speak of attraction but rather of argument, persuasion, and power in their efforts to describe the nature of the church and its mission. The emphasis of such agency theory is on reason and will, whereas the theology of the icon takes into account imagination, perception, and interpretation. The power of the icon, writes Anthony Ugolnik, is in its capacity 'to prepare the believer to look outward, even into the secular world, to find the image of the Creator. This claim on the imagination will allow the very act of interpretation, the structures of meaning that the Christian assigns to the world and experience, to transfigure the culture of his or her people.'"

10. As Donald E. Saliers notes in "Liturgy and Ethics: Some New Beginnings," *JRE* 7 (1979): 174: "The concretization of the moral life requires a vision of a world, and the continuing exercise of recalling, sustaining, and reentering that picture of the cosmos in which norms and practices have meaning and point.... In short, the possibility of religious ethics...rests upon available *mythoi*–stories and narratives of human existence in which a picture of the moral good and associated ideas are expressed."

11. Wadell, 159. Wadell's discussion parallels Ramsey's appropriation of the work of Hans Frei. Ramsey, "Liturgy and Ethics," *JRE* 7 (1979): 147, notes: "Perhaps it is also the task of Christian ethics to 'recreate a universe of discourse' and 'put the reader in the middle of it, instructing him in the use of that language by showing how—extensively, and not only by stating the rules and principles of the discourse.' This seems to me remarkably like the task of 'liturgics' as well." More generally it is held that Christian narratives so learned can be juxtaposed to those of the world, challenging contemporary ideologies and offering an alternative point of departure for construing the world; see, for example, Vigen Guroian, "Seeing Worship as Ethics: An Orthodox Perspective," *JRE* 13 (1985): 354.

12. H. Kathleen Hughes, "Liturgy and Justice: An Intrinsic Relationship," in Hughes and Francis, 45-46. Saliers, "Liturgy and Ethics," 175, notes: "the relations between liturgy and ethics are most adequately formulated by specifying how certain affections and virtues are formed and expressed in the modalities of communal prayer and ritual action. These modalities of prayer enter into the formation of the self in community." In keeping with the formula of *lex orandi lex credendi*, Saliers deems liturgical actions as "the rule-keeping activities of the affections [desires, emotions, attitudes, beliefs, and actions]" (179, 1740; see also Don E. Saliers, "Symbol in Liturgy, Liturgy in Symbol: The Domestication of Liturgical Experience," in *The Awakening Church: 25 Years of Liturgical Renewal*, ed. Lawrence J. Madden (Collegeville, MN: Liturgical Press, 1992), 78. Elsewhere, liturgy is seen to shape character (Dawn, 302), virtues (Guroian, "Seeing Worship as Ethics," 338), moral sensitivies or sensibilities (Pawlikowski, 321; Gurrieri, 24), effect a "change of heart" (Gurrieri, 24), and provide motivation (Weakland, 355).

13. Seasoltz, 54; see also Guroian, "Seeing Worship as Ethics," 343.

14. Seasoltz, 50.

15. Ramsey, 146; see also Ralph A. Kiefer, "Liturgy and Ethics: Some Unresolved Dilemmas," in Hughes and Francis, 69. Likewise, Seasoltz holds, 54: "Liturgical celebration is like a dress rehearsal for the end time. We put on Christ and act and relate to one another as Christ relates to us." For Saliers, "Liturgy and Ethics," 175, 176, 179, 188, it is this dramatic dimension that impacts affectivity: "Beliefs about God and world and self which characterize a religious life are dramatized and appropriated in the mode of the affections and dispositions focused in liturgical occasions.... In the very activity of re-presenting and rehearsing features of existence described in the Scriptures, worshipers articulate their fundamental relations to one another and to the world.... The exercise of such affects requires a continual re-entry of the person in to the narrative and teachings that depict the identity of Jesus Christ.... Liturgy is the non-utilitarian enactment of the drama of the divine-human encounter."

16. Guroian, "Seeing Worship as Ethics," 342-343. This critique ought not suggest that I do not value Guroian's work, which has been so important for my own.

17. Ibid., 343.

18. To what might this oversight be attributed? While a thorough analysis of this issue is beyond the scope of this paper, a number of issues may be compounding traditional suspicions of the body. These

accounts may well presuppose Cartesian or Romantic anthropologies that equate individual identity with mind or feeling. Experiential-expressivist accounts of religion may also be operative as well as accounts of "ethics" that privilege rationality, intention, or will. Moreover, these accounts present precisely the epistemological assumptions criticized by Roberto Goizueta in his article included in this volume, "A Ressourcement from the Margins: U.S. Latino Popular Catholicism as Lived Religion" (see above, 3-37). Over and over again, the language employed presupposes a pre-existent, autonomous realm of beliefs or reality separate from the rites that embody them; the idea is to "get at" what is "behind" the rites. A slight variation on this theme, liturgy is portrayed as the medium that synthesizes or reinte-grates these separated entities insofar as participants narratively or dramaturgically "act out," express, or perform these conceptual orien-tations. This bifurcation between belief/feeling and action belies an epistemological breach between sign and signified, appearance and reality, form and content, truth and meaning. Catherine Bell, *Ritual Theory, Ritual Practice* (New York: Oxford University Press, 1992) like-wise criticizes the field of ritual theory on these same grounds. Ritual theory, Bell argues, is premised on the assumption that thought and action stand in a bifurcated, dichotomous relationship with "thought" being accorded a privileged, autonomous status (19). A danger in such bifurcation, she notes, is that "one might accept beliefs but not the rit-ual activities associated with them...therefore, 'beliefs could exist without rituals; rituals, however, could not exist without beliefs.'" Moreover, as action becomes subordinated to thought, actors (i.e., those who participate in the rituals) become subordinated to the thinkers (i.e., the scholars and analysts).

19. Louis-Marie Chauvet, "Liturgy and the Body: Editorial," in *Liturgy and the Body*, ed. Louis-Marie Chauvet and Francois Kabasele Lumbala, [Concilium 1995/3] (Maryknoll: Orbis, 1995), viii.

20. In making this claim, I do not want to counter reductionisms of the mind and affections with a reductionism of the body. Certainly cogni-tive, affective, and communal dimensions of liturgy, Eucharist, and other Christian practices remain important. My account presumes this but focuses on the body in order to compensate for its erasure else-where. My thanks to Beth Newman for making me clarify this.

21. Two additional analogies are those of music and dance; both can be construed so as to capture the *corps* dimension as outlined below, although they do not present as clearly how the body serves as the site at which power is contested. Paul Connerton details the former in *How Societies Remember* (New York: Cambridge University Press, 1989), 91-

92. As his work suggests, different types of music—jazz, classical, grunge rock—will produce different types of bodies. I am grateful to Philip Thompson for bringing this very useful book to my attention. For a discussion of dance, see Arthur W. Frank, "For a Sociology of the Body: An Analytical Review," in *The Body: Social Process and Cultural Theory*, ed. M. Featherstone, M. Hepworth, and B. Turner (Newbury Park, CA: Sage Publications, 1991), 36-102. Furthermore, ascetic practices remained central to the Christian life beyond the period of persecution in the early Church, but clearly, they served to reconfigure bodies differently as the identity of the Church, and the nature of that which threatened it, changed. For one example, see Patricia Cox Miller, "Desert Asceticism and 'the Body from Nowhere,'" *Journal of Early Christian Studies* 2/2 (1994): 137-153 on how the later practices of desert asceticism, which from one perspective could be construed as rejecting and disfiguring the body, aimed at least in part at producing "angelic" bodies.

22. For an illuminating account of this process see Dave Grossman, *On Killing: The Psychological Cost of Learning to Kill in War and Society*, ed. by G. Kloske (New York: Little Brown and Co., 1996).

23. This analogy shows why it ought to be impossible for Christians to serve in the military, a point brought to my attention by Leslie (Bud) Gerber.

24. This latter "team" dimension is where some athletic analogies will break down, especially those activities that most average, ordinary Americans participate in, such as "working out," aerobics, or (like myself) running. Anyone who takes part in these sorts of activities regularly will recognize how the practices, slowly and over time, produce one's body (we become capable of doing things formerly "impossible"); these sorts of things become second nature. However, as practices of contemporary culture, they are highly individualistic, even if engaged in with a group (e.g., an aerobics class or a running club). Unless, that is, one construes them as supporting the *corps* of the market (aerobics's embodiment of aesthetic standards of consumption) or the state (running's embodiment of fitness as a public health endeavor).

25. Maureen A. Tilley, "The Ascetic Body and the (Un)Making of the World of the Martyr," *Journal of the American Academy of Religion* 59 (1991): 471-474.

26. Ibid., 470. As Dennis Doyle observed, this echoes the breathing training in Lamaze.

27. Ibid., 474. As Tilley notes, voluntary martyrs "tried to run a marathon before learning to walk."

28. Again, I focus solely on bodily practices here simply for purposes of emphasis. Bodies, of course, are situated at the nexus of practices, discourses, and institutions, the latter two of which are likewise crucial to the production of bodies. (See Frank.) A more comprehensive account of bodily production would require consideration of the roles of discourses and institutions, with special attention to the issues of authority and power.

29. De Lubac, *Corpus Mysticum*, 292.

30. Second Vatican Ecumenical Council, 1963. *The Constitution on the Sacred Liturgy (Sacrosanctum Concilium)* in A. Flannery, ed., *Vatican Council II: The Conciliar and Post Conciliar Documents, Study Edition* (Northport, NY: Costello Publishing Co., 1986), no. 2.

31. Ibid., no. 10.

32. Brigid O'Shea Merriman, *Searching for Christ: The Spirituality of Dorothy Day* (Notre Dame: University of Notre Dame Press, 1994), 97, comments on the centrality of the Mass for Day's vision of the Catholic Worker: "Dorothy…in addressing a group of would-be Catholic Workers in the early 1940s admonished them that 'the Mass is the Work!'" Day's own words, as found in "The Council and the Mass," *Catholic Worker* 29 (September 1962): 2, richly resonate the link between liturgy and life, in terms most corporeal: "[The Mass brings] us into the closest of all contacts with our Lord Jesus Christ, enabling us literally to 'put on Christ,' as St. Paul said, and to begin to say with Him, 'Now, not I live but Jesus Christ in me.' With a strong consciousness of this, we remember too those lines 'without Me, ye can do nothing,' and 'with Me you can do all things'…Only by nourishing ourselves as we have been bidden to do by Christ, by eating His body and drinking His blood, can we become Christ and put on the new man" (cited in Merriman, 98). This linkage in her thought and life reflect in part, no doubt, her friendship with Virgil Michel.

33. Bell, 98. As will be clear, this section draws heavily on Bell's work.

34. Ibid., 93.

35. Ibid., 100, citing Roy A. Rappaport, *Ecology, Meaning, and Religion* (Richmond, CA: North Atlantic Books, 1979), 200. Stephen Buckland, in "Ritual, Body and Cultural Memory," in Chauvet and Lumbala, 51, marshals a similar argument in order to challenge the epistemological bifurcation of action and "meaning." Arguing that actions themselves are productive, he maintains: "theories which speak of symbols as 'standing for' or 'representing' something else inevitably suggest that the meaning of a ritual is to be discovered 'behind' the action, in what it 'represents'…. But gestures or postures, like words, do not acquire

meaning simply in the sense of correlating a meaning which lies 'behind' them; their meaning is negotiated in and through the practices in which they are found."

36. I am grateful to Terry Tilley for this example.

37. I am here construing Eucharist in its broadest sense, as the Liturgy of the Word in conjunction with the Liturgy of the Eucharist in the Mass.

38. I include testimony in recognition of our Baptist colleagues of the National Association of Baptist Professors of Religion who greatly enriched this conference by meeting concurrently with the College Theology Society and co-sponsoring this session.

39. Chauvet, 31. Buckland concurs: "From its earliest moments a child is taught how to control and use [its body...] Through such practices which shape its body, a child develops and expresses its own individuality and comes at the same time to incorporate the identity of its family, class, and community.... Through such habitual bodily practices, the experiences of previous generations are 'sedimented' in bodies. Through such practices, a body 're-members' its identity. That is to say, it discovers and reinvents, enforces, and reinforces its identity," 51.

40. At least, for most of us. God, of course, does retain the prerogative of the "instantaneous infusion" method.

41. Bell, 124.

42. Ibid., 221.

43. As Jyoti Sahi, "The Body in Search of Interiority," in Chauvet and Lumbala, 92, notes: "Christian forms of liturgical action have often been dominated by the need to listen to the Word of God. So we note that as the verbal dimension becomes more and more important the physical participation of the worshiper recedes in value. The worshiper is expected just to sit still...it is a passive state, which is meant to allow the individual to listen more attentively to what is spoken. The body, as far as possible, is meant to be ignored."

Part IV
PRAYER AND
TRANSFORMATION

Praying When Troubled: Retrieving Boethius and Aquinas

Edward Jeremy Miller
Professor of Religious Studies
Gwynedd Mercy College

Are there many questions more apropos the theme of our volume, lived Christianity, than that perennially poignant quandary: Why do bad things happen to good people and does it make sense to pray about it? If you do not believe in God, then the matter of bad things afflicting you can feel more stoical than poignant. Why my troubles? "Well, good and bad stuff happens. It's a mixed bag. Chance deals us good cards and bad cards in the game of life, and sometimes we're dealt a very bad hand. So brace up and await fate's next shuffle of the cards." But if you are Christian and trust in God's guidance and loving care, then this stoical sense of an ever-changing fate cannot be your answer.[1]

Perennial quandaries tend to attract to themselves the great minds of a tradition. It behooves us then, as engaged in "lived Christianity" today, to retrieve what astute thinkers of our Christian past have written on such matters. Regarding being afflicted by bad things and believing in God and wondering how praying fits in, I want to invoke Boethius (480-525) and Thomas Aquinas (1225-1274). At the outset I state my conclusion: Boethius articulates the quandary of fate, human freedom, and providence. Even though his answer is, to my mind, only covering God's foreknowledge of earthly affairs, he asserts the need to pray to God in the very last lines of his argument. Everything preceding this abrupt insertion, nevertheless, is argued brilliantly and merits recounting now. Thomas Aquinas adopted key points practically carte blanche. Going beyond Boethius's effort, however, Aquinas treated the matter of God's will and intentionality. If God not only knows the future but wishes good to occur, what use is praying if evil happens notwithstanding, especially those evils called sins? Aquinas offered an answer.

The realization that many readers of this journal are college religion professors was one reason prompting me to select Boethius and Aquinas in the hope these two luminaries can get greater exposure among undergraduates. Aquinas's scholastic terminology has confused and put off readers, and he is seldom read today. Theologians tend to know Boethius through his few theological tractates that gave to the later middle ages celebrated definitions of trinitarian terms such as persona; regrettably, they leave to philosophers to teach Boethius's greatest writing, *The Consolation of Philosophy*. Yet it is the *Consolatio*, the most read book of the middle ages after Jerome's Vulgate Bible, that lays out the issues of evil and divine providence so very well and which I am recommending as a classroom primary text.[2]

I propose to give the main lines of Boethius's argument, its skeletal structure as it were, and I am assuming that the full text will be read to flesh out the argument's cogency. There are other ways to be enlightened by this classic and intoxicating text. For instance, Boethius adopted the genre of a *consolatio*, a philosophic reflection on an illness of soul along with a suggested remedy, and one can analyze the personified figure of healing philosophic insight, Lady Philosophy, who comes to console Boethius as he awaits an unjust execution.[3] Since this text became so seminal to later medieval literature, e.g., Chaucer's *The Canterbury Tales*, one can also analyze the literary forms that were adopted centuries later, such as the wheel of fortune (fate), the dream vision, and the feminine sage figure. It shall be the lineaments of the predominantly Neo-Platonic but occasionally Aristotelian philosophic argument that interest me now.

Boethius structured the *Consolation* into five books, and they provide a useful way to lay out his argument in steps.[4] Book I depicts his predicament, and although Boethius never uses biblical or Christian images throughout the book, his cry is Job's: Woe is me! What have I done to deserve all these troubles? As he tearfully puzzles fortune's[5] "trustless countenance" (35), a woman appears, of wise years but youthful vigor, whose height reached to the heavens. Lady Philosophy is like a nurse come to heal his sickness of soul, and she will question and prod Boethius in the manner of Socratic teaching throughout the five books, wherein insight becomes effective medicine for his kind of soul-sickness. Having gotten Boethius to admit that the world is subject to divine reason, Lady Philosophy concludes Book I with her diagnosis of his illness, amnesia:

> You have forgotten your true nature. And so I have found out in full the reason for your sickness and the way to approach the task of restoring you to health....It is because you don't know the end and purpose of things that you think the wicked and the criminal have power and happiness. And because you have forgotten the means by which the world is governed you believe these ups and downs of fortune happen haphazardly (51).

Throughout Book II Lady Philosophy leads Boethius gently but methodically to the conclusion that true happiness cannot consist in fickle fortune. Fortune has brought him good and bad things in life. Adopting the persona of fortune, the Lady confesses that "inconstancy is my very essence"

(57). Book II's underlying question becomes: What can fortune's ever-turning wheel not budge? "When a being
endowed with a godlike quality in virtue of his rational
nature thinks that his only splendor lies in the possession of
inanimate goods, it is the overthrow of the natural order"
(67). Boethius must look elsewhere for sure footing, and true
to his Neo-Platonic bent, it involves looking within himself.

Having thus reminded Boethius of his true nature, which
is to have a mind made in God's image—recall this is one of
his three amnesias that Lady Philosophy promised to heal—
she embarks upon proving to him that material goods, political power, riches, and pampering one's body cannot bring
true happiness. (To anyone who will use the *Consolation* in
the classroom, I alert you to the text's frequent reference to
the notion of possessing. In Book II, possessing inanimate
things will eventually disappoint you. In Book III, one must
possess the source of happiness to be happy oneself.)

The argument's movement in Book III can be somewhat
difficult to grasp, especially for undergraduates, because its
cogency lies in appreciating the Neo-Platonic principle of
participation, a manner of thinking that does not come readily. This schema should help. What is happiness's cause and
pattern, Book III begins? It must consist in the perfect
expression of whatever is experienced as good and it must
satiate one's questing for it; in other words, it must have the
quality of self-sufficiency. To be without wants, which
wealth seems to provide, to have power, to have fame, and
to possess pleasure seem to be patterns of happiness people
seek, but each of these goals in itself is possessed of fragility.
(I have found undergraduates respond readily to the Socratic
dialogue on 83–4 arguing that wealth cannot bring true happiness.)

If a being existed that is all powerful, universally rever-
enced, without wants, and possessing such qualities all
together and not one after another, it would be supremely
happy, and we would be truly happy if we possessed that

being. Such being cannot be found in our changeable world; it can only be God. As we become just by possessing justice, we become happy by possessing divinity, not becoming gods ourselves by nature but becoming godlike by participation (102). A heady notion to be sure, but it is crucial to the following idea that is a bridge to Book IV. Toward God's goodness all things incline and fall under divinity's sway (112-14); note the Platonic ascent motif in the Orpheus/Eurydice poem supporting Lady Philosophy's contention.

With Book IV we move into the grip of our quandary. In spite of a divinely good helmsman guiding the world, evil exists, goes unchecked, and even tramples the good, objects Boethius; Lady Philosophy retorts that sin gets punished and virtuous people are rewarded (116). (It is not until the final assertion concluding Book V, which I shall quote in full, that I find any warrant, if proof it be, of this step of the argument.)

As she moves towards an important definition, Lady Philosophy lays some groundwork. Good deeds are always rewarded and crimes always punished because "the goal of every action [is] its reward" (124). Does not wicked activity, she asks, make one inhuman, and does not goodness elevate a person to being more godlike? Further, one should not doubt that "a good power rules the world and that everything happens aright" (133). In justification, she clears up a misleading use of words. The causes of events and their mutual influence one on the other spring from the unchanging mind of God. This plan, viewed as rooted in God's knowledge, is called providence. When one views the movement of events themselves within the plan, it is called fate (135). It is a mistake to think of fate (fortune) as chance; rather, it is the working out of God's pervasive plan for everything. Corollaries follow: Providence apprehends what suits each one and applies it to the person (138). All things are created in God's image and are aligned toward their source (141). Finally, all acts of apparent fortune are ultimately a rewarding of virtue and a punishment of vice (142, 144). Recalling Boethius's second amnesia from Book I, that he had lost sight of the goal of all things, we have in Book IV his second cure.

Book V reminds me of Euclid's technique in mathematics. One does not see the upshot of all that has gone before until the last premises are introduced. In the *Consolation* these involve human freedom and apparent coercion. Boethius begins Book V pressing Lady Philosophy to deal with what seem to common sense to be accidental or chance events and therefore the unraveling of any pervasive divine plan. Yes, she responds, people commonly think this way when, for example, one person hides a treasure in a field and another person, digging later, chances upon it.[6] The prior burying and the later digging are coincidences, and viewed at the ground level called common sense are chance events, but viewed from the higher vantage of God's plan these two events proceed from its "inescapable nexus of causation" (148).

Given this web of planned causalities, are people free or are they like manipulated puppets? The third segment of Book V (cf. footnote 2) puts on Boethius's lips all manner of objections why genuine human freedom is incompatible with providence, a divine plan knowing and causing all outcomes. I want to note two of the objections because they mention praying and anticipate prayer's treatment at book's end. If everything is foreordained by a fixed necessity, it makes a mockery of rewards and punishments and of praying in hope (153). If prayer is futile, moreover, it severs our linkage with God (154).

Lady Philosophy supplies the argument's linchpin at the start: the human reasoning process does not manifest the immediacy of God's way of knowing (155), an insight that was anticipated in the beautiful poem which preceded Boethius's litany of objections, comparing God to the sun. "What is, what was, what is to be/ In *one swift glance* His

mind can see" (150, emphasis mine). Some highly philosophic moves now follow, mostly along Aristotelian lines.[7]

There are different levels of knowledge, but the differences are not based upon what is known but upon the different ways of knowing. We are being invited to examine the
knower and not the objects known. The same round ball is
perceived as spherical in one manner by sight and another
manner by touch, and similarly via other levels of human
awareness such as through memory or by intellectual insight
(157). In analogous fashion, there is a way of knowing proper to God, and we are no more privy to it than is an animal
who can also see round things privy to grasping what is the
definition of the spherical, as human reason does.

Human reason informs us of the following fact about
itself: the outcomes of certain natural phenomena can be pre-
dicted, such as this dropped apple will fall straight down;
the outcomes of human choices cannot be forecasted.
Wondering about God, accordingly, "human reason refuses
to believe that divine intelligence can see the future in any
other way except that in which human reason has knowledge. This is how the argument runs: if anything does not
seem to have any certain and predestined occurrence, it cannot be foreknown as a future event" (162). But if a future
event, like a free human choice, is foreknown—and a divine
plan directing the world is foreknowing—then our human
choices are necessitated by some forceful divine sway as
invisible and as ineluctable as gravitation on the proverbial
apple.[8]

God's knowing, however, works differently from human
knowing. God exists eternally, and in eternity God is a
knowing God. The *Consolation*'s most crucial definition follows: "Eternity is the complete, simultaneous and perfect
possession of everlasting life."[9] The Watts translation misses
the mark somewhat. Eternity is the full, all-at-once, perfect
possessing of unending life, a life and therefore a knowing
without before and after. Boethius's eternity is not perpetu-

ity or the unendingness of one moment after another. It is all-
at-onceness! What is future, or past, or now to us is simply
now to God. This insight will undo the conundrum that
foreknowledge of the future implies necessitated outcomes.

Boethius's illustration captures the subtlety of the insight.
A person is mortal. It is necessary that persons die (or that
dropped apples fall), given the nature of matter. These outcomes are necessarily predictable, even by human reason,
for mortals (and apples) are impelled to their outcomes by
what Boethius calls a simple necessity. A person walking
illustrates a quite different necessity in human knowing. I
am viewing the person walking. I necessarily know that the
person is walking, because what is happening is actually
present to my knowing, informing, and necessitating it. But
my necessitated and infallible knowledge of the person
walking, called a conditional necessity by Boethius,[10] does
not impose necessity on the person, who in fact has freely
chosen to walk and easily could have chosen otherwise
(167).

With this distinction we have reached the *Consolation's*
apex, or to use the Euclidean image, the last premise. With
an eternal knowledge, in which past, present, and future
human choices are known in the divine "now," God knows
all and God's plan "with one glance anticipates and
embraces your changes in its constancy" (168). God knows
your future but you remain free to make your future.

We are but a dozen lines from the book's end. Has
Boethius engaged fully the quandary? I think not but here is
what he says to tie matters together:

> And since this is so, man's freedom of will
> remains inviolate and the law does not impose
> reward and punishment unfairly, because the will
> is free from all necessity. God has foreknowledge
> and rests a spectator from on high of all things;
> and as the ever present eternity of His vision dis-
> penses reward to the good and punishment to the

bad, it adapts itself to the future quality of our actions. Hope is not placed in God in vain and prayers are not made in vain, for if they are the right kind they cannot but be efficacious. Avoid vice, therefore, and cultivate virtue; lift up your mind to the right kind of hope, and put forth humble prayers on high. A great necessity is laid upon you, if you will be honest with yourself, a great necessity to be good, since you live in the sight of a judge who sees all things (168–9).

Boethius deals with God's knowledge, Neo-Platonist that he is. The quandary of evil and the value of praying, while touched by what I consider brilliant Boethian reasoning, cut deeper than he goes, because they go to our wondering what God not only is eternally knowing but also is eternally willing. Does God want evil things, by which most people mean, does God tolerate them? Does our praying not only cue us into what God's plan might be—and such is surely one purpose of praying—does it also affect God's will and intentions for us and for the world? I tell my students, "prayer is honest talk." Talking is not only to inform others what we know and ascertain what they know; we talk to influence their behavior, their free will! How, then, does God's will figure in? Boethius does not tread here; Thomas Aquinas does.[11]

About a half-dozen basic concepts underlie the philosophy and theology of Thomas Aquinas,[12] and the concept apropos our topic is causality. Aquinas uses the word cause in a wider and more supple manner than we tend to use it. A hammer causes a nail to enter the wood. Aquinas calls the hammer an efficient cause, an instrumental efficient cause more precisely, and we think of it as a cause in the same way; the carpenter is the real cause, but the hammer helps him. There are three other uses of cause for Aquinas. The artist decides to paint a particular picture; the "idea" of the picture in the artist's imagination, with all its attendant emotional overtones, is the final cause of the picture. The type of brush, the kind of paint, and the texture of the painting surface are material causes for Aquinas. "Human embryos gestate toward becoming viable outside the womb" is an illustration of a formal cause; its very nature, called by Aquinas its "human form," impels and orchestrates billions of events in precise succession to happen in utero and finally to take leave of it. When we use the word cause, we tend to limit it to efficient cause, but to present Aquinas's ideas below, I am using it in the broader manner he did.

Aquinas adopts the central insight of Boethius that reconciled God's knowledge of our past, present, and future with our freedom of choice. God knows in a necessarily true and infallible manner what we will do in the future without causing us to be necessarily programmed to do it, because God exists in eternity as knower. Aquinas was led to coin the technical word "presentiality"[13] to describe how God knows our future, freely decided choices as always present to divine awareness, but Boethius's more poetic "God's one swift glance" retains its own appeal.

If the analysis went only this far, one could charge Boethius[14] (and this portion of Aquinas) with the indictment: your God seems only to know the future but does not seem to create the future; furthermore, I would wish my prayers to shape my future and influence God's purposes, especially regarding my and others' final salvation.

God not only knows the future, writes Aquinas, but also wills it, and the most important instance for human beings is that God wills all people to be saved. This is surely difficult to keep before our mind confidently when evils strike us to such an extent as to doubt whether God is loving and caring or is even present at all. Before hearing Aquinas on whether praying for salvation, or even for "relief," is worthwhile, we must hear him on God's will. Do God's intentions for us impose necessity on our behavior and can they be thwarted?

In the sixth article of question nineteen of the first part of his *Summa Theologiae*, Aquinas begins with the biblical teaching (1 Timothy 2:4) that God wills all persons to be saved, and it would seem that whatever God desires necessarily happens; otherwise, God's will is enfeebled or ineffective.

It is true, he says, that whatever God wills, God causes to come into existence, similar to an artist bringing into existence what was artistically imagined; the realities are synonymous: "what God wills" equals "what God causes to exist." Aquinas phrases it more cryptically: the divine will is causative.

Furthermore the world that God has willed into existence is a non-static world; all reality and especially human reality is active and purposeful and effectual. Therefore the created realities God has willed into existence are imbued with causalities, formal causes, material causes, final causes, whatever. If for Gerard Manley Hopkins "the world is charged with the grandeur of God," for Aquinas it is just as wondrous because the world abounds with causes, with realities exercising causalities. Even more intriguing in Aquinas's vision of creation is that these causes are ever interacting, are situated at different levels of importance and even can "fail" along their causal lines, and all this welter of active creation reflects the goodness and wisdom of its Creator.

Of this welter of causes operating in creation, the category of primary and secondary causes is used in question 19, article 6, to answer the question: Is God's will always fulfilled? I offer my own illustration of this odd-sounding category of primary/secondary causes. A chef cooks a meal. What has to happen? The meat must be tenderized. The fire can't be too hot. The ingredients for the Béarnaise sauce must be added in correct order (the tarragon chopped correctly, the egg yolks added at the right speed and over a correct heat) and so forth, and this is just preparing part of the entrée. The cook is the primary cause, but there are many secondary causes operating: the heat, the freshness of this, the dryness of that, the amount of this or that spice, and on it goes. Could any one of those secondary causes "fail" on the chef? Perhaps not often but from time to time this ingredient or that cooking utensil doesn't work as hoped.

Let me increase the complexity of an illustration, and it will bring us closer to Aquinas's issues in article 6. Take a large economic organization, a business. The primary cause, the one with the vision of the ultimate purpose, is its CEO. Secondary human causes are all of the people working for the company. The CEO directs the employees, a primary cause directing secondary causes. Granted that it is not the mechanistic way the chef "directs" kitchen ingredients, it is a primary/secondary relationship whose secondary causes can "fail." Not only can a person or group not meet expectations, they can actually and intentionally undermine expectations.

In Aquinas's view of God willing salvation to each human being within a providential plan, God is the primary cause and human beings are secondary causes. They are very noble and unique secondary causes because human beings exercise causality in freedom, and they alone within God's material creation are free agents. There is another category Aquinas uses in article 8 of the same question to distinguish causes,[15] and it is apropos this dimension of freedom: necessary causes vs. contingent causes. Human beings are called contingent causes because what they choose freely is not necessitated to a particular outcome. Necessary causes beget determined effects (passing an electric current through water produces oxygen and twice as much hydrogen, always). Contingent causes produce effects but not determinedly. What issues from a free choice is one such contingent effect; events that occur randomly in the realm of nature are other instances.

At the pivotal point of his reflection on God's causative will, Aquinas uses these two categories to express his insight. Salvation comes from God alone. God is its primary cause. God's causative reach stretches throughout a web of secondary causes as it touches me (my parents who taught me, the evangelists who wrote down apostolic preachings, and so forth).[16] I, too, am a secondary cause in a human community to which God is willing (and causing) salvation. Secondary causes can fail, however. One would wish that this web of causalities affecting me and affected by me is where grace and goodness alone exist, but no. Sin happens. My exercise of free choice can consciously resist God's willing of salvation to me, can undermine it, and can be detrimental to others.

Aquinas's next step is subtle. God, as the primary cause, acts on secondary causes according to their nature and not with violence to them. God's saving action on human beings has to be in and through and supportive of freedom, because remaining free is basic to what it means to be human at all. If God has willed into existence so-called contingent causes, such as human beings acting freely, God's primary causality operating on human secondary causes must be in and through their contingency remaining contingent. As enigmatic as such Thomism may sound, remember what Christian faith on this matter demands: God alone saves. I do not save myself. I am not saved against my will. I am not passive to my being saved.

If it were to come to pass that not everyone is saved, it would not mean that God's will was not fulfilled in those who die unsaved. A secondary cause can fail the primary cause's intention, as stated above. God's willing of salvation, which is but the gift of grace, cannot coerce the sinner's freedom to resist grace, even this person's resistance to the very end of life. God's justice must recognize this state of affairs. As it is "owed" human nature that it remain free and uncoerced, even by God, recognition is "owed," even by God, to how individual lives dispose of themselves through lifelong free choices. The salvation of some and not of unrepentant sinners is "owed" the order of God's justice; the salvation of any is "owed" the order of God's mercy. God's will is to be

merciful and just in the plan of salvation, and it is always fulfilled.

Connecting this insight to an eternal plan of salvation that
embraces "in one swift glance" all that happens in our lives
until our deaths, God's unlimited mercy in the will-to-save
expresses itself like "the hound of heaven" in Francis
Thompson's poem. God's saving causative will for us is
never put off by acts of misused freedom (sins); rather, these
sins are countered by the sundry divine measures that also
approach us within our inviolate realms of freedom inviting
repentance and amends. To sum up, if secondary causes can
fail (but need not), that is to say, if persons can misuse their
freedom against God's will to save (but ought not), then this
webbing of various causalities within the plan of salvation is
precisely why praying is needed, why it counts, and why it
works.

In a later part of the *Summa*[17] that discusses multiple
aspects of Christian prayer Aquinas asks whether praying is
worthwhile. His answer incorporates the principle of God's
universal and always effective causality, meaning that nothing is cut off as if sequestered from the imprint of God's
intentions and that the plan of salvation is never "surprised"
by whatever happens, even freely chosen sins. To the intricate and pervasive web of those secondary causes Aquinas
calls acts of human freedom and actions issuing from them,
he includes our choices to have prayed and to have omitted
praying. As every human event is "foreseen" by God in that
every event is eternally "present" to God, so also are present
to God (and thus falling within God's plan) every act of
praying and every gift God has connected to a prayer offered
in hope and devotion.

Does prayer work and "affect" God? Yes it does. "We do
not pray in order to change God's mind. We do pray that we
might secure through prayer that which God has arranged
would have been obtained through prayer." If we are mindful of the many opportunities lost us in our lives due to inac-

tion here or non-communication there, then why cannot there be other giftings of a more salvific nature lost us when we passed up praying even though God had been luring us through our consciences to pray?

It is important that Aquinas's justification for prayer's worthiness not be pushed in rigid fashion to some kind of *reductio ad absurdum*. I refer to a silly implication like "so give up work and give up sleep and pray every waking moment, otherwise you will lose out on something good." Grace builds on nature[18] and the nature of being human is to be reasonable. For Aquinas, the call to grace is never a call to be or to act unreasonably, and this is a principle of the spiritual life not shared by "enthusiasts" but central to Thomistic spirituality. There are times consequently when a Christian ought not to be praying but rather focusing on what is at hand, even if it is quite mundane.

On the other hand, there are moments that particularly invite praying. Moments of savoring God's presence and providence and goodness invite praising. Moments—and some stretch into weeks and months—of feeling troubled invite another style of praying. Does it do anything? The wondering, as I have suggested, has to be directed beyond what God is eternally knowing to what God is eternally willing. Aquinas teaches that the plan of salvation God wills for each one of us takes into account that we must exercise our freedom (to pray or not) and that attached to our choices are outcomes, which from our point of view we effect into existence and from God's eternal vantage had been God's will for us.

We do pray into existence certain gifts of God, that is to say, gifts enter our lives and those of others due to praying. God is the primary cause of gifts, acting in supreme freedom. Our praying has a causal role, too, which does not coerce God into otherwise unintended activity but rather implements what God has both eternally foreseen and eternally willed, as if the plan always and everywhere is taking our free choices into consideration...and always had.[19]

Notes

1. Although I shall use the language of question and answer, as in "Boethius's answer," "Aquinas's answer," etc., divine providence and evil are mysteries. Transcendent realities cannot be squeezed into categorical nomenclatures, except analogously or metaphorically. Thomas R. Heath's book, *In Face of Anguish* (New York: Sheed and Ward, 1966), regrettably out of print, remains one of the finest and most moving reflections on the mystery of evil facing the mystery of God.

2. V. E. Watts has a winning translation of the prose and poetry of the *Consolation of Philosophy* in the Penguin Classics Series (ed. Betty Radice), and my page references are to it. The best Latin text is found in vol. 94 of *Corpus Christianorum Series Latina*, ed. Ludovicus Bieler (Turnholt: Brepols, 1957).

3. See the article of my colleague Donald Duclow, "Perspective and Therapy in Boethius's *Consolation of Philosophy*," *The Journal of Medicine and Philosophy*, 4/3 (1979): 334-342, for a therapeutic interpretation.

4. Boethius's text alternates prose with poetry in the manner of the genre of Menippean satire. Later Latin manuscripts of the text subdivide each chapter into segments, sometimes called *passus* (step) 1, 2, etc., or *metrum* (=the poem) *primum, secundum, et cetera*.

5. The Latin *fortuna* is captured better by the English "fate" or "chance." But given the long history of the "wheel of fortune" (see Watts's footnote on page 56) and such uses as Orff's cantata, *Carmina Burana* [*O Fortuna/velut luna/statu variablis/semper crescis/aut decrescis...* : O fortune, like the changeable moon, ever waxing and waning...], fortune will be kept as the translation.

6. Aquinas takes this same idea but sharpens the lines of causality. Two servants, unaware of each other, are sent to the same place by their master. Their rendezvous seems to them to be by chance, but it was foreseen and caused by their master. See *Summa Theologiae*, I, q.116, a.1. (Henceforth *ST*.)

7. Boethius is a Neo-Platonist, and one senses the shadow of Plotinus throughout the *Consolation*. It must be remembered, however, that Boethius knew Aristotle very well and had intended to translate into Latin the full Aristotelian corpus. He translated a majority of the logical works, and this was the only "Aristotle" known to early medievals.

8. The apple example, and spherical reason before it, are mine but they capture Boethius accurately.

9. The Latin runs: *interminabilis vitae tota simul et perfecta possessio*. The

adverb *simul* is pivotal.

10. I have left the genre of Lady Philosophy as Boethius's alter ego and simply call her insights his.

11. Many are aware that Enlightenment-influenced "modernity" judges the classicism of Boethius and Aquinas to have trodden into areas (the workings of the divine mind) where even angels ought fear to go, and that recent "postmodernism," with its penchant for the pluralism and historicity of thinking, is more hostile to them yet. But these segments of intellectual society are not where common people are. Boethius and Aquinas speak to them if one can peel away the Neo-Platonic and scholastic argot.

12. A very readable introduction to the life of Aquinas and motifs of his writings is Thomas O'Meara, *Thomas Aquinas: Theologian* (Notre Dame, IN: Notre Dame Press, 1997). I, not O'Meara, take responsibility for claiming this or that is fundamental.

13. *ST*, I, q.14, a.13. *"Futura contingentia"* are known by God *secundum suam praesentialitatem*. Rather than saying God knows "future contingents" in this manner, "future freely decided choices" is better even though it loses Aquinas's implication of contingent causality.

14. Boethius does write of God disposing and arranging events in "the plan," but this idea is not developed.

15. *ST* I, 19, 8 asks: Does God's will impose necessity on whatever God has willed into existence? It is with human creatures in their freedom that this article is concerned.

16. If anyone doubts the pervasive web of secondary (human) causes within which we exercise our own humanness, consider this example: A Youngstown man loses his steel job. Why? The company was bought out by another and closed on decision by stockholders. That company is competing against Japanese steel. Japan's market is affected by an economic downturn among Baltic Sea shipbuilders. These are governed by the movement of commodities markets which in turn are constrained by the tariffs created by the U.S. Congress, the EEC, etc. How many decisions made in freedom, driven by noble or selfish reasons, are "connected" to one man's life in northeast Ohio?

17. *ST* II-II, q.83, a.2. These moral and ethical portions of the *Summa Theologiae* reflect Thomas's most mature thought and were composed during his last regency at the University of Paris in the early 1270s.

18. Here is another of what I judge the half dozen or so basic principles undergirding all of Thomas's thinking.

19. The process theism of A. N. Whitehead and his commentators

describes our free actions as being lured by God and that the future unfolds for ourselves and for God. Both these contentions are at strong variance with the theism of Boethius and Aquinas in this paper. Like Aquinas and Boethius, Whitehead is a genius and his insights merit consideration, but in my opinion they do not eviscerate the central insights of classical theism. But this would be the subject of a different essay. I wish to acknowledge the sabbatical support of my college and the Earhart Foundation of Ann Arbor for enabling this effort.

"Do We Drink From An Empty Well?" The Spiritual Exercises and Social Sin

Maria Malkiewicz
Doctoral Candidate in Christian Ethics
University of Notre Dame

When it is necessary to drink so much pain,
when a river of anguish
drowns us,
when we have wept many tears
and they flow like rivers
from our sad eyes,
only then
does the deep hidden sigh of our neighbor
become our own.[1]

State of the Problem and Resources for Renewal

In the last several decades, the language of social sin has
bubbled up from various Latin American liberation theologies, entered into episcopal teaching in Latin America in
Medellin and Puebla, and finally found its way into the mag-
isterial encyclicals of Paul VI and more explicitly in the writings of John Paul II. Although the phrases "social" or
"structural" sin are found in both liberation theology and in

the documents of John Paul II, even a cursory reading of Gustavo Gutiérrez or Jon Sobrino and John Paul II would alert the reader to the fact that these authors are frequently describing different realities and using the phrases with differing theological intent. In fact, in the 1984 "Instruction on Liberation" we see that the concept of sin was one of the major fissures that opened up the debate between liberation theologians and the Vatican, especially the Congregation for the Doctrine of the Faith.[2] Ratzinger, in the 1984 Instruction, argued that the way in which some theologians had described "social sin" appeared to make social sin the primary category and personal sin the derivative and less important category. In response, Ratzinger insisted that social sin is always derivative of personal sin, and that behind every situation of social or structural sinfulness, there are responsible agents committing personal sins.

In this debate over the correct understanding of sin, it appears that the two parties, the magisterium on one hand and liberation theologians on the other, are simply speaking past each other. On the side of the liberation theologians, the use of the language of social sin arises out of concrete experiences of oppression and liberation and responds to a fear that many forms of Catholic devotion have tended to privatize faith, focusing exclusively on the personal dimensions of sin, and thus obscuring or even undermining any political dimension of the Catholic faith. On the side of the magisterium, particularly as represented by John Paul II and Cardinal Ratzinger, there is both a desire to maintain continuity with received tradition and a fear that the liberation theologians have allowed their discourse to be shaped too much by Marxist thought. Related to their worry over the use of Marxist analysis, the magisterium has expressed concern that liberation theologians are in danger of making Christianity into a political movement that replaces the spiritual mission of the church with exclusively temporal demands and promises.[3] For the time being, I would like to begin with the assumption that both of these sets of concerns and fears are legitimate (although it is a separate question as to whether the CDF correctly understood the use of social sin in the writings of the liberation theologians with whom they are concerned).[4]

Theologian Gregory Baum, in an article entitled "Structures of Sin," writes, "It is always surprising to me how quickly certain new theological concepts enter into the church's official social teaching, even though they raise difficult ecclesiological questions for which there are as yet no answers."[5] This observation seems particularly relevant to the increasing attention to social sin and its incorporation into the social encyclicals. Not only has the concept not attained a sufficiently clear and stable theological meaning, but crucial questions, such as the impact that social sin should have on our understanding of baptism and reconciliation, have not been addressed in great detail. In addition, little work has been done to address questions such as: What types of spiritual formation will be necessary to form agents capable of recognizing and responding to social sin? Which of our spiritual traditions are retrievable in light of this heightened awareness of the social dimensions of sin, and how, if at all, should they be altered to take this reality into account? What, if any, are the differences between the way those in the so-called First World and those in the Third should be formed with regard to social sin? These questions seem at least as important to the lived experience of Christians as questions about the precise theological definitions of sin, both personal and social.

Gustavo Gutiérrez, paraphrasing St. Bonaventure, claims that when it comes to spirituality, we all must drink from our own wells, our inherited experiences and traditions.[6] But what does that mean in the U.S. context, particularly in the middle and upper classes of this society, to take seriously both the claims of social sin upon us and the idea that we must drink from our own wells, that we must be willing to hear the gospel in our own context? What are the resources we can reclaim and what insights might we be able to offer out of our own experiences to the understanding of social sin?

This is a rather indirect way to address the debate between liberation theologians and the magisterium, but I would like to suggest that attending to the level of spiritual formation and to the experiences of First World disciples can be fruitful for offering new insights and new challenges to the debate over the appropriate relationship between personal and social sin. In an attempt to show that this is true, I will offer a reading of the First Week of the Spiritual Exercises of St. Ignatius in the hopes that doing this may prove that the Exercises, despite the fact that Ignatius lived centuries before the debate over social sin, are still capable of being life-giving when this new question is put to them. This effort to reread the First Week of the Exercises arises out of a desire to take seriously the critique of Jon Sobrino that the First Week fosters the privatized, non-political notions of sin that he believes we must now challenge.

Sobrino, although he is deeply indebted to the Ignatian tradition and draws heavily from the Second and in his later work the Third Weeks of the Exercises, claims in his book *Christology at the Crossroads*, that while the praxis-oriented nature of the Exercises[7] and the Ignatian focus on disciple-ship are retrievable for modern-day disciples, the First Principle and Foundation "formulates a view of God that could well be called philosophical."[8] He further claims that the First Principle and the First Week as a whole serve to make a cultural appeal to "begin with the radical seriousness of life."[9] Since he interprets this aspect of the Exercises as making an appeal that must be adapted to different cultural conditions if it is to retain its meaning, he recommends that the First Week be altered to reflect an understanding of sin as social, structural, and collective; in place of the First Principle, Sobrino suggests that we reflect on the "absolute necessity of liberating the oppressed masses,"[10] followed by an examination of conscience based on social and structural understandings of sin.[11]

In what follows I argue that Sobrino's suggested alterations will eradicate some of the most important insights to be gained from the First Week of the Exercises; reflection on the need to liberate the oppressed masses, coupled with a heavier emphasis on social sin, will have the opposite effect from the one desired by Sobrino. If these substitutions for the original meditations of the Exercises are the wells from which we must now drink, we will find that our wells are empty; we will be moved to act out of guilt, an unsustainable motivation and a theologically problematic one, rather than out of gratitude, which is the original context for examining sin in Ignatius's First Week. Thus, by offering this re-reading of the First Week in the light of the question of social sin, I hope to show three things: 1) that the Ignatian Spiritual Exercises are a retrievable and life-giving resource for contemporary disciples; 2) that while the challenge Sobrino issues to the First World is absolutely vital (that it must be more conscious of its own sin and more involved in action on behalf of the oppressed), we in the First World must find our own way to attain this goal—we must drink from our own wells to find resources for commitment; 3) a benefit of this rereading of the First Week is that it may prove able to bridge the gap between the liberation theologians, at least as represented by Sobrino, and the magisterium. If it can be shown that a view of sin such as the one offered in the Exercises can retain a profound focus on personal sinfulness and responsibility while fostering a recognition of the larger dimensions of sin and oppression and still provide resources to move retreatants to grateful service on behalf of the oppressed, this reading will indicate some directions for moving the conversation forward. At the end of this essay, I will also return to the insights that I will have drawn out in the reading of the First Week to show that this spiritual tradition can bear fruit for Christian political action.

The First Week

I will now turn to the First Week of the Exercises to suggest that a fresh reading of this spiritual tradition can strike a balance between, or perhaps overcome the opposition between, personal and social sin while simultaneously providing a type of spiritual discipline capable of forming disciples who are capable of recognizing, developing appropriate affections toward, and working to change structural dimensions of sin.[12]

Ignatius defines "Spiritual Exercises" as "every method of examination of conscience, meditation, contemplation, vocal or mental prayer, and other spiritual activities."[13] The Exercises are aimed, first, to "remove disordered affections," and, secondly, to seek and find God's will for the "ordering of our life and for the salvation of our soul."[14] To this end, Ignatius divides the Exercises into four weeks, moving from the "consideration of sins" in the First Week, to the life of Christ through Palm Sunday in the Second, to the Passion in the Third, and finally to an ending with the Resurrection and the Ascension in the Fourth Week.[15] In addition, Ignatius assumes that the one who seeks to enter this process of formation believes in Christ, is a member of the Church, and desires to know and do God's will. The major goal is to elect a way of life that is to the greater glory of God. Ignatius, then, does not design these exercises with atheists, persons of other faiths, or even very seriously lapsed Christians in mind. Thus, the usefulness of the Exercises for these people is limited or at least raises significant challenges. These aims and presuppositions of the Spiritual Exercises place three restrictions on our use of them for the clarification of the theological concept of social sin. First, they can be used well only within a Christian context. Secondly, we must be mindful that we are reflecting theologically on a text that was never intended for academic examination. Finally, although I will focus here on the First Week of the Exercises because it directly addresses sin and because it is an important foundation for understanding the other three weeks, we must keep in mind that the retreat does not end with the First Week's focus on sin, repentance, and gratitude, but moves on to meditations that deal with following Christ through his life, death, and resurrection.

First, then, how does Ignatius understand sin, and how do the Exercises offer resources for understanding the concept of social sin in the spiritual life? At the most basic level, Ignatius understands the end of human life to be the praise, reverence, and service of God.[16] Given this end, he claims that the Christian "ought to desire and elect only the thing which is more conducive to the end for which [he is] created."[17] By implication, sin is any action or inclination that impedes the election of a life conducive to the end of human life. If living according to our proper end is required for the salvation of our souls, then sin, as that which impedes a life according to this end, would have the direct effect of placing the sinner on a path at odds with salvation—namely, the path toward death. "Indifference" names the ascetic discipline that permits the retreatant to discern more clearly the path of salvation by separating selfish desires from desires for the right worship of God. Thus, "indifference," as Ignatius understands it, is neither absolute nor permanent, as it is often misunderstood to be, and it is certainly not indifference to the love, praise, and service of God since indifference to these would prove an impediment to the achievement of our proper end.

With this goal of electing a life in accordance with our proper end, Ignatius sets out a series of reflections that move through four weeks, with the second through the fourth being reflections on the life of Christ from his birth through his resurrection and ascension. Within each week, there is a series of meditations or exercises that generally take the form of reflection on a particular instance in the life of Christ and which usually involve some sort of conversation or colloquy between the retreatant and one person of the Trinity or sometimes Mary. The beginning of the Exercises is the First

Week, which includes the Principle and Foundation, a statement of the purpose of human life ("humans are created to praise, reverence, and serve God our Lord"), an explanation of the requirement of indifference, and the articulation of the goal of the Exercises, namely, the election of a life that is most conducive to the end for which the human is created. Ignatius provides guidelines for a general examination of conscience and general confession, and then enters into the exercises of the First Week, which include a meditation on sin in general, on our own sin, repetitions of these first two meditations, and finally a meditation on hell.

The first meditation of the First Week—the meditation on the first, second, and third sins—is extremely important for a contemporary discussion of social sin. The retreatant begins by asking God for the grace that all her "intentions, actions, and operations may be ordered to the service of his Divine Majesty."[18] Given the focus on the ordering of the intentions and affections of the individual retreatant, one might expect that Ignatius would have had the director lead the retreatant immediately into a meditation on her own personal sin, but this is not the case. Instead, the spiritual director asks the retreatant to begin by reflecting on what I will call the "cosmic" dimension of sin—a dimension that is related to what we have come to call social sin—first by reflecting on the sin of the angels, then the sins of Adam and Eve, and finally, the sin of any human who has "gone to hell because of one mortal sin."[19] Thus, the retreatant, before considering her own sins, begins by exploring the reality of the "sin of the world," and by doing this, her own sins become part of a history of this cosmic sinfulness, this historical rebellion against God.

At the end of the first meditation, the retreatant still does not move directly into a consideration of her own sins. First, she is asked to envisage the crucified Christ and to engage in conversation "in the way one friend speaks to another, or a servant to one in authority."[20] Here Ignatius draws upon human relationships to model how we should speak to Christ, and though servant to master and friend to friend have differing implications, both convey some sort of intimacy and dependence. The retreatant "begs favors," "asks counsel," and tells her concerns to Christ as he is suspended on the cross. She is then directed to ask herself: "What have I done for Christ? What am I doing for Christ? What ought I to do for Christ?" In this first meditation, we find an ideal illustration of the distinction that Gregory Baum makes between the guilt we should feel for our own sins and the mourning or sorrow that we should feel for social sin. While the retreatant cannot exactly feel "guilt" for the sins of the angels, our first parents, or other humans, she is moved first to feel sorrow for their sins and to understand her own sin and guilt within the larger historical context of the sin of the world. She is moved, as Ignatius says, to feel the sorrow felt by the Trinity when they "gazed upon the whole surface...of the world" and decided to "save the human race."[21] The retreatant does not remain, though, in this experience of overwhelming sorrow or guilt, but is moved instead to action for Christ in the world. In this first meditation, we are asked to situate ourselves between life and death, between those who have rebelled and the one who has saved all of humanity, and this placing must provoke both gratitude and desire for action; in fact these sentiments are the signs that one is ready to move forward in the Exercises.

I have already suggested that at least one appropriate feeling in the first meditation would be sorrow for all those who have sinned before me and mourning for their separation from God. I have also emphasized that in the Exercises, the retreatant is moved immediately to take these feelings of sorrow to the foot of the cross and to ask for guidance and the desire to act for Christ in the world. Part of this movement from sorrow to action must be a discernment of responsibility and limitation. I would argue that these two dispositions—responsibility and limitation—must be held closely together in our conception of social sin, since, to put it somewhat simply, if everyone is responsible for everything, no one will be responsible for anything. Fostering an appropriate sense of responsibility and limitation will be necessary in order to make a proper election, that is, to find a way to serve humanity for the greater glory of God; in the second exercise of the First Week, we see that Ignatius makes precisely this move. Turning from cosmic sinfulness to personal sin and then to desire for action in the first exercise of the First Week, he then takes up the cultivation of humility in the second exercise.

The language of the second exercise may sound unduly harsh to the contemporary ear but the point of this exercise cannot be eliminated. The director again leads the retreatant through a reflection that inspires first sorrow and then gratitude. I will focus on two points in this exercise (the third and the fifth point) which, although differing in the responses they are intended to provoke, both aim to foster in the retreatant a sense of her appropriate place in creation and the appropriate limitations of that place. The third point in the second exercise contains a list of questions, and the directions instruct the retreatant to reflect upon herself "using examples which humble" her.[22] By means of comparison, she is led to a sense of "place":

> First, what am I when compared with all other human beings?
> Second, what are they when compared with all the angels and saints in paradise?
> Third, what is all of creation when compared with God? And then I alone—what can I be?
> Fourth, I will look at all the corruption and foulness of my body.
> Fifth, I will look upon myself as a sore or abscess from which have issued such great sins and iniquities and such foul poison.[23]

Again, the language might not translate easily into a contemporary setting, particularly the final two points, but the larger goal here is crucial. The retreatant is moved to a realization of her smallness, her seeming insignificance, and her sinfulness. This, however, is not where the meditation ends, for Ignatius immediately turns this sense of "smallness" into cause for wonder, strength, and gratitude rather than weakness and despair.

The fifth point illustrates this movement from sorrow to gratitude by suggesting that the meditation on sin and insignificance should lead to "an exclamation of wonder and surging emotion, uttered as I reflect on all creatures and wonder how they have allowed me to live and have preserved me in life."[24] Again, the cosmic dimension of the person's life is emphasized, but this time to emphasize all the ways in which the person is sustained through the guidance and prayers of others. The retreatant should develop in this point of the exercise a feeling of gratitude for the mercy bestowed upon him by reflecting on the care and concern of the angels, the saints, and all of creation for him, even in his smallness and sinfulness. Thus, the movement toward the development of a proper sense of humility does not end with either despair or self-abnegation but rather with a prayer of thanksgiving to "God our Lord for giving me life until now, and proposing with his grace, amendment for the future."[25]

The second exercise of the First Week fosters the development of several traits in the formation of the retreatant that I would suggest are key for an appropriate integration of the concept of social sin into the spiritual life. By urging the retreatant to see himself first as small and insignificant in comparison with the whole of creation and with God, and then to see himself as loved and sustained by God and the whole of creation, the dialectic of the third and fifth points of the meditation carve out a balance between "personal" and "social" sin; these exercises aim at an appropriate sorrow for the sin of the world and guilt and promised amendment for the sins for which the retreatant bears responsibility. The

voluntary aspect of sin, then, is retained by the exercises that
cultivate in the retreatant a proper sense of self (humility),
and therefore encourage the person to an acknowledgment
of his own limitations. While retaining a strong focus on personal sin, though, the meditations on the cosmic dimensions
of sin and the even vaster dimensions of God's love for the
world could not help but have the effect of broadening and
deepening the retreatant's desire to serve Christ through the
service of others.

The third exercise of the First Week continues this clarification of the sin of the world and the sin for which the individual bears responsibility. In this exercise, the director
instructs the retreatant to engage in several colloquies, the
first two of which concern the sin for which the person is
responsible:

> First, that I may feel an interior knowledge of my
> sins and also an abhorrence for them.
> Second, that I may perceive the disorder in my
> actions, in order to detest them, amend myself,
> and put myself in order.[26]

After determining "personal" sins, the retreatant asks for the
grace to have a "knowledge of the world, in order to detest
it and rid myself of all that is worldly and vain."[27] The distinction between the "two worlds" is emphasized here; there
is the world as it is in rebellion against God (which is to be
detested) and the world as it is loved by God (which is to be
labored for), mirroring the retreatant's experience of herself
as both insignificant and sinful but also loved and sustained.
The "two worlds," or more appropriately the world looked
at from two directions, also fosters an appropriate dialectical
imagination that enables the retreatant to experience and
recognize all the ways in which the world has fallen and
rebelled and yet simultaneously to see the world as it is
loved and sustained by God. If either aspect of this understanding of the world is missing, the retreatant may either be

tempted to underestimate the evils, sin, and suffering in the world or to condemn the world as merely evil. Both a contempt for the sin of the world and a deep love for the world, mirroring the love of God for the world, set the appropriate context for an integration of the concept of social sin into our spiritual experience.

Several facets of the First Week have emerged in our reading that I have highlighted as relevant for a spiritual grounding of the concept of social sin. First, understanding the cosmic dimensions of sin is a necessary prerequisite for attaining an appropriate understanding of personal sin. To understand the depths of our own sin, we must first see ourselves as players in a drama of sinfulness and rebellion. Second, both our meditations on the sin of all those who have gone before us and the meditations on our own sin are meant finally not to provoke guilt, although guilt will be an important step along the way, but to provoke gratitude. Gratitude is the heart and goal of the First Week of the Exercises, a goal that cannot be met by replacing these meditations with a reflection solely on social sin and the need to liberate the oppressed. Finally, an appropriate sense of place, or humility, is required in order to proceed to the next step of making an election. If one feels despair and overwhelming smallness at the end of this Week, one will not be capable of moving forward to the making of an election or to the living out of the service of God through service of neighbor. These are the three keys then—the interlocking nature of cosmic/historical/social sinfulness and personal sinfulness, gratitude, and humility.

While I have used the terms social, structural, cosmic, and historical sinfulness interchangeably, I am not claiming that social sin and "cosmic" sin are precisely the same thing, although I have suggested that they are related. While attention to structural dimensions of sin—the ways in which institutions and cultures shape our own sinfulness and do violence to others, for example—must be treated in a more detailed fashion if we want to grasp the manifold reality of sin, the question in this essay does not require such precise delineation. The question here is whether the Exercises are capable of fostering the appropriate affections and passions such that an integration of the understanding of social and structural sin can be life-giving rather than deadening. If my reading of the First Week is essentially correct, then Ignatius's understanding of the relationship between cosmic and personal sin is a sufficient spiritual basis on which to construct a notion of social and structural sin adequate to the contemporary situation. Although Ignatius does not give us a "definition" of social or structural sin, the formation offered by this spiritual discipline of the Exercises, with its emphasis on this cosmic/personal dynamic, gratitude, and humility, is a good spiritual foundation on which to build such a definition.

Retrieval of the First Week and Its Significance for Political Commitment and Solidarity

The most critical aspect of the First Week of the Exercises to which I have tried to draw attention is the emphasis on gratitude, a central dimension of the Exercises that must be highlighted when we put the relatively new question of social sin to this spiritual tradition. When gratitude is seen as the heart and goal of the First Week, the meditations on sin will be experienced not necessarily as less painful but certainly will be anything but the overly privatized, moralistic experience so feared by Sobrino. Instead, this profound experience of gratitude and liberation from our own sins can free us for the service of others, to labor for others as God labors for us. As George Aschenbrenner writes in his article, "Consciousness Examen: Becoming God's Heart for the World":

> Mature faith and discipleship cannot happen without this painful transformation in the humiliating experience of guilt and sorrow. As the repentant sinner encounters God's forgiveness in

Jesus, sorrow is transformed into hopeful, vigor-
ous gratitude—and a burning zeal to serve God's
loving justice in our world. In this way, thanksgiving—the central driving force in the heart of
any mature disciple of Jesus Christ—dominates
the daily examen and fuels its impulse toward
loving action.[28]

While Aschenbrenner's immediate concern is the daily examen, the point here is the same. If gratitude is the context for
reflection on sin, the meditations on sin will give way not to
despair but to freedom for love and service in the world. In
addition, the cosmic dimensions of sin or the history of sinfulness emphasized in the First Week will deepen the disciple's capacity for feeling sorrow and for being moved to
respond to those who suffer. Sobrino's suggestion that the
First Week should be replaced with a reflection on social sin
and the need to liberate the oppressed masses might very
well have the opposite effect, particularly in the First World.
Rather than moving retreatants to gratitude and zealous
service, this reflection may very well move them to despair.
Many of us have had the experience, I would suspect, of feeling incapacitated and overwhelmed once we become aware
of the vast dimensions of sin. In the First World, even trips to
the grocery store can become occasions for a devastation of
hope for those who have come to realize the vast dimensions
of social injustice; in this context, finding the hope to sustain
involvement in a political cause can seem nearly impossible.
This is precisely why the insights of the First Week are so
important in our own context. With an appropriate understanding of gratitude as the heart of the First Week and the
heart of our relationship to God, we will be freed from the
temptation of despair. Nonetheless, within this context of
gratitude, the emphases on limit, or humility, and responsibility are equally important.

The need to maintain a primary and well-defined role for
personal responsibility to which I have drawn attention in

this essay is a concern shared by the magisterium in the critiques of liberation theology. When the magisterium fails to ground the notion of personal sin in the more fundamental reality of gratitude, however, these critiques can give the impression that the magisterium has missed the challenge being offered to those of us in the First World by the liberation theologians' attention to social sin. If I am correct, this retrieval of the Exercises can be a life-giving spiritual tradition for First World disciples because it retains the focus on personal responsibility desired by the magisterium while fostering a deeper recognition of the vast social dimensions of sin and the need for action on behalf of the suffering and oppressed. Within the context of the Exercises, there is not only no opposition between personal and social sin, but one is required to understand the other.

If we are able to drink deeply from this tradition, I would suggest that we will not find that our wells are empty with despair, but rather that there is a continuous supply of gratitude for God's love for us that will enable us to remain committed and engaged in even the most overwhelming situations. As the poem by Julia Esquivel suggests, once we have drunk deeply from the rivers of our own anguish, we will be able to make the deep hidden sigh of our neighbor our own. Hearing the neighbor's sigh as our own is the beginning of all true solidarity, and it is the beginning of any genuine commitment to political change. If the Exercises help us to hear that sigh, then they will continue to be a source that guides us to the election of a life conducive to the end of human life, namely, the praise, reverence, and service of God.

Notes

1. Julia Esquivel, "The Sigh," from *The Certainty of Spring: Poems by a Guatemalan in Exile*, trans. Anne Woehrle (Washington, DC: EPICA, 1993).

2. See especially the Sacred Congregation for the Doctrine of the Faith

(henceforth CDF), "Instruction on Certain Aspects of the 'Theology of Liberation,'" (1984), 12-13 (section IV, paragraphs 13-15).

3. Ibid., 15-16 (Section VI).

4. This would have to involve a separate treatment and one that cannot be addressed adequately in the confines of this paper. It should be noted, however, that one of the main impediments to adjudicating whether the CDF has fairly represented the views of liberation theologians is that liberation theology is treated as a single entity. No names or works are given when a position is questioned, and given the breadth of liberation theology and the significant differences between theologians, it is very difficult to judge whether the readings are simply unfair or whether they are only based on problems in one or several authors, rather than representative of problems in liberation theology as a whole.

5. Gregory Baum, "Structures of Sin," in *The Logic of Solidarity*, ed. Gregory Baum and Robert Ellsberg (Maryknoll, NY: Orbis Books, 1989), 110.

6. Gustavo Gutiérrez, *We Drink From Our Own Wells: The Spiritual Journey of a People*, trans. Matthew J. O'Connell (Maryknoll, NY: Orbis Books, 1984).

7. Jon Sobrino, *Christology at the Crossroads*, trans. John Drury (Maryknoll, NY: Orbis Books, 1978), 399.

8. Ibid., 413.

9. Ibid., 416-417.

10. Ibid.

11. It is important to note that Sobrino does develop a concept of personal sin in other works. He does not return, however, to reevaluate the First Week of the Exercises in light of his understanding of personal sin. This paper is intended less as a critique of Sobrino than as a sympathetic attempt to take Sobrino's critiques seriously and yet to suggest that he could indeed retrieve the First Week of the Exercises in a far less negative and much more fruitful manner. For more on Sobrino's understanding of personal sin, see especially his article, "Personal Sin, Forgiveness, and Liberation," in *The Principle of Mercy: Taking the Crucified People from the Cross*, ed. Robert R. Barr (Maryknoll, NY: Orbis Books, 1995), 83-104.

12. The value in seeking a better understanding of structural sin from the Exercises is that they can provide clarification from a spiritual tradition, and they are thus oriented toward the praxis of Christian life. It must be noted, however, that at least in the context of a strictly aca-

demic discussion of social sin, the genre of the Exercises may be seen also as a hindrance. Because I am concerned in this essay about the role of the concept of social sin in a community of those who try to follow Christ, the disadvantages of drawing from a spiritual tradition are not insurmountable, but we should at least point out the limits of trying to draw out a theological concept from a text that was not devised to set out doctrine or provide a systematic presentation of theology but rather to offer guidance for individuals seeking to follow Christ. The limitations of the genre primarily stem from the aims and presuppositions of the Exercises.

13. Ignatius of Loyola, *Spiritual Exercises* in *Ignatius of Loyola: Spiritual Exercises and Selected Works*, ed. George E. Ganss (New York: Paulist Press, 1991), 121. Citations refer to the page numbers in this volume, not to the paragraph numbers in the Exercises.

14. Ibid.

15. Ibid., 122.

16. Ibid., 130.

17. Ibid.

18. Ibid., 136.

19. Ibid., 138. I will not explore in this essay some of the problems raised by Ignatius's understanding of damnation and mortal sin, but a fuller treatment of this would be important for a consideration of how the First Week might be brought into conversation with contemporary belief and practice.

20. Ibid.

21. Ibid.

22. Ibid., 139.

23. Ibid.

24. Ibid.

25. Ibid., 140.

26. Ibid.

27. Ibid.

28. George A. Aschenbrenner, "Consciousness Examen: Becoming God's Heart for the World," in *Ignatian Exercises: Contemporary Annotations*, ed. David L. Fleming (St. Louis, MO: Review for Religious, 1996), 115.

Past CTS Volumes

Volume 41 • 1996
Religion, Ethics, & the Common Good
James Donahue and M. Theresa Moser, R.S.C.J., Editors

Here sixteen members of the College Theology Society contribute essays covering a wide range of perspectives on some of today's most basic theological questions: "What is the common good?" "What are individual rights?" and "What role does the church and its theology have in addressing these issues?"

ISBN: 0-89622-701-4, 272 pages, $14.95

Volume 43 • 1998
Theology: Expanding the Borders
Roberto S. Goizueta and Marla Pilar Aquino, Editors

In *Theology: Expanding the Borders,* sixteen members of the College Theology Society invite readers to join the discussion about the notion of "borders" to come to a deeper understanding of both the destructive nature of as well as the potential good of borders—not only territorial or national borders, but epistemological, ethnic, racial, gender, disciplinary, and ecclesial.

ISBN: 0-89622-933-5, 352 pages, $14.95